RESEARCHES INTO
THE EARLY HISTORY OF MANKIND

CLASSICS IN ANTHROPOLOGY
Paul Bohannan, Editor

RESEARCHES INTO THE EARLY HISTORY OF MANKIND AND THE DEVELOPMENT OF CIVILIZATION

By Edward B. Tylor
Edited and abridged with an Introduction
by Paul Bohannan

PHOENIX BOOKS

THE UNIVERSITY OF CHICAGO PRESS / CHICAGO & LONDON

042439

Library of Congress Catalog Card Number: 64-23416

The University of Chicago Press, Chicago & London
The University of Toronto Press, Toronto 5, Canada

NOTE

Strong opinions are held about the advisability of abridging "classics." In my opinion, the practice depends on two factors: (1) if the original author of the book conceived it as a structured unity and argued closely, it is probably not advisable; but if such is not the case, it depends on (2) whether the prospective readers are interested in the *culs-de-sac* of history or in the vitality of the facts and arguments.

Tylor specifically says that his book, herewith set forth in abridged form, was not conceived as an entity, but is rather a collection of essays. Moreover, the reader is not primarily the professional historian but rather the anthropologist who wants to know something of the origins of the ideas and concepts with which he works. Twenty or thirty years from now, a new edition, with still a new introduction and perhaps different deletions, may be useful.

Two chapters of the original were omitted from this book since other writers more or less contemporary with Tylor could be said to have covered the ground more fully. Chapter 8 in the original book, called "The Stone Age—Past and Present," was made obsolete in the very year of its publication (1865) by Sir John Lubbock's *Prehistoric Times,* and chapter 10 in the original book, called "Some Remarkable Customs" (discussions of couvade, marriage prohibitions, totemism, and some other matters), was made obsolete by the writings of MacLennan, Morgan, Maine, and others, not to mention the sociologists of the late nineteenth century.

Once chapters 8 and 10 were deleted, chapter 9 stood starkly alone in a book about the history and processes of symbolization. Unlike the other two, it could not be omitted because it is still one of the best general summaries on its subject, "Fire, Cooking, and Vessels." Therefore, that chapter is printed as an appendix.

The remaining ten chapters belie Tylor's claim that the book is no more than a collection of essays; they reveal a structured argument and a unity that is probably more apparent to modern readers than it was to Tylor. Tylor's original unity was based on his view of culture, stated in preliminary form in the first sentence of this book and in more finished form in the first sentence of *Primitive Culture*. With twentieth-century separation (derived from French sources) of ideal culture from traitlike manifestations of culture, a deeper unity and structure are revealed; here is a book about the history and institutionalization of the processes of communication and the formation of values.

A few minor deletions have been made in the chapters that are retained; all of them are indicated. Deletions of parts of paragraphs are indicated by four periods, passages of a paragraph or more by four asterisks. Two sorts of passages were excised: (1) a few in which examples are needlessly multiplied from what twentieth-century readers would consider inadequate ethnographic sources and (2) those in which analogies or other images seemed to endanger immediate communication with readers lacking a century of background. The guiding principle throughout was to maintain the flow of Tylor's argument; it is my opinion that occasional paring has best served that principle.

Writing a book is an exercise in communication. That so little of this book is dated is an indication of what vital communication was in fact achieved, and that anthropology is indeed firmly based.

PAUL BOHANNAN

EDITOR'S INTRODUCTION

With each rereading, it becomes more obvious how right Tylor's contemporaries were when they referred to anthropology, either disparagingly or proudly, as "Mr. Tylor's science." It is still Mr. Tylor's science. Within the literature available even in his time on the exotic peoples of the world, he discerned a design for comprehending the human condition and reducing that comprehension to the certitude of science.

Tylor's fundamental premise was, like all the premises of science, simple: in order for people to communicate with one another there must be repeated activities and shared ideas. The factors that made for predictability in behavior could also make for certainty in science. His most difficult task came with the resolution that the resultant common understandings and shared techniques must be made overt and their systematic interrelationships demonstrated. These common understandings, plus the linguistic and material phenomena which form their idiom, and the psychic and emotional phenomena that underlie them, Tylor called "culture," borrowing the term from German historians for his new purpose. Anthropology became, in Tylor's hands, the science of culture.

That premise still stands. Tylor's fundamental problem, on the other hand, was to recapture in the greatest possible detail the history of the development of that culture. The problem is, in some forms, still with us. But, as we shall see, it has undergone considerable change with the turn in the twentieth century from genetic explanations to analytical explanations.

Like so many men since, Tylor came to anthropology in search of a means for making an honest man of himself. In 1855, he was told that he must, for his health, travel in warmer and sunnier places. At that time 23 years old, he accompanied an older friend, the amateur archaeologist and collector Henry Christy, to Mexico. The undiluted color of the Mexicans and the potential of self-realization (always dormant in fascination with strange peoples) caught the imagination of this cultured but uncommitted man. His first book, *Anahuac,* was published in 1861. It was only a little more than a travel book about Mexico. Yet that "little more" contained the seed of what was to become modern anthropology.

Tylor did not merely travel and write. Something of a more fundamental nature emerged from his Mexican experience. He wanted to know not merely how Mexican life looked to a modestly well-to-do English Quaker like himself, but also how it looked to Mexican Indians. It would be going too far to claim that Tylor's experiences in Mexico constituted "field work." They did, however, provide one residuum of field work in this scientist—the personal experience of exotic culture that allows one to turn a comparative glance upon one's self.

Tylor spent the next few years examining the world around him, the vast literature of history and the classics, and the equally vast travel literature about so-called "savages." The result was the book that is republished here—*Researches into the Early History of Mankind and the Development of Civilization.* The book was published in 1865 and went through several printings. Tylor himself edited the book for a new edition (called the "Third" although the "Second" was no more than a reprint of the first) in 1878.

In addition to his many papers, Tylor wrote two important books after he had finished *The Early History of Mankind. Primitive Culture* was published in 1871 and his popular and penetrating *Anthropology* a decade later. Tylor occupied Britain's first recognized university post in anthropology when he became Keeper of the University Museum of Oxford in 1883, and the next year he was named Reader in Anthropology. A personal professorship was proffered him in 1896. He retired in 1909 to Somerset where he lived quietly until his death in 1917.

The fact that Tylor's life does not provide a biography abounding in exciting incidents and famous people is no more than a reflection of this strong but still man, happily married for nearly sixty years and happily employed for almost as many. Nevertheless, his quiet, persevering need to know changed the direction of thought of the scientific and philosophical worlds.

The Early History of Mankind is not merely a landmark in the early history of anthropology, although that reason alone would merit its republication. It stands, moreover, as a sort of primer to which social scientists can go back and back again in search of the origins of the problems with which they are concerned today, to the fresh statement of the axioms on which their science proceeds. Nowhere has the creed of the anthropologist been better stated than in the first two sentences of the Introduction to the *Early History:*

> In studying the phenomena of knowledge and art, religion and mythology, law and custom, and the rest of the complex whole which we call Civilization it is not enough to have in view the more advanced races and to know their history so far as direct records have preserved it for us. The explanation of the state of things in which we live has often to be sought in the condition of rude and early tribes; and without a knowledge of this to guide us, we may miss the meaning even of familiar thoughts and practices.

TYLOR A CENTURY AFTER

The range of Tylor's interests, his taste for facts of global provenience, and his capacity for combining synthesis and originality mean that the whole of anthropology would have to be ransacked to provide in full measure any statement of the modern outgrowth of his contributions. Yet in order to fit Tylor's work into the era almost precisely a century after he wrote, it is necessary to take cognizance of the fate of the ideas that have been set forth in this, his first professional book.

Signs, Symbols, and Communication.—The first five chapters of this book provide detailed accounts (later summarized in chapters 4 and 5 of *Anthropology*) on the basic arts of communication. Tylor's investigation of communication among deaf-mutes is a veritable model for examining strange and exotic modes of communication. His insights into the nature of the process of symbolization and its importance to human life lie at the foundation of all later work on the subject.

A number of major fields of specialization have developed since Tylor's time. The art of communicating with the deaf has been brought to a high plane.[1] The processes of symbol formation and the place of symbols in thought processes have been studied more fully, and a philosophical and scientific revolution has proceeded from such studies.[2] The covert, indeed emotional, meaning of gestures has been analyzed.[3] Philology has become linguistics.[4] The semantics of painting and the communication elements in art styles have come under scrutiny,[5] vastly enlarging the field with which Tylor worked.

The arts of communication have, in our own day, made dramatic progress. Tylor's spirit remains; the central issue still lies in learning the modes by which men perceive in symbols and communicate their imprinted perceptions.

Images and Names.—It is difficult, in the years after Whitehead and his followers have made the "subject-object confusion" a part of the armory of every analytical mind, to appreciate how far along the path Tylor had proceeded in his discussion of "this confusion of objective with subjective connexion" (p. 111). Tylor was certainly among the first social scientists to point out the difficulty in distinguishing subject and object (pp. 100 ff.).

[1] See *American Annals of the Deaf,* especially CIII (March, 1958), 207–433, which contains summary articles on many aspects of the subject. See also Helmer R. Myklebust, *The Psychology of Deafness* (New York: Grune & Stratton, 1960), especially chap. 9.

[2] Charles W. Morris, *Signs, Language, and Behavior* (New York: Prentice-Hall, 1946); Ernst Cassirer, *The Philosophy of Symbolic Forms,* trans. Ralph Manheim (New Haven: Yale University Press, 1953–57).

[3] Raymond L. Birdwhistell, *Introduction to Kinesics* (Washington: Foreign Service Institute, 1952); George F. Mahl, Burton Danet, and Nea Norton, "Reflection of Major Personality Characteristics in Gestures and Body Movements," paper read before American Psychological Association, Annual Meeting, 1959.

[4] Ferdinand de Saussure, *A Course in General Linguistics* (New York: Philosophical Library, 1959); Leonard Bloomfield, *Language* (New York: Holt, 1933); H. A. Gleason, Jr., *An Introduction to Descriptive Linguistics* (New York: Holt, Rinehart, and Winston, 1961).

[5] Meyer Schapiro, "Style" in A. L. Kroeber (ed.), *Anthropology Today* (Chicago: University of Chicago Press, 1953), pp. 287–312.

He was even able, occasionally, to point out that social scientists were unable to maintain the distinction. Yet, for all that, Tylor lived in an age devoted to genetic rather than to analytical explanations—an age before it was possible to turn the full glare of analysis onto the self. He knew that savages confused subject and object, even some civilized men did—perhaps even he himself did. But in his time he did not have the tools to sustain the self-examination necessary to bring the scientist's viewpoints into the data, thereby creating a real theory of social, psychic, and cultural analysis. We still may not have that capacity, but we are much closer to it than was Tylor—and we know that this capacity is what a real theory in the social sciences demands. It was Tylor who took a giant step toward its realization.

Tylor's basic mistake has been revealed by Evans-Pritchard[6] in dealing with Tylor's premises concerning primitive religion: Tylor sought to discover what was "in the mind" of another man rather than the substantive statements and the social and psychic background of communications. Many wasted words about prejudice for or against "psychological methods" and for or against "sociological methods" will continue to obscure the point. Tylor's method was not faulty because it was psychological or sociological, but precisely because it was *not* psychological or sociological. To say that it was cultural is true, but beside this particular point. Tylor imputed thoughts and psychic conditions and (to a lesser extent) values and social conditions on the basis of evidence that was only cultural. For all that he created the science of culture, he could not be wholly cultural in his approach.

In short, Tylor's mistake was that he tackled the problem of images and names as if it were a problem in "certain processes of the human mind." Today we would tackle the same range of problems in terms of symbolic representation, learning theory, and social structure.

Whereas Tylor said, "Man . . . very commonly believes that between the object and the image of it there is a real connexion, which does not arise from a mere subjective process in the mind of the observer," a twentieth-century anthropologist would say,

6 E. E. Evans-Pritchard, "The Intellectualist (English) Interpretation of Magic," *Bulletin of the Faculty of Arts* (Cairo), vol. I, part 2 (1933).

'In some cultures there is a postulate of mystical connection between an object and an image of it." Instead of proceeding, "It is
accordingly possible to communicate an impression to the original through the copy," a twentieth-century American would proceed, "Such men claim that, through mystical means, a connection exists or can be established between the object and the
image." The word "claim" is important—this idea has been communicated to the field worker. The word "mystical" is also important. It refers to what is a mystery to the actors, not to the social
scientists to whom a "mystery" need not be mysterious.

When Tylor's ideas are restated in this way, we can see that his
confusion was one between perception and communication. What
he was studying was communication, for the simple reason that
perception *cannot* be studied without the intermediacy of communication. The truths that Tylor clothed in untruths about
"perception" stand revealed if they are clothed rather in truths
concerning communication. Tylor, indeed, paved the way to
Sapir and Whorf,[7] to psychological anthropology,[8] to social anthropology,[9] and to an increased awareness of the nature of metaphor and ambiguity.[10] Tylor wrote before psychoanalysis and
philosophy taught us that mere discovery of error was not
enough, but that we must learn what it is that error portends.

We can vouchsafe that Tylor, read in such a way, was not
"wrong." Rather, he took a step which we had to take to understand such problems, but which has since been obscured by the
achievements over a century in symbolic theory, learning theory,
psychoanalysis, and social theory.

[7] Edward Sapir, *Selected Writings of Edward Sapir*, ed. D. G. Mandelbaum
(Berkeley: University of California Press, 1949); Benjamin L. Whorf, *Language,
Thought, and Reality* (New York: John Wiley & Sons, 1956).

[8] Francis L. K. Hsu, *Psychological Anthropology* (Homewood, Ill.: Dorsey
Press, 1962); Anthony F. C. Wallace, *Culture and Personality* (New York:
Random House, 1961).

[9] E. E. Evans-Pritchard, *Social Anthropology* (London: Cohen and West,
1951); Raymond Firth, *Elements of Social Organization* (2d ed.; London:
Watts, 1956); Paul Bohannan, *Social Anthropology* (New York: Holt, Rinehart, and Winston, 1963).

[10] William Empson, *The Structure of Complex Words* (London: Chatto
and Windus, 1951).

Early History.—Tylor's self-assigned task was the recovery of the early history, "lost" before written documentation was possible. This task became unfashionable in the early twentieth century as the result of a series of attacks, most of them well founded, on the concept and methods of "reconstruction of history" and by brilliant polemics that all but discredited the idea of "survivals."

Yet, Tylor's goal of discovering "the many ways of bringing indirect evidence to bear on the problem" of cultural development (p. 137) was never totally lost, and in the 1960's it has again become one of the dominant goals of anthropology.[11] In order to read Tylor to best advantage in the 1960's, two points must be kept in mind: (1) Tylor used genetic explanations of history that we in the twentieth century do not favor, and (2) "survivals" is a useful concept in the tug-of-war between proponents of evolution and those of degeneration, but misleading in any other context.

Being a widely read man of the nineteenth century, Tylor used a genetic mode of explanation—an explanation of what something is by exhaustive delineation of how it came to be. Genetic explanation, which is standard in geometry (a circle is a line connecting all points equidistant from a given point) and which has paid off handsomely in biology, was ultimately shown to be extraordinarily tricky when applied to the field of culture, where confusion of phylogenesis and history can be devastating. We now realize that we cannot say, as Tylor said, "It is hard to imagine" so-and-so (p. 164) and then, for lack of the imaginable, use the unimaginable as data. In short, our idea of history and our proficiency in historiography have come a long way. We do, however, still use all the sources which Tylor used and some besides: linguistic evidence; the distribution of techniques, ideas, and themes across the surface of the earth; musical characteristics; sculpture styles; the themes of tales; and intricacies of myth. Indeed, most of these sources of information have developed into

11 Jan Vansina, "Recording the Early History of the Bakuba," *Journal of African History,* vol. I (1960), No. 1; A. Irving Rouse, "The Strategy of Culture History" in A. L. Kroeber (ed.), *Anthropology Today* (Chicago: University of Chicago Press, 1953), pp. 57–76.

specialties: linguistics, ethnomusicology, and the study of "narrative." There are also, today, means for reconstructing the historical record that Tylor would obviously have embraced with enthusiasm: dating of objects by analysis of the radioactive chemicals they contain, paleobotany and paleozoology, the application of genetics, and the more difficult inferences to be drawn from sociology and social anthropology. Tylor would, in fact, have every reason to be pleased with the way we have stuck to his guns; we have not "lost" any of the techniques known to Tylor, and we have gained others—a situation that fits neatly into his general theory.

There is one dispute, however, that often obscures the direct line that links him and his work to us. Today we are no longer interested in the central problem of Tylor's age: the confrontation of theories of evolution with theories of degeneration. In Tylor's day, the opposite of evolution was degeneration. In our day, the opposite of evolution is functionalism. Just as the earlier dispute left in its wake both useful conceptual tools and some prejudices, so the modern one is now disappearing, leaving a conceptual armory of great potential and some foolish bickering between the partisans of one system or the other. The obscuring point is, however, the theory of "survivals" on which Tylor and his contemporaries leaned so heavily. This concept was transferred more or less intact from the use made of the geological record by such biologists as Darwin to the use made of nonfunctional culture traits to explain apparent anomalies. When irreversible changes in culture took place, the theory went, and created new and more nearly modern modes of living, other traits of culture that were peripheral to the central change were brought willy-nilly into the new situation. So much is undeniable. But it is also undeniable that the "progressive" evolutionists used the idea of "survivals" to explain what they considered to be inadequate, weak, or inconsistent parts of the culture; exactly the same technique was used by the proponents of a theory of degeneration, who said that anything good, strong, efficient, and inconsistent with other parts of the culture was left from the days before degeneration had reduced the population to its present miserable state.

There is probably just enough to the notion of decline that one cannot throw it out, but one must understand it in a new way. Individual cultures wax and wane. They grow and decline. Culture, on the other hand, tends to grow; that is, once the ideas are present, human society adapts to them to insure their continued presence. Evolutionary theory is based on the latter fact; decline theory is based on the former, improperly understood and too broadly generalized.

Tylor's technique—and it is one which was taken further, indeed driven into the ground, by Tylor's American contemporary Lewis H. Morgan—involved the assumption that from these survivals of earlier times, it was possible to reconstruct the society and culture of earlier times. Such an assumption is questionable in some degree for two reasons: (1) the symbolic nature of culture (which Tylor understood) makes it possible for one act or one thing to mean many different things and (2) the assumptions applied to degeneration were in fact in search of a functional theory. Therefore, although the evolution of material culture can sometimes be traced backward from the present to the past, any effort to do the same thing with ideas is fraught with difficulties and probably doomed to failure.

The last chapter of Tylor's book gives a beautifully concise statement of the difficulties inherent in deciding whether similarities in different parts of the world have resulted from independent invention, from migration of peoples, or from diffusion of culture traits. Although our tools have become very much more precise and our concepts more developed, that problem is still the fundamental one.

It should be noted that in almost no place is Tylor himself chargeable with evolutionary overstatement. He did not carry the method to the length of incredibility, let alone absurdity, as some of his successors did. Tylor was first of all a careful and reasonable man: "It is safest to ascribe [similarities] to independent invention unless the coincidence passes the limits of ordinary probability" (p. 148). Tylor did not often go beyond his data. It is no accident that modern studies in social and cultural evolution have had to reject most of what appeared after Tylor and begin again with his work.[12]

Contained within the Tylorian analogies is the seed not merely of evolutionary theory but also of diffusion theory, functional theory, and indeed of structural theory.

Myth.—We have probably learned more about myth since Tylor's time than we have about most other subjects with which he dealt. Yet the illusion persists that we know little about it. Tylor, in dealing with myth, was intent on one problem: separating the "fact" from the "fiction" and using the so-called fact to discover ancient connections between peoples. That use of myth is still to be found, and its problems are still valid. However, many other aspects of myth are recognized today. A masterly correlation remains to be made of the uses of myth and the types of incident used.[13]

Surely a myth is as good as its equivocality. Any myth that can be used to explain cosmography, history, society, the origin of custom, the tensions in family and community life, the pressure of morality, and the uncertain and lonely experiences of the psychic life is a very handy myth indeed. What we have learned is that myth is a means of culturally organizing "facts" perceived and communicated into economical statements for purposes of explanation, entertainment, or both. The creation of the world can, by myth, be made real in psychic experiences. The origin of custom can be made consonant with the moral certitude expressed by one's peers. Myth is, indeed, a handy device for simplifying nature, culture, and psyche into a realizable whole.

A myth is, in short, a narrative substitute for a theory. The difference lies in the form and in the standards for verifiability. Myths are constantly verified by culturally dictated perception of experience. Theories must be verified according to "scientific"

12 Leslie A. White, *The Science of Culture* (New York: Farrar, Straus, 1949); Marshall D. Sahlins and Elman B. Service, *Evolution and Culture* (Ann Arbor: University of Michigan Press, 1960).

13 Bronislaw Malinowski, *The Myth in Primitive Psychology* (New York: W. W. Norton, 1926); Ernst Cassirer, *An Essay on Man* (New Haven: Yale University Press, 1944).

canons. Indeed, myths must be "true" or they could not be told, but they are simply not verifiable by historical or scientific canons of "truth." The main difficulty in Tylor's conception of myth is that he applies more or less scientific canons of verifiability to it. He realizes only dimly that a myth is an elegant arrangement of facts in the form of a narrative.

Since the days of psychoanalysis it is no longer fashionable to seek different sorts of error, which was Tylor's method and which was followed by such later scholars as Frazer and Levy-Bruhl. Rather, today we seek to know different kinds of truth: historical truth, social truth, psychic truth, and artistic truth.

All myths can be explained in each of these various dimensions, and no doubt many others, and all the dimensions lead ultimately to a sort of truth. Sorting out these explanations comes less from the subject matter of the myth (although such is still important for historical leads) than from the purpose to which the myth is put by the people who tell it, and the more or less systematic skewing by the people who record it.

To distinguish (or interrelate) myth and metaphor seems to be Tylor's most excruciating difficulty. That difficulty is found in statements such as "to them, as to the higher races, the idea is familiar that the stars are men" (p. 195). Metaphorically, stars may be men; mythically, stars may be made to stand, like quipu, as mnemonics for the customs, the history, and the morality of men.

Chapter 8 deals with myth as history and is almost modern. Chapter 9 deals with myth as historical evidence and is dated, although the problem of the myth as historical evidence has recently been attacked again.

Anthropology has come a long way; but it is still Mr. Tylor's science, because he set it on the right road.

CONTENTS

1   I   Introduction

9   II   The Gesture-Language

27   III The Gesture-Language—*Continued*

48   IV   Gesture-Language and Word-Language

69   V   Picture-Writing and Word-Writing

91   VI   Images and Names

128   VII Growth and Decline of Culture

167   VIII Historical Traditions and Myths of Observation

193   IX   Geographical Distribution of Myths

232   X   Concluding Remarks

243   Appendix

291   Index

CHAPTER I

INTRODUCTION

In studying the phenomena of knowledge and art, religion and mythology, law and custom, and the rest of the complex whole which we call Civilization, it is not enough to have in view the more advanced races, and to know their history so far as direct records have preserved it for us. The explanation of the state of things in which we live has often to be sought in the condition of rude and early tribes; and without a knowledge of this to guide us, we may miss the meaning even of familiar thoughts and practices. . . .

It is indeed hardly too much to say that Civilization, being a process of long and complex growth, can only be thoroughly understood when studied through its entire range; that the past is continually needed to explain the present, and the whole to explain the part. . . .

Though, however, the Early History of Man is felt to be an attractive subject, and great masses of the materials needed for working it out have long been forthcoming, they have as yet been turned to but little account. The opinion that the use of facts is to illustrate theories, the confusion between History and Mythology, which is only now being partly cleared up, an undue confidence in the statements of ancient writers, whose means of information about times and places remote from themselves were often much narrower than those which are, ages later, at our own command, have been among the hindrances to the growth of sound knowledge in this direction. The time for writing a systematic treatise on the subject does not seem yet to have come; certainly nothing of the kind is attempted in the present series of essays, whose contents, somewhat miscellaneous as they are, scarcely come into contact with great parts of the most important problems involved, such as the relation of the bodily characters of the various races, the question of their origin and descent, the development of morals, religion, law, and many others. The matters discussed have been chosen, not so much for their absolute importance, as because, while they are among the easiest and most inviting parts of the subject, it is possible so to work them as to bring into view certain general lines of argument, which apply not only to them, but also to the more complex and difficult problems involved in a complete treatise on the History of Civilization. These lines of argument, and their relation to the different essays, may be briefly stated at the outset.

In the first place, when a general law can be inferred from a group of facts, the use of detailed history is very much superseded. When we see a magnet attract a piece of iron, having come by experience to the general law that magnets attract iron, we do not take the trouble to go into the history of the particular magnet in question. To some extent this direct reference to general laws may be made in the study of Civilization. The four next chapters of the present book treat the various ways in which man utters his thoughts, in Gestures, Words, Pictures, and Writing. Here, though Speech and Writing must be investigated historically, depending as they do in so great measure on the words and characters which were current in the world thousands of years ago, on the other hand the Gesture-Language and Picture-Writing may be mostly explained without the aid of history, as direct products of the human mind. In the chapter on "Images and Names," an attempt is made to refer a great part of the beliefs and practices included under the general name of magic, to one very simple mental law, as resulting from a condition of mind which we of the more advanced races have almost outgrown, and in doing so have undergone one of the most notable changes which we can trace as having happened to mankind. And lastly, a particular habit of mind accounts for a class of stories which are here grouped together as "Myths of Observation," as distinguished from the tales which make up the great bulk of the folk-lore of the world, many of which latter are now being shown by the new school of Comparative Mythologists in Germany and England to have come into existence also by virtue of a general law, but a very different one.

But it is only in particular parts of Human Culture, where

the facts have not, so to speak, travelled far from their causes, that this direct method is practicable. Most of its phenomena have grown into shape out of such a complication of events, that the laborious piecing together of their previous history is the only safe way of studying them. It is easy to see how far a theologian or a lawyer would go wrong who should throw history aside, and attempt to explain, on abstract principles, the existence of the Protestant Church or the Code Napoléon. A Romanesque or an Early English cathedral is not to be studied as though all that the architect had to do was to take stone and mortar and set up a building for a given purpose. The development of the architecture of Greece, its passage into the architecture of Rome, the growth of Christian ceremony and symbolism, are only part of the elements which went to form the state of things in which the genius of the builder had to work out the requirements of the moment. . . .

As, however, the earlier civilization lies very much out of the beaten track of history, the place of direct records has to be supplied in great measure by indirect evidence, such as Antiquities, Language, and Mythology. This makes it generally difficult to get a sound historical basis to work on, but there happens to be a quantity of material easily obtainable, which bears on the development of some of the more common and useful arts. . . .

In the remote times and places where direct history is at fault, the study of Civilization, Culture-History as it is conveniently called in Germany, becomes itself an important aid to the historian, as a means of re-constructing the lost records of early or barbarous times. But its use as contributing to the early history of mankind depends mainly on the answering of the following question, which runs through all the present essays, and binds them together as various cases of a single problem.

When similar arts, customs, beliefs, or legends are found in several distant regions, among peoples not known to be of the same stock, how is this similarity to be accounted for? Sometimes it may be ascribed to the like working of men's minds under like conditions, and sometimes it is a proof of blood relationship or of intercourse, direct or indirect, between the races among whom it is found. In the one case it has no historical value whatever, while in the other it has this value in a high degree, and the ever-recurring problem is how to distinguish between the two. An example on each side may serve to bring the matter into a clearer light.

The general prevalence of a belief in the continuance of the soul's existence after death, does not prove that all mankind have inherited such a belief from a common source. It may have been so, but the historical argument is made valueless by the fact that certain natural phenomena may have suggested to the mind of man, while in a certain stage of development, the idea of a future state, and this not once only but again and again in different regions and in different times. These phenomena may prove nothing of the kind to us, but that is not the question. The reasoning of the savage is not to be judged by the rules which belong to a higher education; and what the ethnologist requires in such a case, is not to know what the facts prove to his own mind, but what inference the very differently trained mind of the savage may draw from them.

The belief that man has a soul capable of existing apart from the body it belongs to, and continuing to live, for a time at least, after the body is dead and buried, fits perfectly in such a mind with the fact that the shadowy forms of men and women do appear to others, when the men and women themselves are at a distance, and after they are dead. We call these apparitions dreams or phantasms, according as the person to whom they appear is asleep or awake, and when we hear of their occurrence in ordinary life, set them down as subjective processes of the mind. We do not think that the phantom of the dark Brazilian who used to haunt Spinoza was a real person; that the head which stood before a late distinguished English peer, whenever he was out of health, was a material object; that the fiends which torment the victim of delirium tremens, are what and where they seem to him to be; that any real occurrence corresponds to the dreams of the old men who tell us they were flogged last night at school. It is only a part of mankind, however, who thus disconnect dreams and visions from the objects whose forms they bear. Among the less civilized races, the separation of subjective and objective impressions, which in this, as in several other matters, makes the most important difference between the educated man and the savage, is much less fully carried out. This is indeed true to some extent among the higher nations, for no Greenlander or Kaffir ever mixed up his subjectivity with the evidence of his senses into a more hopeless confusion than the modern spiritualist.

* * * *

Mr. St. John says that the Dayaks regard dreams as actual occurrences. They think that in sleep the soul sometimes remains in the body, and sometimes leaves it and travels far away, and that both when in and out of the body it sees and hears and talks, and altogether has a prescience given to it, which, when the body is in its natural state, it does not enjoy. Fainting fits, or a state of coma, are thought to be caused by the departure or absence of the soul on some distant expedition of its own. When a European dreams of his distant country, the Dayaks think his soul has annihilated space, and paid a flying visit to Europe during the night.[1] Very many tribes believe in this way that dreams are incidents which happen to the spirit in its wanderings from the body, and the idea has even expressed itself in a superstitious objection to waking a sleeper, for fear of disturbing his body while his soul is out.[2] Father Charlevoix found both the theories in question current among the Indians of North America. A dream might either be a visit from the soul of the object dreamt of, or it might be one of the souls of the dreamer going about the world, while the other—for every man has two —stayed behind with the body. Dreams, they think, are of supernatural origin, and it is a religious duty to attend to them. That the white men should look upon a dream as a matter of no consequence is a thing they cannot understand.[3]

How like a dream is to the popular notion of a soul, a shade, a spirit, or a ghost, need not be said. But there are facts which bring the dream and the ghost into yet closer connection than

[1] St. John, 'Forests of the Far East'; London, 1862, vol. i. p. 189.

[2] Bastian, 'Der Mensch in der Geschichte'; Leipzig, 1860, vol. ii. p. 318, etc.

[3] Charlevoix, 'Hist. et Descr. Gén. de la Nouvelle-France'; Paris, 1744, vol. vi. p. 78.

follows from mere resemblance. Thus the belief is found among
the Finnish races that the spirits of the dead can plague the living in their sleep, and bring sickness and harm upon them.[4]
Herodotus relates that the Nasamones practise divination in the
following manner:—they resort to the tombs of their ancestors,
and after offering prayers, go to sleep by them, and whatever
dream appears to them they take for their answer.[5] In modern
Africa, the missionary Casalis says of the Basuto, "Persons who
are pursued in their sleep by the image of a deceased relation,
are often known to sacrifice a victim on the tomb of the defunct,
in order, as they say, to calm his disquietude."[6] Clearly, then,
a man who thinks he sees in sleep the apparitions of his dead
relatives and friends has a reason for believing that their spirits
outlive their bodies, and this reason lies in no far-fetched induc-
tion, but in what seems to be the plain evidence of his senses.

* * * *

It appears then, from these considerations, that when we find
dim notions of a future state current in the remotest regions of
the world, we must not thence assume that they were all diffused
from a single geographical centre. The case is one in which any
one plausible explanation from natural causes is sufficient to bar
the argument from historical connexion. On the other hand,
there is nothing to hinder such an argument in the following
case, which is taken as showing the opposite side of the problem.

The great class of stories known as Beast Fables have of late
risen much in public estimation. In old times they were listened
to by high and low with the keenest enjoyment for their own
sake. Then they were wrested from their proper nature into
means of teaching little moral lessons, and at last it came to be
the most contemptuous thing that could be said of a silly, point-
less tale, to call it a "cock and bull story." In our own day,
however, a generation among whom there has sprung up a new
knowledge of old times, and with it a new sympathy with old

---

[4] Castrén, 'Vorlesungen über die Finnische Mythologie'; (Tr. and Ed. Schief-
ner); St. Petersburgh, 1853, p. 120.

[5] Herod. iv. 172. See Mela, i. 8.

[6] Casalis, 'The Basutos'; London, 1861, p. 245.

thoughts and feelings, not only appreciate the beast fables for themselves, but find in their diffusion over the world an important aid to early history.

* * * *

As it happens, we know from other sources enough to explain the appearance in South Africa of stories from Reynard and the Arabian Nights by referring them to European or Moslem influence. But even without such knowledge, the tales themselves prove an historical connexion, near or remote, between Europe, Egypt, and South Africa. To try to make such evidence stand alone is a more ambitious task. In the chapter on the Geographical Distribution of Myths, I have compared a series of stories collected on the American Continent with their analogues elsewhere, endeavouring thereby to show an historical connexion between the mythology of America and that of the rest of the world, but with what success the reader must decide. . . .

For the errors which no doubt abound in the present essays, and for the superficial working of a great subject, a word may be said in apology. In discussing questions in which sometimes the leading facts have never before been even roughly grouped, it is very difficult not only to reject the wrong evidence, but to reproduce the right with accuracy, and the way in which new information comes in, which quite alters the face of the old, does not tend to promote over-confidence in first results. For instance, after having followed other observers in setting down as peculiar to the South Sea Islands, in or near the Samoan group, an ingenious little drilling instrument which will be hereafter described, I found it kept in stock in the London tool shops; mistakes of this kind must be frequent till our knowledge of the lower civilization is much more thoroughly collected and sifted. More accuracy might indeed be obtained by keeping to a very small number of subjects, but our accounts of the culture of the lower races, being mostly unclassified, have to be gone through as a whole, and up to a certain point it is a question whether the student of a very limited field might not lose more in largeness of view than he gained by concentration. Whatever be the fate of my arguments, any one who collects and groups a mass of evidence, and makes an attempt to turn it to account which may lead to something better, has, I think, a claim to be exempt from any very harsh criticism of mistakes and omissions. As the Knight says in the beginning of his Tale:—

> I have, God wot, a largë feeld to ere;
> And waykë ben the oxen in my plough.

[Note to 2d Edition, 1870. . . . I am indebted to Dr. W. R. Scott, Director of the Deaf and Dumb Institution at Exeter, for much of the assistance which has enabled me to write about the Gesture-Language with something of the confidence of an "expert"; and I have to thank Prof. Pott, of Halle, and Prof. Lazarus, of Berlin, for personal help in several difficult questions. Among books, I have drawn largely from the philological works of Prof. Steinthal, of Berlin, and from the invaluable collection of facts bearing on the history of civilization in the "Allgemeine Cultur-Geschichte der Menschheit," and "Allgemeine Culturwissenschaft," of the late Dr. Gustav Klemm, of Dresden.]

CHAPTER II

THE GESTURE-LANGUAGE

The power which man possesses of uttering his thoughts is one of the most essential elements of his civilization. Whether he can even think at all without some means of outward expression is a metaphysical question which need not be discussed here. Thus much will hardly be denied by any one, that man's power of utterance, so far exceeding any that the lower animals possess, is one of the principal causes of his immense pre-eminence over them.

Of the means which man has of uttering or expressing that which is in his mind, speech is by far the most important, so much so, that when we speak of *uttering* our thoughts, the phrase is understood to mean expressing them in words. But when we say that man's power of utterance is one of the great differences between him and the lower animals, we must attach to the word utterance a sense more fully conformable to its etymology. As Steinthal admits, the deaf-and-dumb man is the living refutation of the proposition, that man cannot think without speech, unless we allow the understood notion of speech as the utterance of thought by articulate sounds to be too narrow.[1] To *utter* a thought is literally to put it outside us, as to *express* is to squeeze it out. Grossly material as these metaphors are they are the best terms we have for that wonderful process by which a man, by some bodily action, can not only make other men's minds reproduce more or less exactly the workings of his own, but can even receive back from the outward sign an impression similar to theirs, as though not he himself but some one else had made it.

Besides articulate speech, the principal means by which man can express what is in his mind are the Gesture-Language, Picture-Writing, and Word-Writing. If we knew now, what we hope

[1] Steinthal, 'Ueber die Sprache der Taubstummen' (in Prutz's 'Deutsches Museum.' Jan. to June, 1851, p. 904, etc.).

to know some day, how Language sprang up and grew in the world, our knowledge of man's earliest condition and history would stand on a very different basis from what it now does. But we know so little about the Origin of Language, that even the greatest philologists are forced either to avoid the subject altogether, or to turn themselves into metaphysicians in order to discuss it. The Gesture-Language and Picture-Writing, however, insignificant as they are in practice in comparison with Speech and Phonetic Writing, have this great claim to consideration, that we can really understand them as thoroughly as perhaps we can understand anything, and by studying them we can realize to ourselves in some measure a condition of the human mind which underlies anything which has as yet been traced in even the lowest dialect of Language if taken as a whole. Though, with the exception of words in which we can trace the effects either of direct emotion, as in interjections, or of imitative formation, as in "peewit" and "cuckoo," we cannot at present tell by what steps man came to express himself by words, we can at least see how he still does come to express himself by signs and pictures, and so get some idea of the nature of this great movement, which no lower animal is known to have made or shown the least sign of making. The idea that the Gesture-Language represents a distinct separate stage of human utterance, through which man passed before he came to speak, has no support from facts. But it may be plausibly maintained, that in early stages of the development of language, while as yet the vocabulary was very rude and scanty, gesture had an importance as an element of expression, which in conditions of highly organized language it has lost.

The Gesture-Language, or Language of Signs, is in great part a system of representing objects and ideas by a rude outline-gesture, imitating their most striking features. It is, as has been well said by a deaf-and-dumb man, "a picture-language." Here at once its essential difference from speech becomes evident. Why the words *stand* and *go* mean what they do is a question to which we cannot as yet give the shadow of an answer, and if we had been taught to say "stand" where we now say "go," and "go" where we now say "stand," it would be practically all the same to us. No doubt there was a sufficient reason for these words receiving the meanings they now bear, as indeed there is a sufficient reason for everything; but so far as we are concerned, there might as well have been none, for we have quite lost sight of the connexion between the word and the idea. But in the gesture-language the relation between idea and sign not only always exists, but is scarcely lost sight of for a moment. When a deaf-and-dumb child holds his two first fingers forked like a pair of legs, and makes them stand and walk upon the table, we want no teaching to show us what this means, nor why it is done.

This definition of the gesture-language is, however, not complete. Such objects as are actually in the presence of the speaker, or may be supposed so, are brought bodily into the conversation by touching, pointing, or looking towards them, either to indicate the objects themselves or one of their characteristics. Thus if a deaf-and-dumb man touches his underlip with his forefinger, the context must decide whether he means to indicate the lip itself or the colour "red," unless, as is sometimes done, he shows by actually taking hold of the lip with finger and thumb, that it is the lip itself, and not its quality, that he means. Under the two classes "pictures in the air" and things brought before the mind by actual pointing out, the whole of the sign-language may be included.

It is in Deaf-and-Dumb Institutions that the gesture-language may be most conveniently studied, and what slight practical knowledge I have of it has been got in this way in Germany and in England. In these institutions, however, there are grammatical signs used in the gesture-language which do not fairly belong to it. These are mostly signs adapted, or perhaps invented, by teachers who had the use of speech, to express ideas which do not come within the scope of the very limited natural grammar and dictionary of the deaf-and-dumb. But it is to be observed that though the deaf-and-dumb have been taught to understand these signs and use them in school, they ignore them in their ordinary talk, and will have nothing to do with them if they can help it.

By dint of instruction, deaf-mutes can be taught to communicate their thoughts, and to learn from books and men in nearly the same way as we do, though in a more limited degree. They learn to read and write, to spell out sentences with the finger-alphabet, and to understand words so spelt by others; and besides this, they can be taught to speak in articulate language, though in a hoarse and unmodulated voice, and when another speaks, to follow the motions of his lips almost as though they could hear the words uttered.

It may be remarked here, once for all, that the general public often confuses the real deaf-and-dumb language of signs, in which objects and actions are expressed by pantomimic gestures, with the deaf-and-dumb finger-alphabet, which is a mere substitute for alphabetic writing. It is not enough to say that the two things are distinct; they have nothing whatever to do with one another, and have no more resemblance than a picture has to a writen description of it. Though of little scientific interest, the finger-alphabet is of great practical use. It appears to have been invented in Spain, to which country the world owes the first systematic deaf-and-dumb-teaching, by Juan Pablo Bonet, in whose work a one-handed alphabet is set forth, differing but little from that now in use in Germany, or perhaps by his predecessor, Pedro de Ponce. The two-handed or French alphabet, generally used in England, is of newer date.[2]

The mother-tongue (so to speak) of the deaf-and-dumb is the language of signs. The evidence of the best observers tends to prove that they are capable of developing the gesture-language out of their own minds without the aid of speaking men. Indeed, the deaf-mutes in general surpass the rest of the world in their power of using and understanding signs, and for this simple reason, that though the gesture-language is the common property of all mankind, it is seldom cultivated and developed to so high a degree by those who have the use of speech, as by those who cannot speak, and must therefore have recourse to other means of communication. The opinions of two or three practical observers may be cited to show that the gesture-language is not, like the finger-alphabet, an art learnt in the first instance from the teacher, but an independent process originating in the mind of the deaf-

2 Bonet, 'Reduction de las Letras, y Arte para enseñar á ablar los Mudos'; Madrid, 1620; pp. 128, etc. Schmalz, 'Ueber die Taubstummen'; Dresden and Leipzig, 1848; pp. 214, 352.

mute, and developing itself as his knowledge and power of reasoning expand under instruction.

Samuel Heinicke, the founder of deaf-and-dumb teaching in Germany, remarks:—"He (the deaf-mute) prefers keeping to his pantomime, which is simple and short, and comes to him fluently as a mother-tongue."[3] Schmalz says:—"Not less comprehensible are many signs which we indeed do not use in ordinary life, but which the deaf-and-dumb child uses, having no means of communicating with others but by signs. These signs consist principally in drawing in the air the shape of objects to be suggested to the mind, indicating their character, imitating the movement of the body in an action to be described, or the use of a thing, its origin, or any other of its notable peculiarities."[4] "With regard to signs," says Dr. Scott, of Exeter, "the (deaf-and-dumb) child will most likely have already fixed upon signs by which it names most of the objects given in the above lesson (pin, key, etc.), and which it uses in its intercourse with its friends. These signs had always better be retained (by the child's family), and if a word has not received such a sign, endeavour to get the child to fix upon one. It will do this most probably better than you."[5]

The Abbé Sicard, one of the first and most eminent of the men who have devoted their lives to the education and "humanizing" of these afflicted creatures, has much the same account to give. "It is not I," he says, "who am to invent these signs. I have only to set forth the theory of them under the dictation of their true inventors, those whose language consists of these signs. It is for the deaf-and-dumb to make them, and for me to tell how they are made. They must be drawn from the nature of the objects they are to represent. It is only the signs given by the mute himself to express the actions which he witnesses, and the objects which are brought before him, which can replace articulate language." Speaking of his celebrated deaf-and-dumb pupil, Massieu, he says:—"Thus, by a happy exchange, as I taught him the written signs of our language, Massieu taught me the mimic signs of his. . . . So it must be said that it is neither I nor my admirable

---

3 Heinicke, 'Beobachtungen über Stumme,' etc.; Hamburg, 1778, p. 56.

4 Schmalz, p. 267.

5 Scott, 'The Deaf and Dumb'; London, 1844, p. 84.

master (the Abbé de l'Epée) who are the inventors of the deaf-and-dumb language. And as a foreigner is not fit to teach a Frenchman French, so the speaking man has no business to meddle with the invention of signs, giving them abstract values."[6] All these are modern statements; but long before the days of Deaf-and-Dumb Institutions, Rabelais' sharp eye had noticed how natural and appropriate were the untaught signs made by born deaf-mutes. When Panurge is going to try by divination from signs what his fortune will be in married life, Pantagruel thus counsels him:—"Pourtant, vous fault choisir ung mut sourd de nature, affin que ses gestes vous soyent naifuement propheticques, non fainctz, fardez, ne affectez."

Nor are we obliged to depend upon the observations of ordinary speaking men for our knowledge of the way in which the gesture-language develops itself in the mind of the deaf-and-dumb. The educated deaf-mutes can tell us from their own experience how gesture-signs originate. The following account is given by Kruse, a deaf-mute himself, and a well-known teacher of deaf mutes, and author of several works of no small ability:—"Thus the deaf-and-dumb must have a language, without which no thought can be brought to pass. But here nature soon comes to his help. What strikes him most, or what . . . makes a distinction to him between one thing and another, such distinctive signs of objects are at once signs by which he knows these objects, and knows them again; they become tokens of things. And whilst he silently elaborates the signs he has found for single objects, that is, whilst he describes their forms for himself in the air, or imitates them in thought with hands, fingers, and gestures, he developes for himself suitable signs to represent ideas, which serve him as a means of fixing ideas of different kinds in his mind and recalling them to his memory. And thus he makes himself a language, the so-called gesture-language (*Geberden-sprache*) ; and with these few scanty and imperfect signs, a way for thought is already broken, and with his thought as it now opens out, the language cultivates and forms itself further and further."[7]

I will now give some account of the particular dialect (so to

6 Sicard, 'Cours d'Instruction d'un Sourd-muet'; Paris, 1803, pp. xlv. 18.

7 Kruse, 'Ueber Taubstummen,' etc.; Schleswig, 1853, p. 51.

speak) of the gesture-language, which is current in the Berlin Deaf-and-Dumb Institution.[8] I made a list of about 500 signs, taking them down from my teacher, Carl Wilke, who is himself deaf-and-dumb. They talk of 5000 signs being in common use there, but my list contains the most important. First, as to the signs themselves, the following, taken at random, will give an idea of the general principle on which all are formed.

To express the pronouns "I, thou, he," I push my forefinger against the pit of my stomach for "I;" push it towards the person addressed for "thou;" point with my thumb over my right shoulder for "he;" and so on.

When I hold my right hand flat with the palm down, at the level of my waist, and raise it towards the level of my shoulder, that signifies "great;" but if I depress it instead, it means "little."

The sign for "man" is the motion of taking off the hat; for "woman," the closed hand is laid upon the breast; for "child," the right elbow is dandled upon the left hand.

The adverb "hither" and verb "to come" have the same sign, beckoning with the finger towards oneself.

To hold the first two fingers apart, like a letter V, and dart the finger tips out from the eyes, is to "see." To touch the ear and tongue with the fore-finger, is to "hear" and to "taste." Whatever is to be pointed out, the fore-finger, so appropriately called "index," has to point out or indicate. . . .

To "speak" is to move the lips as in speaking (all the deaf-and-dumb are taught to speak in articulate words in the Berlin establishment), and to move the lips thus, while pointing with the fore-finger out from the mouth, is "name," or "to name," as though one should define it to "point out by speaking."

The outline of the shape of roof and walls done in the air with two hands is "house;" with a flat roof it is "room." To smell as at a flower, and then with the two hands make a horizontal circle before one, is "garden."

[8] Whether the "dialects" of the different deaf-and-dumb institutions have received any considerable proportion of natural signs from one another, as, for instance, by the spreading of the system of teaching from Paris, I am unable to say; but there is so much in each that differs from the others in detail, though not in principle, that they may, I think, be held as practically independent, except as regards grammatical signs.

To pull up a pinch of flesh from the back of one's hand is "flesh" or "meat." Make the steam curling up from it with the fore-finger, and it becomes "roast meat." Make a bird's bill with two fingers in front of one's lips and flap with the arms, and that means "goose"; put the first sign and these together, and we have "roast goose."

How natural all these imitative signs are. They want no elaborate explanation. To seize the most striking outline of an object, the principal movement of an action, is the whole secret, and this is what the rudest savage can do untaught, nay, what is more, can do better and more easily than the educated man. "None of my teachers here who can speak," said the Director of the Institution, "are very strong in the gesture-language. It is difficult for an educated speaking man to get the proficiency in it which a deaf-and-dumb child attains to almost without an effort. It is true that I can use it perfectly; but I have been here forty years, and I made it my business from the first to become thoroughly master of it. To be able to speak is an impediment, not an assistance, in acquiring the gesture-language. The habit of thinking in words, and translating these words into signs, is most difficult to shake off; but until this is done, it is hardly possible to place the signs in the logical sequence in which they arrange themselves in the mind of the deaf-mute."

As new things come under the notice of the deaf-and-dumb, of course new signs immediately come up for them. So to express "railway" and "locomotive," the left hand makes a chimney, and the steam curling almost horizontally out is imitated with the right fore-finger. The tips of the fingers of the half-closed hand coming towards one like rays of light, is "photograph."

But the casual observer, who should take down every sign he saw used in class by masters and pupils, as belonging to the natural gesture-language, would often get a very wrong idea of its nature. Teachers of the deaf-and-dumb have thought it advisable for practical purposes, not merely to use the independent development of the language of signs, but to add to it and patch it so as to make it more strictly equivalent to their own speech and writing. For this purpose signs have to be introduced for many words, of which the pupil mostly learns the meaning through their use in writing, and is taught to use the sign where he would use the word. Thus, the clenched fists, pushed forward with the thumbs up, mean "yet." To throw the fingers gently open from the temple means "when." To move the closed hands with the thumbs out, up and down upon one's waistcoat, is to "be." All these signs may, it is true, be based upon natural gestures. Dr. Scott, for instance, explains the sign "when" as formed in this way. But this kind of derivation does not give them a claim to be included in the pure gesture-language; and it really does not seem as though it would make much difference to the children if the signs for "when" were used for "yet," and so on.

The Abbé Sicard has left us a voluminous account of the sign-language he used, which may serve as an example of the curious hybrid systems which grow up in this way, by the grafting of the English, or French, or German grammar and dictionary on the gesture-language. Sicard was strongly impressed with the necessity of using the natural signs, and even his most arbitrary ones may have been based on such; but he had set himslf to make gestures do whatever words can do, and was thereby often driven to strange shifts. Yet he either drew so directly from his deaf-and-dumb scholars, or succeeded so well in learning to think in their way; that it is often very hard to say exactly where the influence of spoken or written language comes in. For instance, the deaf-mute borrows the signs of space, as we do similar words, to express notions of time; and Sicard, keeping to these real signs, and only using them with a degree of analysis which has hardly been attained to but by means of words, makes the present tense of his verb by indicating "here" with the two hands held out, palm downward, the past tense by the hand thrown back over the shoulder, "behind," the future by putting the hand out, "forward." But when he takes on his conjugation to such tenses as "I should have carried," he is merely translating words into more or less appropriate signs. Again, by the aid of two fore-fingers hooked together,—to express, I suppose, the notion of dependence or connection,—he distinguishes between *moi* and *me,* and by translating two abstract grammatical terms from words into signs, he introduces another conception quite foreign to the pure gesture-language. If something that has been signed is a substantive, he puts the right hand under the left, to show that it is that which stands underneath; while if it is an adjective, he puts the right hand on the top, to show that it is the quality which lies upon or is added to the substantive below.[9]

These partly artificial systems are probably very useful in teaching, but they are not the real gesture-language, and what is more, the foreign element so laboriously introduced seems to have little power of holding its ground there. So far as I can learn, few or none of the factitious grammatical signs will bear even the short journey from the schoolroom to the playground, where there is no longer any verb "to be," where the abstract conjunctions are unknown, and where mere position, quality, action, may serve to describe substantive and adjective alike.

At Berlin, as in all deaf-and-dumb institutions, there are numbers of signs which, though most natural in their character, would not be understood beyond the limits of the circle in which they are used. These are signs which indicate an object by some accidental peculiarity, and are rather epithets than names. My deaf-and-dumb teacher, for instance, was named among the children by the action of cutting off the left arm with the edge of the right hand; the reason of this sign was, not that there was anything peculiar about his arms, but that he came from Spandau, and it so happened that one of the children had been at Spandau, and had seen there a man with one arm; thence this epithet of "one-armed" came to be applied to all Spandauers, and to this one in particular. Again the Royal residence of Charlottenburg was named by taking up one's left knee and nursing it, in allusion apparently to the late king having been laid up with the gout there.

In like manner, the children preferred to indicate foreign countries by some characteristic epithet, to spelling out their names on their fingers. Thus England and Englishmen were aptly alluded to by the action of rowing a boat, while the signs of chopping off a head and strangling were used to describe France and Russia, in allusion to the deaths of Louis XVI and the Emperor Paul, events which seem to have struck the deaf-and-

9 Sicard, 'Théorie des Signes pour l'Instruction des Sourds-muets'; Paris, 1808, vol. ii. p. 562, etc. A really possible distinction appears in "lip," "red," *ante,* p. 11.

dumb children as the most remarkable in the history of the two countries. These signs are of much higher interest than the grammatical symbols, which can only be kept in use, so to speak, by main force, but these, too, never penetrate into the general body of the language, and are not even permanent in the place where they arise. They die out from one set of children to another, and new ones come up in their stead.

The gesture-language has no grammar, properly so called; it knows no inflections of any kind, any more than the Chinese. The same sign stands for "walk," "walkest," "walking," "walked," "walker." Adjectives and verbs are not easily distinguished by the deaf-and-dumb; "horse-black-handsome-trot-canter," would be the rough translation of the signs by which a deaf-mute would state that a handsome black horse trots and canters. Indeed, our elaborate systems of "parts of speech" are but little applicable to the gesture-language, though, as will be more fully said in another chapter, it may perhaps be possible to trace in spoken language a Dualism, in some measure resembling that of the gesture-language, with its two constituent parts, the bringing forward objects and actions in actual fact, and the mere suggestion of them by imitation.

It has however a syntax, which is worthy of careful examination. The syntax of speaking man differs according to the language he may learn, "equus niger," "a black horse"; "hominem amo," "j'aime l'homme." But the deaf-mute strings together the signs of the various ideas he wishes to connect, in what appears to be the natural order in which they follow one another in his mind, for it is the same among the mutes of different countries, and is wholly independent of the syntax which may happen to belong to the language of their speaking friends. For instance, their usual construction is not "black horse," but "horse black"; not "bring a black hat," but "hat black bring"; not "I am hungry, give me bread," but "hungry me bread give." The essential independence of the gesture-language may indeed be brought very clearly into view, by noticing that ordinary educated men, when they first begin to learn the language of signs, do not come naturally to the use of its proper syntax, but, by arranging their gestures in the order of the words they think in, make sentences which are unmeaning or misleading to a deaf-mute, unless he can reverse the process, by translating the gestures into words, and considering what such a written sentence would mean. Going once into a deaf-and-dumb school, and setting a boy to write words on the black board, I drew in the air the outline of a tent, and touched the inner part of my under-lip to indicate "red," and the boy wrote accordingly "a red tent." The teacher remarked that I did not seem to be quite a beginner in the sign-language, or I should have translated my English thought *verbatim*, and put the "red" first.

The fundamental principle which regulates the order of the deaf-mute's signs seems to be that enunciated by Schmalz, "that which seems to him the most important he always sets before the rest, and that which seems to him superfluous he leaves out. For instance, to say, 'My father gave me an apple,' he makes the sign for 'apple,' then that for 'father,' and that for 'I,' without adding that for 'give.' "[10] The following remarks, sent to me by Dr. Scott, seem to agree with this view. "With regard to the two sentences you give (I struck Tom with a stick, Tom struck me with a stick), the sequence in the introduction of the particular parts would, in some measure, depend on the part that most attention was wished to be drawn towards. If a mere telling of the fact was required, my opinion is that it would be arranged so, 'I-Tom-struck-a-stick,' and the passive form in a similar manner, with the change of Tom first. But these sentences are not generally said by the deaf-and-dumb without their having been interested in the fact, and then, in coming to tell of them, they first give that part they are most anxious to impress upon their hearer. Thus if a boy had struck another boy, and the injured party came to tell us; if he was desirous to impress us with the idea that a particular boy did it, he would point to the boy first. But if he was anxious to draw attention to his own suffering, rather than to the person by whom it was caused, he would point to himself and make the sign of striking, and then point to the boy; or if he was wishful to draw attention to the cause of his suffering, he might sign the striking first, and then tell afterwards by whom it was done."

*   *   *   *

10 Schmalz, p. 274.

A look of inquiry converts an assertion into a question, and fully serves to make the difference between "The master is come," and "Is the master come?" The interrogative pronouns, "who?" "what?" are made by looking or pointing about in an inquiring manner; in fact, by a number of unsuccessful attempts to say, "he," "that." The deaf-and-dumb child's ways of asking, "Who has beaten you?" would be, "You beaten; who was it?" Though it is possible to render a great mass of simple statements or questions, almost gesture for word, the concretism of thought which belongs to the deaf-mute whose mind has not been much developed by the use of written language, and even to the educated one when he is thinking and uttering his thoughts in his native signs, commonly requires more complex phrases to be re-cast. A question so common amongst us as, "What is the matter with you?" would be put, "You crying? you been beaten?" and so on. The deaf-and-dumb child does not ask, "What did you have for dinner yesterday?" but "Did you have soup? did you have porridge?" and so forth. A conjunctive sentence he expresses by an alternative or contrast; "I should be punished if I were lazy and naughty," would be put, "I lazy, naughty, no!—lazy, naughty, I punished, yes!" Obligation may be expressed in a similar way; "I must love and honour my teacher," may be put, "teacher, I beat, deceive, scold, no!—I love, honour, yes!" As Steinthal says in his admirable essay, it is only the certainty which speech gives to a man's mind in holding fast ideas in all their relations, which brings him to the shorter course of expressing only the positive side of the idea, and dropping the negative.[11]

What is expressed by the genitive case, or a corresponding preposition, may have a distinct sign of holding in the gesture-language. The three signs to express "the gardener's knife," might be the knife, the garden, and the action of grasping the knife, pressing it to his breast, putting it into his pocket, or something of the kind. But the mere putting together of the possessor and the possessed may answer the purpose, as is well shown by the way in which a deaf-and-dumb man designates his wife's daughter's husband and children in making his will by signs. The

11 Kruse, p. 56, etc. Steinthal, 'Spr. der T.,' p. 923.

following account is taken from the "Justice of the Peace," October 1, 1864:—

John Geale, of Yateley, yeoman, deaf, dumb, and unable to read or write, died leaving a will which he had executed by putting his mark to it. Probate of this will was refused by Sir J. P. Wilde, Judge of the Court of Probate, on the ground that there was no sufficient evidence of the testator's understanding and assenting to its provisions. At a later date, Dr. Spinks renewed the motion upon the following joint affidavit of the widow and the attesting witnesses:—"The signs by which deceased informed us that the will was the instrument which was to deal with his property upon his death, and that his wife was to have all his property after his death in case she survived him, were in substance, so far as we are able to describe the same in writing, as follows, viz.:—The said John Geale first pointed to the said will itself, then he pointed to himself, and then he laid the side of his head upon the palm of his right hand with his eyes closed, and then lowered his right hand towards the ground, the palm of the same hand being upwards. These latter signs were the usual signs by which he referred to his own death or the decease of some one else. He then touched his trousers pocket (which was the usual sign by which he referred to his money) , then he looked all round and simultaneously raised his arms with a sweeping motion all round (which were the usual signs by which he referred to all his property or all things) . He then pointed to his wife, and afterwards touched the ring-finger of his left hand, and then placed his right hand across his left arm at the elbow, which latter signs were the usual signs by which he referred to his wife. The signs by which the said testator informed us that his property was to go to his wife's daughter, in case his wife died in his lifetime, were . . . as follows:—He first referred to his property as before, he then touched himself, and pointed to the ring-finger of his left hand, and crossed his arm as before (which indicated his wife) ; he then laid the side of his head on the palm of his right hand (with his eyes closed) , which indicated his wife's death; he then again, after pointing to his wife's daughter, who was present when the said will was executed, pointed to the ring-finger of his left hand, and then placed his right hand across his left arm at the elbow as before. He then put his forefinger to his mouth, and immediately touched his breast, and moved his arms in such a manner as to indicate a child, which were his usual signs for indicating his wife's daughter. He always indicated a female by crossing his arm, and a male person by crossing his wrist. The signs by which the said testator informed us that his property was to go to William Wigg (his wife's daughter's husband), in case his wife's daughter died in his lifetime, were . . . as follows:—He repeated the signs indicating his property and his wife's daughter, then laid the side of his head on the palm of his right hand with his eyes closed, and lowered his hand towards the ground as before (which meant her death); he then again repeated the signs indicating his wife's daughter, and crossed his left arm at the wrist with his right hand, which meant her husband, the said William Wigg. He also communicated to us by signs, that the said William Wigg resided in London. The said William Wigg is in the employ of and superintends the goods department of the North-Western Railway Company at Camden Town. The signs by which the said testator informed us that his property was to go to the children of his wife's daughter and son-in-law, in case they both died in his lifetime, were . . . as follows, namely:—He repeated the signs indicating the said William Wigg and his wife, and their death before him, and then placed his right hand open a short distance from the ground, and raised it by degrees, and as if by steps, which were his usual signs for pointing out their children, and then swept his hand round with a sweeping motion, which indicated that they were all to be brought in. The said testator always took great notice of the said children, and was very fond of them. After the testator had in manner aforesaid expressed to us what he intended to do by his said will, the said R. T. Dunning, by means of the before-mentioned signs, and by other motions and signs by which we were accustomed to converse with him, informed the said testator what were the contents and effect of the said will."

Sir J. P. Wilde granted the motion.

The deaf-mute commonly expresses past and future time in a concrete form, or by implication. To say "I have been ill," he may convey the idea of his being ill by looking as though he were so, pressing in his cheeks with thumb and finger to give himself a lantern-jawed look, putting his hand to his head, etc., and he may show that this event was "a day behind," "a week behind," that is to say yesterday or a week ago, and so he may say that he is going home "a week forward." That he would of himself make the abstract past or future, as the Abbé Sicard has it, by throwing the hand back or forward, without specifying any particular period, I am not prepared to say. The difficulty may be avoided by signing "my brother sick done" for "my brother has been sick," as to imply that the sickness is a thing finished and done with. Or the expression of face and gesture may often tell what is meant. The expression with which the sign for eating dinner is made will tell whether the speaker has had his dinner or is going to it. When anything pleasant or painful is mentioned by signs, the look will commonly convey the distinction between remembrance of what is past, and anticipation of what is to come.

Though the deaf-and-dumb has, much as we have, an idea of the connexion of cause and effect, he has not, I think, any direct means of distinguishing causation from mere sequence or simultaneity, except a way of showing by his manner that two events belong to one another, which can hardly be described in words, though if he sees further explanation necessary, he has no difficulty in giving it. Thus he would express the statement that a man died of drinking, by saying that he "died, drank, drank, drank." If the inquiry were made, "died, did he?" he could put the causation beyond doubt by answering, "yes, he drank, and drank, and drank!" If he wished to say that the gardener had poisoned himself, the order of his signs would be, "gardener dead, medicine bad drank."

To "make" is too abstract an idea for the deaf-mute; to show that the tailor makes the coat, or that the carpenter makes the table, he would represent the tailor sewing the coat, and the carpenter sawing and planing the table. Such a proposition as "Rain makes the land fruitful" would not come into his way of thinking; "rain falls, plants grow," would be his pictorial expression.[12]

As an example of the structure of the gesture-language, I give the words roughly corresponding to the signs by which the Lord's

12 Steinthal, 'Spr. der T.,' p. 923.

Prayer is acted every morning at the Edinburgh Institution. They were carefully written down for me by the Director, and I made notes of the signs by which the various ideas were expressed in this school. "Father" is represented in the prayer as "man old," though in ordinary matters he is generally "the man who shaves himself;" "name" is, as I have seen it elsewhere, touching the forehead and imitating the action of spelling on the fingers, as to say, "the spelling one is known by." To "hallow" is to "speak good of" ("good" being expressed by the thumb, while "bad" is represented by the little finger, two signs of which the meaning lies in the contrast of the larger and more powerful thumb with the smaller and less important little finger). "Kingdom" is shown by the sign for "crown"; "will" by placing the hand on the stom-ach, in accordance with the natural and wide-spread theory that desire and passion are located there, to which theory such expres-sions belong as "to have no stomach to it." "Done" is "worked," shown by hands as working. The phrase "on earth as it is in heaven" was, I believe, put by signs for "on earth" and "in heav-en," and then by putting out the two forefingers side by side, the sign for sameness and similarity all the world over, so that the whole would stand "earth on, heaven in, just the same." "Trespass" is "doing bad"; to "forgive" is to rub out, as from a slate; "temptation" is plucking one by the coat, as to lead him slily into mischief. The alternative "but" is made with the two fore-fingers, not alongside of one another as in "like," but op-posed point to point, Sicard's sign for "against." "Deliver" is to "pluck out," "glory" is "glittering," "for ever" is shown by mak-ing the fore-fingers held horizontally turn round and round one another.

The order of the signs is much as follows:—"Father our, heaven in—name thy hallowed—kingdom thy come—will thy done—earth on, heaven in, as. Bread give us daily—trespasses our forgive us, them trespass against us, forgive, as. Temptation lead not—but evil deliver from—kingdom power glory thine for ever."

When I write down descriptions in words of the deaf-and-dumb signs, they seem bald and weak, but it must be remembered that I can only write down the skeletons of them. To see them is something very different, for these dry bones have to be covered with flesh. Not the face only, but the whole body joins in giving expression to the sign. Nor are the sober, restrained looks and gestures to which we are accustomed in our daily life sufficient for this. He who talks to the deaf-and-dumb in their own language, must throw off the rigid covering that the Englishman wears over his face like a tragic mask, that never changes its expression while love and hate, joy and sorrow, come out from behind it.

Religious service is performed in signs in many deaf-and-dumb schools. In the Berlin Institution, the simple Lutheran service, a prayer, the gospel for the day, and a sermon, is acted every Sunday morning in the gesture-language for the children in the school and the deaf-and-dumb inhabitants of the city, and it is a very remarkable sight. No one could see the parable of the man who left the ninety and nine sheep in the wilderness, and went after that which was lost, or of the woman who lost the one piece of silver, performed in expressive pantomime by a master in the art, without acknowledging that for telling a simple story and making simple comments on it, spoken language stands far behind acting. The spoken narrative must lose the sudden anxiety of the shepherd when he counts his flock and finds a sheep wanting, his hurried penning up the rest, his running up hill and down dale, and spying backwards and forwards, his face lighting up when he catches sight of the missing sheep in the distance, his carrying it home in his arms, hugging it as he goes. We hear these stories read as though they were lists of generations of antediluvian patriarchs. The deaf-and-dumb pantomime calls to mind the "action, action, action!" of Demosthenes.

CHAPTER III

THE GESTURE-LANGUAGE (*Continued*)

There is another department of the gesture-language which has reached nearly as high a development as that in use among the deaf-mutes. Men who do not know one another's language are to each other as though they were dumb. Thus Sophocles uses αγλωσσος, "tongueless," for "barbarian," as contrasted with "Greek"; and the Russians, to this day, call their neighbours the Germans, "Njemez,"—that is, speechless, *njemou* meaning dumb. When men who are thus dumb to one another have to communicate without an interpreter, they adopt all over the world the very same method of communication by signs, which is the natural language of the deaf-mutes.

Alexander von Humboldt has left on record, in the following passage, his experiences of the gesture-language among the Indians of the Orinoco, in districts where it often happens that small, isolated tribes speak languages of which even their nearest neighbours can hardly understand a word:—" 'After you leave my mission,' said the good monk of Uruana, 'you will travel like mutes.' This prediction was almost accomplished; and, not to lose all the advantage that is to be had from intercourse even with the most brutalized Indians, we have sometimes preferred the language of signs. As soon as the native sees that you do not care to employ an interpreter, as soon as you ask him direct questions, pointing the object out to him, he comes out of his habitual apathy, and displays a rare intelligence in making himself understood. He varies his signs, pronounces his words slowly, and repeats them without being asked. His *amour-propre* seems flattered by the consequence you accord to him by letting him instruct you. This facility of making himself understood is above all remarkable in the independent Indian, and in the Christian missions I should recommend the traveller to address himself in preference to those of the natives who have been but lately *re-*

duced, or who go back from time to time to the forest to enjoy their ancient liberty."[1]

It is well known that the Indians of North America, whose nomad habits and immense variety of languages must continually make it needful for them to communicate with tribes whose language they cannot speak, carry the gesture-language to a high degree of perfection, and the same signs serve as a medium of converse from Hudson's Bay to the Gulf of Mexico. Several writers make mention of this "Indian pantomime," and it has been carefully described in the account of Major Long's expedition, and more recently by Captain Burton.[2] The latter traveller considers it to be a mixture of natural and conventional signs, but so far as I can judge from the one hundred and fifty or so which he describes, and those I find mentioned elsewhere, I do not believe that there is a really arbitrary sign among them. There are only about half-a-dozen of which the meaning is not at once evident, and even these appear on close inspection to be natural signs, perhaps a little abbreviated or conventionalized. I am sure that a skilled deaf-and-dumb talker would understand an Indian interpreter, and be himself understood at first sight, with scarcely any difficulty. The Indian pantomime and the gesture-language of the deaf-and-dumb are but different dialects of the same language of nature. Burton says that an interpreter who knows all the signs is preferred by the whites even to a good speaker. "A story is told of a man, who, being sent among the Cheyennes to qualify himself for interpreting, returned in a week and proved his competence: all that he did, however, was to go through the usual pantomime with a running accompaniment of grunts."

In the Indian pantomime, actions and objects are expressed very much as a deaf-mute would show them. The action of beckoning towards oneself represents to "come"; darting the two first

1 Humboldt and Bonpland, 'Voyage'; Paris, 1814, etc. vol. ii. p. 278.

2 Edwin James, 'Major Stephen H. Long's Exped. Rocky Moun.'; Philadelphia, 1823, i. p. 378, etc. Capt. R. F. Burton, 'The City of the Saints,' London, 1861, p. 150, etc. See also Prinz Maximilian von Wied-Neuwied, 'Voyage dans l'Intérieur de l'Amérique du Nord'; Paris, 1840–3, vol. iii. p. 389. Buschmann, 'Spuren der Azt. Spr., etc.'; (Abh. der K. Akad. der Wissensch. 1854) Berlin, 1859, p. 641.

fingers from the eyes is to "see"; describing in the air the form of the pipe and the curling smoke is to "smoke"; thrusting the hand under the clothing of the left breast is to "hide, put away, keep secret." "Enough to eat" is shown by an imitation of eating, and the forefingers and thumb forming a C, with the points towards the body, are raised upward as far as the neck; "fear," by putting the hands to the lower ribs, and showing how the heart flutters and seems to rise to the throat; "book," by holding the palms together before the face, opening and reading, quite in deaf-and-dumb fashion, and as the Moslems often do while they are reciting prayers and chapters of the Koran.

One of our accounts says that "fire" is represented by the Indian by blowing it and warming his hands at it; the other that flames are imitated with the fingers. The latter sign was in use at Berlin, but I noticed that the children in another school did not understand it till the sign of blowing was added. The Indian and the deaf-mute indicate "rain" by the same sign, bringing the tips of the fingers of the partly-closed hand downward, like rain falling from the clouds, and the Indian makes the same sign do duty for "year," counting years by annual rains. The Indian indicates "stone," if light, by picking it up, if heavy, by dropping it. The deaf-mute taps his teeth with his finger-nail to show that it is something hard, and then makes the gesture of flinging it. The Indian sign for mounting a horse is to make a pair of legs of the two first fingers of the right hand, and to straddle them across the left fore-finger; a similar sign among the deaf-and-dumb means to "ride."

Among the Indians the sign for "brother" or "sister" is, according to Burton, to put the two first finger-tips (that is, I suppose, the fore-fingers of both hands) into the mouth, to show that both fed from the same breast; the deaf-mute makes the mere sign of likeness or equality suffice, holding out the forefingers of both hands close together, a sign which, according to James, also does duty to indicate "husband" or "companion." This sign of the two forefingers is understood everywhere, and some very curious instances of its use in remote parts of the world are given by Marsh[3] in illustration of Fluellen's "But 'tis all one, 'tis so like

3 Marsh, 'Lectures on the English Language'; London, 1862, p. 486.

as my fingers is to my fingers." It belongs, too, to the sign-language of the Cistercian monks.

Animals are represented in the Indian pantomime very much as the deaf-and-dumb would represent them, by signs character-izing their peculiar ears, horns, etc., and their movements. Thus the sign for "stag" among the deaf-and-dumb, namely, the thumbs to both temples, and the fingers widely spread out, is almost identical with the Indian gesture. For the dog, however, the Indians have a remarkable sign, which consists in trailing the two first fingers of the right hand, as if they were poles dragged along the ground. Before the Indians had horses, the dogs were trained to drag the lodge-poles on the march in this way, and in Catlin's time the work was in several tribes divided between the dogs and horses; but it appears that in tribes where the trailing is now done by horses only, the sign for "dog" derived from the old custom is still kept up.

One of the Indian signs is curious as having reflected itself in the spoken language of the country. "Water" is represented by an imitation of scooping up water with the hand and drinking out of it, and "river" by making this sign, and then waving the palms of the hands outward, to denote an extended surface. It is evident that the first part of the sign is translated in the western Americanism which speaks of a river as a "drink," and of the Mississippi, *par excellence,* as the "Big Drink."[4] It need hardly be said that spoken language is full of such translations from gestures, as when one is said to wink at another's faults, an ex-pression which shows us the act of winking accepted as a gesture-sign, meaning to pretend not to see. But the Americanism is interesting as being caught so near its source.

I noted down a few signs from Burton as not self-evident, but it will be seen that they are all to be explained. They are, "yes," wave the hands straightforward from the face; "no," wave the hand from right to left as if motioning away. These signs corre-spond with the general practice of mankind, to nod for "yes," and shake the head for "no." The idea conveyed by nodding seems to correspond with the deaf-and-dumb sign for "truth,"

[4] J. R. Bartlett, 'Dictionary of Americanisms,' 2nd edit., Boston, 1859, *s.v.* "Drink."

made by moving the finger straightforward from the lips, apparently with the sense of "straightforward speaking," while the finger is moved to one side to express "lie," as "sideways speaking." The understanding of nodding and shaking the head as signs of assent and denial appears to belong to uneducated deaf-and-dumb children, and even to those who are only one degree higher than idiots. In a very remarkable dissertation on the art of thrusting knowledge into the minds of such children, Schmalz assumes that they can always make and understand these signs.[5] It is true they may have learnt them from the people who take care of them.

This explanation is, however, somewhat complicated by the Indian signs for "truth," and "lie," given by Burton, who says that the fore-finger extended from the mouth means to "tell truth," "one word"; but two fingers mean to "tell lies," double tongue." So to move two fingers before the left breast means, "I don't know," that is to say, "I have two hearts." I found that deaf-and-dumb children understood this Indian sign for "lie" quite as well as their own.

"Good," wave the hand from the mouth, extending the thumb from the index, and closing the other three fingers. This is like kissing the hand as a salutation, or what children call "blowing a kiss," and it is clearly a natural sign, as it is recognized by the deaf-and-dumb language. Dr. James gives the Indian sign as waving the hand with the back upward, in a horizontal curve outwards, the well-known gesture of benediction. At Berlin, a gesture like that of patting a child on the head, accompanied, as of course all these signs are, with an approving smile, is in use. Possibly the ideas of stroking or patting may lie at the bottom of all these signs of approving and blessing.

"Think," pass the fore-finger sharply across the breast from right to left, meaning of course that a thought passes through one's heart.

"Trade, exchange, swop," cross the fore-fingers of both hands before the breast. This sign is also used, Captain Burton says, to denote Americans, or indeed any white men, who are generally called by the Indians west of the Rocky Mountains, "shwop,"

5 Schmalz, pp. 267–277. See Wedgwood, p. 91.

from their trading propensities. As given by Burton, the sign is hardly intelligible. But Dr. James describes the gesture of which this is a sort of abridgment, which consists in holding up the two fore-fingers, and passing them by each other transversely in front of the breast so that they change places, and nothing could be clearer than this.

The sign in the Berlin gesture-language for "day" is made by opening out the palms of the hands. I supposed it to be an arbitrary and meaningless sign, till I found the Indian sign for "this morning" to consist in the same gesture. It refers, perhaps to awaking from sleep, or to the opening out of the day.

As a means of communication, there is no doubt that the Indian pantomime is not merely capable of expressing a few simple and ordinary notions, but that, to the uncultured savage, with his few and material ideas, it is a very fair substitute for his scanty vocabulary. Stansbury mentions a discourse delivered in this way in his presence, which lasted for some hours occupied in continuous narration. The only specimen of a connected story I have met with is a hunter's simple history of his day's sport, as Captain Burton thinks that an Indian would render it in signs. The story to be told is as follows:—"Early this morning, I mounted my horse, rode off at a gallop, traversed a kanyon or ravine, then over a mountain to a plain where there was no water, sighted bison, followed them, killed three of them, skinned them, packed the flesh upon my pony, remounted, and returned home." The arrangement of the signs described is as follows:— I—this morning—early—mounted my horse—galloped—a kanyon— crossed—a mountain—a plain—drink—no!—sighted—bison—killed— three—skinned—packed flesh—mounted—hither." There is perhaps nothing which would strike a deaf-and-dumb man as peculiar in the sequence of these signs; but it would be desirable for a real discourse, delivered by an Indian in signs, to be taken down, especially if its contents were of a more complex nature.

Among the Cistercian monks there exists, or existed, a gesture-language. As a part of their dismal system of mortifying the deeds of the body, they held speech, except in religious exercises, to be sinful. But for certain purposes relating to the vile material life that they could not quite shake off, communication among the brethren was necessary, so the difficulty was met by the use of pantomimic signs. Two of their written lists or dictionaries are printed in the collected edition of Leibnitz's works,[6] one in Latin, the other in Low German; they are not identical, but appear to be mostly or altogether derived from a list drawn up by authority.

A great part of the Cistercian gesture-signs are either just what the deaf-and-dumb would make, or are so natural that they would at once understand them. Thus, to make a roof with the fingers is "house;" to grind the fists together is "corn;" to "sing" is indicated by beating time; to "bathe" is to imitate washing the breast with the hollow of the hand; "candle," or "fire," is shown by holding up the fore-finger and blowing it out like a candle; a "goat" is indicated by the fingers hanging from the chin like a beard; "salt," by taking an imaginary pinch and sprinkling it; "butter," by the action of spreading it in the palm of the hand. The deaf-and-dumb sign used at Berlin and other places to indicate "time" by drawing the tip of the fore-finger up the arm, is in the Cistercian list "a year;" it is Sicard's sign for "long," and the idea it conveys is plainly that of "a length" transferred from space to time. To "go" is to make the two first fingers walk hanging in the air (Hengestu se dahl und rörest se, betekend *Gahen*), while the universal sign of the two fore-fingers stands for "like" (Hölstu se even thosamen, dat betekent *like*). The sign for "beer" is to put the hand before the face and blow into it, as if blowing off the froth (Thustu de hand vor dem anschlahe dat du darin pustest, dat bedüdt *gut Bier*). Wiping your mouth with the whole hand upwards (cum omnibus digitis terge buccam sursum), means a country clown (rusticus).

To put the fore-finger against the closed lips is "silence," but the finger put in the mouth means a "child." These are two very natural and distinct signs; but then the finger to the lips for "silence" may serve also quite fitly to show that a child so represented is an *infant*, that is, that it cannot speak. The confusion of the signs of "childhood" and "silence" once led to a curious misunderstanding. The infant Horus, god of the dawn, was appropriately represented by the Egyptians as a child with his fingers to his lips, and his name as written in the hieroglyphics (Fig. 1)

6 Leibnitz, Opera Omnia, ed. Dutens; Geneva, 1768, vol. vi. part ii. p. 207, etc.

may be read Har- (p) -chrot, "Horus- (the) -son."[7] The Greeks mistook the meaning of the gesture, and (as it seems) Grecizing this name into Harpokrates, adopted him as the god of silence.

To conclude, the Cistercian lists contain a number of signs which at first sight seem conventional, but yet a meaning may be discerned in most or all of them. Thus, it seems foolish to make two fingers at the right side of one's nose stand for "friend;" but when we see that placed on the left side, they stand for "enemy," it becomes clear that it is the opposition of right and left that is meant. So the little finger to the tip of the nose means "fool," which seemingly poor sign is explained by the fore-finger being put there for "wise man." The fact of such a contrast as wise and foolish being made between the forefinger and the little finger, corresponds with the use of the thumb and little finger for "good"

FIG. 1

and "bad" by the deaf-and-dumb, and makes it likely that both pairs of signs may be natural, and independent of one another. The sign of grasping the nose with the crooked fore-finger for "wine," suggests that the thought of a jolly red nose was present even in so unlikely a place. The sign for "the devil," gripping one's chin with all five fingers, shows the enemy seizing a victim. In a mediaeval picture, an angel may be seen taking a man by the chin with one hand, and pointing up to heaven with the other. Thus, in a Hindoo tale, Old Age in person comes to claim his own. "In time then, when I had grown grey with years, Old Age took me by the chin, and in his love to me said kindly, 'My son, what doest thou yet in the house?' "[8]

[7] Coptic *khroti* (ni) = filii, liberi, *hroti* = cognatus, filius. Old Eg. in Rosetta Ins. Compare S. Sharpe, Hist. of Egypt, 4th ed. vol. ii. p. 148. Wilkinson, 'Popular Account of the Ancient Egyptians'; London, 1854 vol. ii. p. 182.

[8] 'Mährchensammlung des Somadeva Bhatta' (trans. by Dr. H. Brockhaus); Leipzig, 1843, ii. p. 96.

There is, yet another development of the gesture-language to be noticed, the stage performances of the professional mimics of Greece and Rome, the pantomime *par excellence.* To judge by two well-known anecdotes, the old mimes had brought their art to great perfection. Macrobius says it was a well-known fact that Cicero used to try with Roscius the actor, which of them could express a sentiment in the greater variety of ways, the player by mimicry or the orator by speech, and that these experiments gave Roscius such confidence in his art, that he wrote a book comparing oratory with acting.[9] Lucian tells a story of a certain barbarian prince of Pontus, who was at Nero's court, and saw a pantomime performed so well, that though he could not understand the songs which the player was accompanying with his gestures, he could follow the performance from the acting alone. When Nero afterwards asked the prince to choose what he would have for a present, he begged to have the player given to him, saying that it was difficult to get interpreters to communicate with some of the tribes in his neighbourhood who spoke different languages, but that this man would answer the purpose perfectly.[10]

It would seem from these stories that the ancient pantomimes generally used gestures so natural that their meaning was self-evident, but a remark of St. Augustine's intimates that signs understood only by regular playgoers were also used. "For all those things which are valid among men, because it pleases them to agree that they shall be so, are human institutions. . . . So if the signs which mimes make in their performances had their meaning from nature, and not from the agreement and ordinance of men, the crier in old times would not have given out to the Carthaginians at the play what the actor meant to express, a thing still remembered by many old men by whom we use to hear it said; which is readily to be believed, seeing that even now, if any one who is not learned in such follies goes into the theatre, unless some one else tells him what the signs mean, he can make nothing of them. All men, indeed, desire a certain likeness in sign-making, that the signs should be as like as may be to that which is signi-

9 Macrob. Saturn. lib. ii. c. x.

10 Lucian. De Saltatione, 64.

fied; but seeing that things may be like one another in many ways, such signs are not constant among men, unless by common consent."[11]

Knowing what we do of mimic performances from other sources, we can, I think, only understand by this that natural gestures were very commonly conventionalized and abridged to save time and trouble, and not that arbitrary signs were used; and such abridgments, like the simplified sign for trading or swopping among the Indians, as well as the whole class of epithets and allusions which would grow up among mimics addressing their regular set of playgoers, would not be intelligible to a stranger. Christians, of course, did not frequent such performances in St. Augustine's time, but looked upon them as utterly abominable and devilish; nor can we accuse them of want of charity for this, when we consider the class of scenes that were commonly chosen for representation.

There seem to have been written lists of signs used to learn from, which are now lost.[12] The mimic, it should be observed, had not the same difficulties to contend with as an Indian interpreter. In the first place, the stories represented were generally mythological, very usually love-passages of the gods and heroes, with which the whole audience was perfectly familiar; and, moreover, appropriate words were commonly sung while the mimic acted, so that he could apply all his skill to giving artistic illustrations of the tale as it went on. The pantomimic performances of Southern Europe may be taken as representing in some degree the ancient art, but it is likely that the mimicry in the modern ballet and the Eastern pantomimic plays falls much below the classical standard of excellence.

I have now noticed what I venture to call the principal dialects of the gesture-language. It is fit, however, that, gesture-signs having been spoken of as forming a complete and independent language by themselves, something should be said of their use as an accompaniment to spoken language. We in England make comparatively little use of these signs, but they have been and are in use in all quarters of the world as highly important aids to con-

11 Aug. Doct. Chr. ii. 25.

12 Grysar, in Ersch and Gruber, art. 'Pantomimische Kunst der Alten.'

versation. Thus, Captain Cook says of the Tahitians, after mentioning their habit of counting upon their fingers, that "in other instances, we observed that, when they were conversing with each other, they joined signs to their words, which were so expressive that a stranger might easily apprehend their meaning;"[13] and Charlevoix describes, in almost the same words, the expressive pantomime with which an Indian orator accompanied his discourse.[14]

Gesticulation goes along with speech, to explain and emphasize it, among all mankind. Savage and half-civilized races accompany their talk with expressive pantomime much more than nations of higher culture. The continual gesticulation of Hindoos, Arabs, Greeks, as contrasted with the more northern nations of Europe, strikes every traveller who sees them; and the colloquial pantomime of Naples is the subject of a special treatise.[15] But we cannot lay down a rule that gesticulation decreases as civilization advances, and say, for instance, that a Southern Frenchman, because his talk is illustrated with gestures, as a book with pictures, is less civilized than a German or an Englishman.

We English are perhaps poorer in the gesture-language than any other people in the world. We use a form of words to denote what a gesture or a tone would express. Perhaps it is because we read and write so much, and have come to think and talk as we should write, and so let fall those aids to speech which cannot be carried into the written language.

The few gesture-signs which are in common use among ourselves are by no means unworthy of examination; but we have lived for so many centuries in a highly artificial state of society, that some of them cannot be interpreted with any certainty, and the most that we can do is to make a good guess at their original meaning. Some, it is true, such as beckoning or motioning away with the hand, shaking the fist, etc., carry their explanation with them; and others may be plausibly explained by a comparison with analogous signs used by speaking men in other parts of the world, and by the deaf-and-dumb. Thus, the sign of "snapping

13 Cook, First Voyage, in Hawkesworth's Voyages; London, 1773, vol. ii. p. 228.

14 Charlevoix, vol. i. p. 413.

15 Wiseman, 'Essays'; London, 1853, vol. iii. p. 531.

one's fingers" is not very intelligible as we generally see it; but when we notice that the same sign made quite gently, as if rolling some tiny object away between the finger and thumb, or the sign of flipping it away with the thumb-nail and fore-finger, are usual and well-understood deaf-and-dumb gestures, denoting anything tiny, insignificant, contemptible, it seems as though we had exaggerated and conventionalized a perfectly natural action so as to lose sight of its original meaning. There is a curious mention of this gesture by Strabo. At Anchiale, he writes, Aristobulus says there is a monument to Sardanapalus, and a stone statue of him as if snapping his fingers, and this inscription in Assyrian letters: —"Sardanapallus, the son of Anacyndaraxes, built in one day Anchiale and Tarsus. Eat, drink, play; the rest is not worth *that!*"[16]

Shaking hands is not a custom which belongs naturally to all mankind, and we may sometimes trace its introduction into countries where it was before unknown. The Fijians, for instance, who used to salute by smelling or sniffing at one another, have learnt to shake hands from the missionaries.[17] The Wa-nika, near Mombaz, grasp hands; but they use the Moslem variety of the gesture, which is to press the thumbs against one another as well,[18] and this makes it all but certain that the practice is one of the many effects of Moslem influence in East Africa.

It is commonly thought that the Red Indians adopted the custom of shaking hands from the white men.[19] This may be true; but there is reason to suppose that the expression of alliance or friendship by clasping hands was already familiar to them, so that they would readily adopt it as a form of salutation, if they had not used it so before the arrival of the Europeans. More than a century ago, Charlevoix noticed in the Indian picture-writing the expression of alliance by the figure of two men holding each

[16] Strabo, xiv. 5, 9.

[17] Rev. Thos. Williams, 'Fiji and the Fijians,' 2nd ed.; London, 1860, vol. i. p. 153.

[18] Krapf, 'Travels, etc., in East Africa'; London, 1860, p. 138.

[19] H. R. Schoolcraft, 'Historical and Statistical Information respecting the History, etc., of the Indian Tribes of the U.S.'; Philadelphia, 1851, etc., part iii. pp. 212, 244. Burton, 'City of the Saints,' p. 144. But see also Schoolcraft, part iii. p. 263.

other by one hand, while each grasped a calumet in the other hand.[20] In one of the Indian pictures given by Schoolcraft, close affection is represented by two bodies united by a single arm (see Fig. 6) ; and in a pictorial message sent from an Indian tribe to the President of the United States, an eagle, which represents a chief, is holding out a hand to the President, who also holds out a hand.[21] The last of these pictured signs may be perhaps ascribed to European influence, but hardly the first two.

We could scarcely find a better illustration of the meaning of the gesture of joining hands than in its use as a sign of the marriage contract. One of the ceremonies of a Moslem wedding consists in the bridegroom and the bride's proxy sitting upon the ground, face to face, with one knee on the ground, and grasping each other's right hands, raising the thumbs and pressing them against each other,[22] or in the almost identical ceremony in the Pacific Islands, in which the bride and bridegroom are placed on a large white cloth, spread on the pavement of a marae, and join hands.[23] This as evidently means that the man and wife are joined together, as the corresponding ceremony in the ancient Mexican and the modern Hindu wedding, in which the clothes of the parties are tied together in a knot. Among our own Aryan race, the taking hands was a usual ceremony in marriage in the Vedic period.[24] The idea which shaking hands was originally intended to convey, was clearly that of fastening together in peace and friendship; and the same thought appears in the probable etymology of *peace, pax,* Sanskrit *pac,* to bind, and in *league* from *ligare.*

Cowering or crouching is so natural an expression of fear or inability to resist, that it belongs to the brutes as well as to man. Among ourselves this natural sign of submission is generally used in the modified forms of bowing and kneeling; but the analogous gestures found in different countries not only give us the intermediate stages between an actual prostration and a slight bow,

20 Charlevoix, vol. v. p. 440.

21 Schoolcraft, part i. pp. 403, 418.

22 E. W. Lane, 'Modern Egyptians'; London, 1837, vol. i. p. 219.

23 Rev. W. Ellis, 'Polynesian Researches'; London, 1830, vol. ii. p. 569.

24 Ad. Pictet, 'Origines Indo-Européennes'; Paris, 1859–63, part ii. p. 336.

but also a set of gestures and ceremonies which are merely suggestive of a prostration which is not actually performed. The extreme act of lying with the face in the dust is not only usual in China, Siam, etc., but even in Siberia the peasant grovels on the ground and kisses the dust before a man of rank. The Arab only suggests such a humiliation by bending his hand to the ground and then putting it to his lips and forehead—a gesture almost identical with that of the ancient Mexican, who touched the ground with his right hand and put it to his mouth.[25] Captain Cook describes the way of doing reverence to chiefs in the Tonga Islands, which was in this wise:—When a subject approached to do homage, the chief had to hold up his foot behind, as a horse does, and the subject touched the sole with his fingers, thus placing himself, as it were, under the sole of his lord's foot. Every one seemed to have the right of doing reverence in this way when he pleased; and chiefs got so tired of holding up their feet to be touched, that they would make their escape at the very sight of a loyal subject.[26] Other developments of the idea are found in the objection made to a Polynesian chief going down into the ship's cabin,[27] and to images of Buddha being kept there[28] in Siam, namely, that they were insulted by the sailors walking over their heads, and in the custom, also among the Tongans, of sitting down when a chief passed.[29] The ancient Egyptian may be seen in the sculptures abbreviating the gesture of touching the ground, by merely putting one hand down to his knee in bowing before a superior. A slight inclination of the body indicates submission or reverence, and becomes at last a mere act of politeness, not involving any sense of inferiority at all. This is brought about by that common habit of civilized man, of pretending to a humility that he does not feel, which leads the Chinese to allude to himself in conversation as "the blockhead" or "the thief," and makes our own high official personages write themselves, Sir, your most

[25] A. v. Humboldt, 'Vues des Cordillères'; Paris, 1810, p. 83.

[26] Cook, Third Voyage, 2nd ed.; London, 1785, vol. i. pp. 267, 409.

[27] Cook, Third Voyage, vol. i. p. 265.

[28] Sir J. Bowring, 'Siam'; London, 1857, vol. i. p. 125.

[29] Cook, ib. p. 409.

obedient humble servant, to persons whom they really consider their inferiors.

With regard to the position of the hands in prayer, there seems to have been a confusion of gestures distinct in their origin. With hands held out as if to touch or embrace a protector, to receive a gift, to ward off a blow, to present a helpless suppliant, unresisting or even offering his wrists for the cord,[30] the worshipper has means of expression which, when meaning becomes stiff in ceremony, he often misapplies. It is not unnatural that mercy or protection should be looked upon as a gift, and that the rustic Phidyle should hold out her supine hands to ask that her vines should *not* feel the pestilent south-west wind; but the conventionalizing process is carried much further when the hands clasped or with the finger-tips set together can be used to ask for a benefit which they cannot even catch hold of when it comes.

It is easy enough to give a plausible reason for the custom of taking off the hat as an expression of reverence or politeness, by referring it to times when armour was generally worn. To take off the helmet would be equivalent to disarming, and would indicate, in the most practical manner, either submission or peace. The practice of laying aside arms on entering a house appears in a quotation from the 'Boke of Curtayse,' which shows that in the Middle Ages visitors were expected to leave their weapons with the porter at the outer gate, and when they came to the hall door to take off hoods and gloves.

> When thou come tho hall dor to,
> Do of thy hode, thy gloves also.[31]

That women are not required to uncover their heads in church or on a visit, is quite consistent with such an origin of the custom, as their head-dresses were not armour; and the same consistency may be observed in the practice of ladies keeping the glove on in shaking hands, while men very commonly remove it. When a knight's glove was a steel gauntlet, such a distinction would be reasonable enough.

[30] Wedgwood, 'Origin of Language'; London, 1866, p. 146. Grimm, D. M. p. 1200. Meiners, 'Allg. Gesch. der Religionen'; Hanover, 1806–7, vol. ii. p. 280.

[31] Wright, 'History of Domestic Manners,' etc.; London, 1862, p. 141.

This may indeed be fanciful. The practice of women having the head covered in church belongs to the earliest period of Christianity, and the reasons for adopting it were clearly specified. And the usage of men praying with the head uncovered, may have been an intentional reversal of the practice of covering the head in offering sacrifice among the Romans, and among the Jews in their prayers then and now. It does not seem to have been universal, and is even now not followed in the Coptic and Abyssinian churches, in which the Semitic custom of uncovering not the head but the feet is still kept up. This latter ceremony is of high antiquity, and may be plausibly explained as having been done at first merely for cleanliness, as it is now among the Moslems in their baths and houses, as well as in their mosques, that the ground may not be defiled.

There are, moreover, a number of practices found in different parts of the world, which throw doubt on these off-hand explanations of the customs of uncovering the head and feet, and would almost lead us to include both, as particular cases of a general class of reverential uncoverings of the body. Saul strips off his clothes to prophesy, and lies down so all that day and night.[32] Tertullian speaks against the practice of praying with cloaks laid aside, as the heathen do.[33] There was a well-known custom in Tahiti, of uncovering the body down to the waist in honour of gods or chiefs, and even in the neighbourhood of a temple, and on the sacred ground set apart for royalty, with which may be classed a very odd ceremony, which was performed before Captain Cook on his first visit to the island.[34]

The regulations concerning the *fow* or turban in the Tonga Islands are very curious, from their partial resemblance to European usages. The turban, Mariner says, may only be worn by warriors going to battle, or at sham fights, or at night-time by chiefs and nobles, or by the common people when at work in the fields or in canoes. On all other occasions, to wear a head-dress would be disrespectful, for although no chief should be present,

[32] 1 Sam. xix. 24.

[33] Tert., 'De Oratione,' xii.

[34] Cook, 'First Voy. II.,' vol. ii. pp. 125, 153. Ellis, 'Polyn. Res.,' vol. ii. pp. 171, 352–3.

some god might be at hand unseen. If a man were to wear a turban except on these occasions, the first person of superior rank who met him would knock him down, and perhaps even an equal might do it. Even when the turban is allowed to be worn, it must be taken off when a superior approaches, unless in actual battle, but a man who is not much higher in rank will say, "Toogo ho fow," that is, Keep on your turban.[35]

During the administration of the ordeal by poison in Madagascar, Ellis says that no one is allowed to sit on his long robe, nor to wear the cloth round the waist, and females must keep their shoulders uncovered.[36] A remarkable statement is made by Ibn Batuta, in his account of his journey into the Soudan, in the fourteenth century. He mentions as an evil thing which he has observed in the conduct of the blacks, that women may only come unclothed into the presence of the Sultan of Melli, and even the Sultan's own daughters must conform to the custom. He notices also, that they threw dust and ashes on their heads as a sign of reverence,[37] which makes it appear that the stripping was also a mere act of humiliation. With regard to the practice of uncovering the feet, when we find the Damaras, in South Africa, taking off their sandals, before entering a stranger's house,[38] the idea of connecting the practice with the ancient Egyptian custom, or of ascribing it to Moslem influence, at once suggests itself, but the taking off the sandals as a sign of respect seems to have prevailed in Peru. No common Indian, it is said, dared go shod along the Street of the Sun, nor might any one, however great a lord he might be, enter the houses of the sun with shoes on, and even the Inca himself went barefoot into the Temple of the Sun.[39]

In this group of reverential uncoverings, the idea that the subject presents himself naked, defenceless, poor, and miserable before his lord, seems to be dramatically expressed, and this view is

---

[35] Mariner, 'Tonga Islands'; vol. i. p. 158.

[36] Rev. W. Ellis, 'Hist. of Madagascar'; London, 1838, vol. i. p. 464.

[37] Ibn Batuta in 'Journal Asiatique,' 4me Série, vol. i. p. 221. Waitz, 'Introd. to Anthropology,' E. Tr. ed. by J. F. Collingwood; part i., London, 1863, p. 301.

[38] C. J. Andersson, 'Lake Ngami,' etc., 2nd ed.; London, 1856, p. 231.

[39] Prescott, 'History of the Conquest of Peru,' 2nd ed.; London, 1847, vol. i. pp. 97, 78.

borne out by the practice of stripping, or uncovering the head and feet, as a sign of mourning,[40] where there can hardly be anything but destitution and misery to be expressed.

The lowest class of salutations, which merely aim at giving pleasant bodily sensations, merge into the civilities which we see exchanged among the lower animals. Such are patting, stroking, kissing, pressing noses, blowing, sniffing, and so forth. The often described sign of pleasure or greeting of the Indians of North America, by rubbing each other's arms, breasts, and stomachs, and their own,[41] is similar to the Central African custom, of two men clasping each other's arms with both hands, and rubbing them up and down,[42] and that of stroking one's own face with another's hand or foot, in Polynesia;[43] and the pattings and slappings of the Fuegians belong to the same class. Darwin describes the way in which noses are pressed in New Zealand, with details which have escaped less accurate observers.[44] It is curious that Linnæus found the salutation by touching noses in the Lapland Alps. People did not kiss, but put noses together.[45] The Andaman Islanders salute by blowing into another's hand with a cooing murmur.[46] Charlevoix speaks of an Indian tribe on the Gulf of Mexico, who blew into one another's ears;[47] and Du Chaillu describes himself as having been blown upon in Africa.[48] Sir S. Baker describes the expression of thanks among the Kytch of the White Nile, by holding their benefactor's hand and pretending to spit upon it.[49] Natural expressions of joy, such as clapping

[40] Micah i. 8. Ezekiel xxiv. 17. Herod. ii. 85. Rev. J. Roberts, 'Oriental Illustrations of the Sacred Scriptures,' 2nd ed. London, 1844, p. 492, etc.

[41] Charlevoix, vol. iii. p. 16; vol. vi. p. 189, etc.

[42] Burton, 'Lake Regions of Central Africa'; London, 1860, vol. ii. p. 69.

[43] Cook, 'Third Voy.,' vol. i. p. 179.

[44] Darwin, 'Journal of Res.,' etc.; London, 1860, pp. 205, 423. See W. v. Humboldt, 'Kawi-Spr.' vol. i. p. 77.

[45] Linnaeus, 'Tour in Lapland'; London, 1811, vol. i. p. 315. See Kotzebue, 'Voyage,' vol. i. p. 192 (Esquimaux).

[46] Mouat, 'Andaman Islanders'; London, 1863, pp. 279–80.

[47] Charlevoix, vol. iii. p. 16.

[48] Du Chaillu, 'Equatorial Africa'; London, 1861, pp. 393, 430.

[49] Baker, 'Albert Nyanza'; London, 1866, vol. i. p. 72.

hands in Africa,[50] and jumping up and down in Tierra del Fuego,[51] are made to do duty as signs of friendship or greeting.

There are a number of well-known gestures which are hard to explain. Such are various signs of hatred and contempt, such as lolling out the tongue, which is a universal sign, though it is not clear why it should be so, biting the thumb, making the sign of the stork's bill behind another's back (*ciconiam facere*), and the sign known as "taking a sight," which was as common at the time of Rabelais as it is now.

In modern India, as in ancient Rome, only a part of the signs we find described are such as can be set down at once to their proper origin.[52] One of the common gestures in India, especially, has puzzled many Europeans. This is the way of beckoning with the hand to call a person, which looks as though it were the reverse of the movement which we use for the purpose. I have heard, on native authority, that the apparent difference consists in the palm being outwards instead of inwards, but a remark made about the natives of the south of India by Mr. Roberts, who seems to have been an extremely good observer, suggests another explanation: "The way in which the people beckon for a person, is to lift up the right hand to its extreme height, and then bring it down with a sudden sweep to the ground."[53] It is evident that to make a sort of abbreviation of this movement, as by doing it from the wrist or elbow instead of from the shoulder, would be a natural sign, and yet would be liable to be taken for our gesture of motioning away. It is possible that something of this kind has led to the following description of the way of beckoning in New Zealand:—"In signals for those some way off to come near, the arm is waved in an exactly opposite direction to that adopted by Englishmen for similar purposes, and the natives in giving silent assent to anything, elevate the head and chin in place of nodding acquiescence."[54] The contrast between yes and no is variously

[50] Burton, 'Central Africa,' vol. ii. p. 69.

[51] Wilkes, U.S. Exploring Exp.; London, 1845, vol. i. p. 127.

[52] Plin. xi. 103. Roberts, 'Oriental Illustr.,' pp. 87, 90, 285, 293, 461, 475, 491.

[53] 'Oriental Illustr.' p. 396.

[54] A. S. Thomson, 'The Story of New Zealand'; London, 1859, vol. i. p. 209. See Cook, 'First Voy. H.,' vol. ii. p. 311.

made by different nations. The ancient Greeks used to nod (κατα-νένω, ἐπινεύω) for yes, but to throw back the head (ἀνανένω) for no; these signs may still be seen in Italy.[55] The Turk throws his head back with a cluck to express no, but can express yes by a movement like our shaking the head.[56] The Siamese priest's gestures in giving evidence, are raising his hat or fan to express yes, and lowering it to express no.[57]

Of signs used to avert the evil eye, some are connected with the ancient counter-charms, and others are of uncertain meaning, such as the very common one represented in old Greek and Roman amulets, the hand closed all but the fore-finger and little finger, which are held out straight. When King Ferdinand I, of Naples used to appear in public, he might be seen to put his hand from time to time into his pocket. Those who understood his ways knew that he was clenching his fist with the thumb stuck out between the first and second fingers, to avert the effect of a glance of the evil eye that some one in the street might have cast on him.

Enough has now been said to show that gesture-language is a natural mode of expression common to mankind in general. Moreover, this is true in a different sense to that in which we say that spoken language is common to mankind, including under the word language many hundreds of mutually unintelligible tongues, for the gesture-language is essentially one and the same in all times and all countries. It is true that the signs used in different places, and by different persons, are only partially the same; but it must be remembered that the same idea may be expressed in signs in very many ways, and that it is not necessary that all should choose the same. How the choice of gesture-signs is influenced by education and habit of life is well shown by a story told somewhere of a boy, himself deaf-and-dumb, who paid a visit to a Deaf-and-Dumb Asylum. When he was gone, the inmates expressed to the master their disgust at his ways. He talked an ugly language, they said; when he wanted to show that something was black, he pointed to his dirty nails.

---

55 Liddell and Scott; Liebrecht in Heidelb. Jahrb., 1868, p. 325.

56 Bastian, vol. i. p. 395.

57 Low in Journ. Ind. Archip., vol. i. p. 356.

The best evidence of the unity of the gesture-language is the ease and certainty with which any savage from any country can understand and be understood in a deaf-and-dumb school. A native of Hawaii is taken to an American Institution, and begins at once to talk in signs with the children, and to tell about his voyage and the country he came from. A Chinese, who had fallen into a state of melancholy from long want of society, is quite revived by being taken to the same place, where he can talk in gestures to his heart's content. A deaf-and-dumb lad named Collins is taken to see some Laplanders, who were carried about to be exhibited, and writes thus to his fellow-pupils about the Lapland woman:—"Mr. Joseph Humphreys told me to speak to her by signs, and she understood me. When Cunningham was with me, asking Lapland woman, and she frowned at him and me. She did not know we were deaf-and-dumb, but afterwards she knew that we were deaf-and-dumb, then she spoke to us about reindeers and elks and smiled at us much."[58]

The study of the gesture-language is not only useful as giving us some insight into the workings of the human mind. We can only judge what other men's minds are like by observing their outward manifestations, and similarity in the most direct and simple kind of utterance is good evidence of similarity in the mental processes which it communicates to the outer world. As, then, the gesture-language appears not to be specifically affected by differences in the race or climate of those who use it, the shape of their skulls and the colour of their skins, its evidence, so far as it goes, bears against the supposition that specific differences are traceable among the various races of man, at least in the more elementary processes of the mind.

[58] Dr. Orpen, 'The Contrast,' p. 177.

CHAPTER IV

GESTURE-LANGUAGE
AND WORD-LANGUAGE

We know very little about the origin of language, but the subject has so great a charm for the human mind that the want of evidence has not prevented the growth of theory after theory; and all sorts of men, with all sorts of qualifications, have solved the problem, each in his own fashion. We may read, for instance, Dante's treatise on the vulgar tongue, and wonder, not that, as he lived in mediæval times, his argument is but a mediæval argument, but that in the 'Paradiso,' seemingly on the strength of some quite futile piece of evidence, he should have made Adam enunciate a notion which even in this nineteenth century has hardly got fairly hold of the popular mind, namely, that there is no primitive language of man to be found existing on earth.

> La lingua ch' io parlai fu tutta spenta
> Innanzi che all' ovra inconsumabile
> Fosse la gente di Nembrotte attenta.
> Chè nullo affetto mai raziocinabile
> Per lo piacere uman che rinnovella,
> Seguendo 'l cielo, sempre fu durabile.
> Opera naturale è ch' uom favella:
> Ma cosi, o cosi, natura lascia
> Poi fare a voi secondo che v' abbella.
> Pria ch' oi scendessi all' infernale ambascia
> EL s' appellava in terra il sommo Bene
> Onde vien la letizia che mi fascia
> ELI si chiamò poi: e ciò conviene:
> Chè l' uso de' mortali è come fronda
> In ramo, che sen va, ed altra viene.

In Mr. Pollock's translation:—

> The language, which I spoke, was quite worn out
> Before unto the work impossible
> The race of Nimrod had their labour turned;
> For no production of the intellect

Which is renewed at pleasure of mankind,
Following the sky, was durable for aye.
It is a natural thing that man should speak;
But whether this or that way, nature leaves
To your election, as it pleases you.
Ere I descended on the infernal road,
Upon earth, EL was called the Highest Good,
From whom the enjoyment flows that me surrounds;
And was called ELI after; as was meet:
For mortal usages are like a leaf
Upon a bough, which goes, and others come.

Since Dante's time, how many men of genius have set the whole power of their minds against the problem, and to how little purpose. Steinthal's masterly summary of these speculations in his 'Origin of Language' is quite melancholy reading. It may indeed be brought forward as evidence to prove something that matters far more to us than the early history of language, that it is of as little use to be a good reasoner when there are no facts to reason upon, as it is to be a good bricklayer when there are no bricks to build with.

At the root of the problem of the origin of language lies the question, why certain words were originally used to represent certain ideas, or mental conditions, or whatever we may call them. The word may have been used for the idea because it had an evident fitness to be used rather than another word, or because some association of ideas, which we cannot now trace, may have led to its choice. That the selection of words to express ideas was ever purely arbitrary, that is to say, such that it would have been consistent with its principle to exchange any two words as we may exchange algebraic symbols, or to shake up a number of words in a bag and re-distribute them at random among the ideas they represented, is a supposition opposed to such knowledge as we have of the formation of language. And not in language only, but in the study of the whole range of art and belief among mankind, the principle is continually coming more and more clearly into view, that man has not only a definite reason, but very commonly an assignable one, for everything that he does and believes.

In the only departments of language of whose origin we have any certain notion, as for instance in the class of pure imitative words such as *"cuckoo," "peewit,"* and the like, the connection between word and idea is not only real but evident. It is true that different imitative words may be used for the same sound, as for instance the *tick* of a clock is called also *pick* in Germany; but both these words have an evident resemblance to the unwriteable sound that a clock really makes. So the Tahitian word for the crowing of cocks, *aaoa,* might be brought over as a rival to "cock-a-doodle-do!" There is, moreover, a class of words of undetermined extent, which seem to have been either chosen in some measure with a view to the fitness of their sound to represent their sense, or actually modified by a reflection of sound into sense. Some such process seems to have made the distinction between to *crash,* to *crush,* to *crunch,* and to *craunch,* and to have differenced to *flip,* to *flap,* to *flop,* and to *flump,* out of a common root. Some of these words must be looked for in dictionaries of "provincialisms," but they are none the less English for that. In pure interjections, such as *oh! ah!* the connection between the actual pronunciation and the idea which is to be conveyed is perceptible enough, though it is hardly more possible to define it than it is to convey in writing their innumerable modulations of sound and sense.

But if there was a living connection between word and idea outside the range of these classes of words, it seems dead now. We might just as well use "inhabitable" in the French sense as in that of modern English. In fact Shakespeare and other writers do so, as where Norfolk says in 'Richard the Second,'

> Even to the frozen ridges of the Alps,
> Or any other ground inhabitable.

It makes no practical difference to the world at large, that our word to "rise" belongs to the same root as Old German *rîsan,* to fall, French *arriser,* to let fall, whichever of the two meanings may have come first, nor that *black, blanc, bleich,* to *bleach,* to *blacken,* Anglo-Saxon *blæc, blac* = black, *blâc* = pale, white, come so nearly together in sound. It has been plausibly conjectured that the reversal of the meaning of to "rise" may have happened through a preposition being prefixed to change the sense, and dropping off again, leaving the word with its altered meaning,[1] while if *black* is related to German *blaken,* to burn, and has the sense of "charred, burnt to a coal," and *blanc* has that of shining,[2] a common origin may possibly be forthcoming for both sets among the family of words which includes *blaze, fulgeo, fla-gro,* φλέγω, φλόξ, Sanskrit *bhrâg,* and so forth. But explanations of this kind have no bearing on the practical use of such words by mankind at large, who take what is given them and ask no questions. Indeed, however much such a notion may vex the souls of etymologists, there is a great deal to be said for the view that much of the accuracy of our modern languages is due to their having so far "lost consciousness" of the derivation of their words, which thus become like counters or algebraic symbols, good to represent just what they are set down to mean. Archæology is a very interesting and instructive study, but when it comes to exact argument, it may be that the distinctness of our apprehension of what a word means, is not always increased by a misty recollection hovering about it in our minds, that it or its family once meant something else. For such purposes, what is required is not so much a knowledge of etymology, as accurate definition, and the practice of checking words by realizing the things and actions they are used to denote.

It is as bearing on the question of the relation between idea and word that the study of the gesture-language is of particular interest. We have in it a method of human utterance independent of speech, and carried on through a different medium, in which, as has been said, the connection between idea and sign has hardly ever been broken, or even lost sight of for a moment. The gesture-language is in fact a system of utterance to which the description of the primæval language in the Chinese myth may be applied; "Suy-jin first gave names to plants and animals, and these names were so expressive, that by the name of a thing it was known what it was."[3]

To speak first of the comparison of gesture-signs with words, it has been already observed that the gesture-language uses two

1 Jacob Grimm, 'Geschichte der Deutschen Sprache'; Leipzig, 1848, p. 664.

2 See J. and W. Grimm, 'Deutsches Wörterbuch,' s. vv. *black, blaken, blick,* etc. Diez, Wörterb., s. v. *bianco.*

3 Goguet, 'De l'Origine des Loix,' etc.; Paris, 1758, vol. iii. p. 322.

different processes. It brings objects and actions bodily into the conversation, by pointing to them or looking at them, and it also suggests by imitation of actions, or by "pictures in the air," and these two processes may be used separately or combined. This division may be clumsy and in some cases inaccurate, but it is the best I have succeeded in making. I will now examine more closely the first division, in which objects are brought directly before the mind.

When Mr. Lemuel Gulliver visited the school of languages in Lagado, he was made acquainted with a scheme for improving language by abolishing all words whatsoever. Words being only names for things, people were to carry the things themselves about, instead of wasting their breath in talking about them. The learned adopted the scheme, and sages might be seen in the streets bending under their heavy sacks of materials for conversation, or unpacking their loads for a talk. This was found somewhat troublesome. "But for short conversations, a man may carry implements in his pockets, and under his arms, enough to supply him; and in his house, he cannot be at a loss. Therefore the room where the company meet who practise this art, is full of all things, ready at hand, requisite to furnish matter for this kind of artificial converse."

The traveller records that this plan did not come into general use, owing to the ignorant opposition of the women and the common people, who threatened to raise a rebellion if they were not allowed to speak with their tongues after the manner of their forefathers. But this system of talking by objects is in sober earnest an important part of the gesture-language, and in its early development among the deaf-and-dumb, perhaps the most important. Is there then anything in spoken language that can be compared with the gestures by which this process is performed? Quintilian incidentally answers the question. "As for the hands indeed, without which action would be maimed and feeble, one can hardly say how many movements they have, when they almost follow the whole stock of words; for the other members help the speaker, but they, I may almost say, themselves speak." . . . *"Do they not in pointing out places and persons, fulfil the purpose of adverbs and pronouns?* so that in so great a diversity of tongues among all people and nations this seems to me the common language of all mankind?" . . .[4]

Where a man stands is to him the centre of the universe, and he refers the position of any object to himself, as before or behind him, above or below him, and so on; or he makes his fore-finger issue, as it were, as a radius from this imaginary centre, and, pointing in any direction into space, says that the thing he points out is *there*. He defines the position of an object somewhat as it is done in Analytical Geometry, using either a radius vector, to which the demonstrative pronoun may partly be compared, or referring it to three axes, as, in front or behind, to the right or left, above or below. His body, however, not being a point, but a structure of considerable size, he often confuses his terms, as when he uses *here* for some spot only comparatively near him, instead of making it come towards the same imaginary centre whence *there* started. He can in thought shift his centre of co-ordinates and the position of his axes, and imagining himself in the place of another person, or even of an inanimate object, can describe the position of himself or anything else with respect to them. Movement and direction come before his mind as a real or imaginary going from one place to another, and such movement gives him the idea of time which the deaf-and-dumb man expresses by drawing a line with his finger along his arm from one point to another, and the speaker by a similar adaptation of prepositions or adverbs of place.

I do not wish to venture below the surface of this difficult subject, for an elaborate examination of which I would especially refer to the researches of Professor Pott, of Halle.[5] But it may be worthwhile to call attention to an apparent resemblance of two divisions of the root-words of our Aryan languages to the two great classes of gesture-signs. Professor Max Müller divides the Sanskrit root-forms into two classes, the *predicative* roots, such as

---

[4] Quint., Inst. Orat., lib. xi. 3, 85, *seq.* "Luther führt an *das ist mein leib* und bemerkt dabei folgendes, 'das ist ein pronomen und lautet der buchstab a drinnen stark und lang, als wäre es geschrieben also, dahas, wie ein schwäbisch oder algauwisch daas lautet, und wer es höret, dem ist als stehe ein finger dabei der darauf zeige' " (Grimm, 'D. W.,' *s. r.* "der").

[5] Pott, 'Etymologische Forschungen,' new ed.; Lemgo and Detmold, 1859, etc., vol. i.

to *shine,* to *extend,* and so forth; and the *demonstrative* roots, "a small class of independent radicals, not predicative in the usual sense of the word, but simply pointing, simply expressive of existence under certain more or less definite, local or temporal prescriptions."[6] If we take from among the examples given, *here, there, this, that, thou, he,* as types, we have a division of the elements of the Sanskrit language to which a divison of the signs of the deaf-mute into *predicative* and *demonstrative* would at least roughly correspond. Many centuries ago the Indian grammarians made desperate efforts to bring pronouns and verbs, as the Germans say, "under one hat." They deduced the demonstrative *ta* from *tan,* to stretch, and the relative *ya* from *yaǵ,* to worship. Unity is pleasant to mankind, who are often ready to sacrifice things of more consequence than etymology for it. But perhaps, after all, the world may not have been constructed for the purpose of providing for the human mind just what it is pleased to ask for. Of course, any full comparison of speech and the gesture-language would have to go into the hard problem of the relation of prepositions to adverbs and pronouns on the one hand, and to verb-roots on the other. As to this matter, I can only say that the educated deaf-mute puts his right fore-finger into the palm of his left hand to say "in," takes it out again to say "out," puts his right hand above or below his left to say "above" or "below," etc., which are imitative signs, very likely learnt from the teacher. But the natural gestures with which he shows that anything is "above me," "behind me," and so on, are of a more direct character, and are rather demonstrative than predicative.

The class of imitative and suggestive signs in the gesture-language corresponds in some measure with the Chinese words which are neither verbs, substantives, adjectives, nor adverbs, but answer the purpose of all of them, as, for instance, *ta,* meaning great, greatness, to make great, to be great, greatly;[7] or they may be compared with what Sanskrit roots would be if they were used as they stand in the dictionaries, without any inflections. In the gesture-language there seems no distinction between the adjective, the adverb which belongs to it, the substantive, and the verb.

---

[6] Müller, Lectures, 3rd ed.; London, 1862, p. 272.

[7] Endlicher, 'Chin. Gramm.'; Vienna, 1845, p. 168.

To say, for instance, "The pear is green," the deaf-and-dumb child first eats an imaginary pear, and then using the back of the flat left hand as a ground, he makes the fingers of the right hand grow up on the edge of it like blades of grass. We might translate the signs as "pear-grass;" but they have quite as good a right to be classed as verbs, for they are signs of eating in a peculiar way, and growing.

It is not necessary to have recourse to Asiatic languages for analogies of this kind with the gesture-language. The substantive-adjective is common enough in English, and indeed in most other languages. In such compounds as *chestnut-horse, spoon-bill, iron-stone, feather-grass,* we have the substantive put to express a quality which distinguishes it. Our own language, which has gone so far towards assimilating itself to the Chinese by dropping inflection and making syntax do its work, has developed to a great extent a concretism which is like that of the Chinese, who makes one word do duty for "stick" and "to beat with a stick," or of the deaf-mute, whose sign for "butter" or the act of "buttering" is the same, the imitation of spreading with his finger on the palm of his hand. To *butter* bread, to *cudgel* a man, to *oil* machinery, to *pepper* a dish, and scores of such expressions, involve action and instrument in one word, and that word a substantive treated as the root or crude form of a verb. Such expressions are concretisms, picture-words, gesture-words, as much as the deaf-and-dumb man's one sign for "butter" and "buttering." To separate these words, and to say that there is one *butter,* a noun, and another *butter,* a verb, may be convenient for the dictionary; but to pretend that there is a real distinction between the words is a mere grammatical juggle, like saying that the noun *man* has a nominative case *man,* and an objective case which is also *man,* and much of the rest of the curious system of putting new wine into old bottles, and stretching the organism of a live language upon a dead framework, which is commonly taught as English Grammar.

The reference of substantives to a verb-root in the Aryan languages and elsewhere is thoroughly in harmony with the spirit of the gesture-language. Thus, the horse is the *neigher;* stone is what *stands,* is *stable;* water is that which *waves, undulates;* the mouse is the *stealer;* an age is what *goes on;* the oar is what *makes to go;* the serpent is the *creeper;* and so on; that is to say, the etymologies of these words lead us back to the actions of neighing, standing, waving, stealing, etc. Now, the deaf-and-dumb Kruse tells us that even to the mute who has no means of communication but signs, "the bird is what flies, the fish what swims, the plant what sprouts out of the earth."[8] It may be said that action, and form resulting from action, form the staple of that part of the gesture-language which occupies itself with suggesting to the mind that which it does not bring bodily before it. But, though there is so much similarity of principle in the formation of gesture-signs and words, there is no general correspondence in the particular idea chosen to name an object by in the two kinds of utterance.

In the second place, with regard to the syntax of the gesture-language, it is hardly possible to compare it with that of inflected languages such as Latin, which can alter the form of words to express their relation to one another. With Chinese and some other languages of Eastern Asia, and with English and French, etc., where they have thrown off inflection, it may be roughly compared, though all these languages use at least grammatical particles which have nothing corresponding to them in the gesture-language. Now, it is remarkable to what an extent Chinese and English agree in doing just what the gesture-language does not. Both put the attribute before the subject, *pe ma,* "white horse;" *shing jin,* "holy man;" both put the actor and action before the object, *ngo ta ni,* "I strike thee," *tien sang in,* "heaven destroys me." The practice of the gesture-language is opposed both to Chinese and English construction, as these examples show. "It seems," says Steinthal, "that the speech of the Chinese hastens toward the conclusion, and brings the end prominently forward. In the described position of the three relations of speech the more important member stands last."[9] A more absolute contradiction of the leading principle of the gesture-syntax could hardly have been formulated in words.

The theory that the gesture-language was the original language

[8] Kruse, p. 53.

[9] Steinthal, 'Charakteristik der hauptsächlichsten Typen des Sprachbaues'; Berlin, 1860, p. 114, etc.

of man, and that speech came afterwards, has been already mentioned. We have no foundation to build such a theory upon, but there are several questions bearing upon the matter which are well worth examining. Before doing so, however, it will be well to look a little more closely into the claim of the gesture-language to be considered as a means of utterance independent of speech.

In the first place, an absolute separation between the two things is not to be found within the range of our experience. Though the deaf-mute may not speak himself, yet the most of what he knows, he only knows by means of speech, for he learns from the gestures of his parents and companions what they learnt through words. We speak conventionally of the uneducated deaf-and-dumb, but every deaf-and-dumb child is educated more or less by living among those who speak, and this education begins in the cradle. And on the other hand, no child attains to speech independently of the gesture-language, for it is in great measure by means of such gestures as pointing, nodding, and so forth, that language is first taught.

* * * *

Though, however, the deaf-and-dumb prove clearly to us that a man may have human thought without being able to speak, they by no means prove that he can think without any means of physical expression. Their evidence tends the other way. We may read with profit an eloquent passage on this subject by a German professor, as, transcendental as it is, it is put in such clear terms, that we may almost think we understand it.

"Herein lies the necessity of utterance, the representation of thought. Thought is not even present to the thinker, till he has set it forth out of himself. Man, as an individual endowed with sense and with mind, first attains to thought, and at the same time to the comprehension of himself, in setting forth out of himself the contents of his mind, and in this his free production, he comes to the knowledge of himself, his thinking 'I.' He comes first to himself in uttering himself."[10]

This view is not contradicted, but to some extent supported, by what we know of the earliest dawnings of thought among the

---

10 Heyse, 'System der Sprachwissenschaft'; Berlin, 1856, p. 39.

deaf-and-dumb. But we must take the word "utterance" in its larger sense to include not speech alone, as Heyse seems to do, but all ways by which man can express his thoughts. *Man* is essentially, what the derivation of his name among our Aryan race imports, not "the speaker," but he who thinks, he who *means*.

*   *   *   *

Whether the human mind is capable of exercising at all any of its peculiarly human functions without any means of utterance, or not, we shall all admit that it could have gone but very little way, could only just have passed the line which divides beast from man. All experience concurs to prove, that the mental powers and the stock of ideas of those human beings who have but imperfect means of utterance, are imperfect and scanty in proportion to those means. The manner in which we can see such persons accompanying their thought with the utterance which is most convenient to them, shows to how great a degree thought is "talking to oneself." The deaf-and-dumb gesticulate as they think. Laura Bridgman's fingers worked, making the initial movements for letters of the finger-alphabet, not only during her waking thought, but even in her dreams.

Spoken language, though by no means the exclusive medium of thought and expression, is undoubtedly the best. In default of this, it is only by means of a substitute for it, namely, alphabetic writing, that we succeed in giving more than a very low development to the minds of the deaf-and-dumb; and they of course connect the idea directly with the written word, not as we do, the writing with the sound, and then the sound with the idea. When they think in writing, as they often do, the image of the written words which correspond to their ideas, must rise up before them in the "mind's eye." The Germans, who are strong advocates of the system of teaching the deaf-and-dumb to articulate, believe that the power of connecting ideas with actual or imaginary movements of the organs of speech, gives an enormous increase of mental power, which I am, however, inclined to think is a good deal exaggerated. Heinicke gives a description of the results of his teaching his pupils to articulate, their delight at being able to communicate their ideas in this new way, and the increased intelligence which appeared in the expression of their faces. As soon, he says, as the born-mute is sufficiently taught to enable him to increase his stock of ideas by the power of naming them, he begins to talk aloud in his sleep, and when this happens, it shows that the power of thinking in words has taken root. . . .[11]

It is quite clear that the loss of the powers of hearing and speech is a loss to the mind which no substitute can fully replace. Children who have learnt to speak and afterwards become deaf, lose the power of thinking in inward language, and become to all intents and purposes the same as those who could never hear at all, unless great pains are taken to keep up and increase their knowledge by other means. "And thus even those who become hard of hearing at an age when they can already speak a little, by little and little lose all that they have learnt. Their voices lose all cheerfulness and euphony, every day wipes a word out of the memory, and with it the idea of which it was the sign."[12]

Spoken words appear to be, in the minds of the deaf-mutes who have been artificially taught to speak, merely combined movements of the throat and other vocal organs, and the initial movement made by them in calling words to mind has been compared to a tickling in the throat. People wanting a sense often imagine to themselves a resemblance between it and one of the senses which they possess. The old saying of the blind man, that he thought scarlet was like the sound of the trumpet, is somewhat like a remark made by Kruse, that though he is "stock-deaf" he has a bodily feeling of music, and different instruments have different effects upon him. Musical tones seem to his perception to have much analogy with colours. The sound of the trumpet is yellow to him, that of the drum red; while the music of the organ is green, and of the bass-viol blue, and so on. Such comparisons are, indeed, not confined to those whose senses are incomplete. Language shows clearly that men in general have a strong feeling of such analogies among the impressions of the different senses. Expressions such as "schreiend roth," and the use of "loud," as applied to colours and patterns, are superficial examples of analogies which have their roots very deep in the human mind.

11 Heinicke, p. 103, etc.

12 Schmalz, pp. 2, 32.

It is a very notable fact bearing upon the problem of the Origin of Language, that even born-mutes, who never heard a word spoken, do of their own accord and without any teaching make vocal sounds more or less articulate, to which they attach a definite meaning, and which, when once made, they go on using afterwards in the same unvarying sense. Though these sounds are often capable of being written down more or less accurately with our ordinary alphabets, their effect on those who make them can, of course, have nothing to do with the sense of hearing, but must consist only in particular ways of breathing, combined with particular positions of the vocal organs.

Teuscher, a deaf-mute, whose mind was developed by education to a remarkable degree, has recorded that, in his uneducated state, he had already discovered the sounds which were inwardly blended with his sensations (innig verschmolzen mit meiner Empfindungsweise). So, as a child, he had affixed a special sound to persons he loved, his parents, brothers and sisters, to animals, and things for which he had no sign (as water) ; and called any person he wished with one unaltered voice.[13] Heinicke gives some remarkable evidence, which we may, I think, take as given in entire good faith, though the reservation should be made, that through his strong partiality for articulation as a means of educating the deaf-and-dumb, he may have given a definiteness to these sounds in writing them down which they did not really possess. The following are some of his remarks:—"All mutes discover words for themselves for different things. Among over fifty whom I have partly instructed or been acquainted with, there was not one who had not uttered at least a few spoken names, which he had discovered himself, and some were very clear and well defined. I had under my instruction a born deaf-mute, nineteen years old, who had previously invented many writeable words for things, some three, four, and six syllables long." For instance, he called to eat "mumm," to drink "schipp," a child "tutten," a dog "beyer," money "patten." He had a neighbour who was a grocer, and him he called "patt" a name, no doubt, connected with his name for money, for buying and selling is indicated by the deaf-and-dumb by the action of counting out

[13] Steinthal, Spr. der T., p. 917.

coin. The grocer's son he called by a simple combination "pat-tutten." For the two first numerals, he had words—1, "gä;" 2, "schuppatter." In his language, "riecke" meant "I will not;" and when they wanted to force him to do anything, he would cry "naffet riecke schito." An exclamation which he used was "hesch-befa," in the sense of God forbid.[14]

Some of these sounds, as "mumm" and "schipp," for eating and drinking, and perhaps "beyer," for the dog, are mere vocalizations of the movements of the mouth, which the deaf-and-dumb make in imitating the actions of eating, drinking, and barking, in their gesture-language. Besides, it is a common thing for even the untaught deaf-and-dumb to speak and understand a few words of the language spoken by their associates. Though they cannot hear them, they imitate the motions of the lips and teeth of those who speak, and thus make a tolerable imitation of words containing labial and dental letters, though the gutturals, being made out of sight, can only be imparted to them by proper teaching, and then only with difficulty and imperfectly. It is scarcely necessary to say that when the deaf-and-dumb are taught to speak in articulate language, this is done merely by developing and systematizing the lip-imitation which is natural to them. As instances of the power which deaf-mutes have of learning words by sight without any regular teaching, may be given the cases mentioned by Schmalz of children born stone-deaf, who learnt in this way to say "papa," "mamma," "muhme" (cousin), "puppe" (doll), "bitte" (please).[15] All the sounds in these words are such as deaf persons may imitate by sight.

* * * *

The vocal sounds used by Laura Bridgman are of great interest from the fact that, being blind as well as deaf-and-dumb, she could not even have imitated words by seeing them made. Yet she would utter sounds, as *"ho-o-ph-ph"* for wonder, and a sort of chuckling or grunting as an expression of satisfaction. When she did not like to be touched, she would say *f!* Her teachers used to restrain her from making inarticulate sounds, but she felt a

14 Heinicke, p. 137, etc.

15 Schmalz, p. 216 *a*.

great desire to make them, and would sometimes shut herself up
and "indulge herself in a surfeit of sounds." But this vocal faculty of hers was chiefly exercised in giving what may be called
name-sounds to persons whom she knew, and which she would
make when the persons to whom she had given them came near
her, or when she wanted to find them, or even when she was
thinking of them. She had made as many as fifty or sixty of these
name-sounds, some of which have been written down, as *foo, too,
pa, fif, pig, ts,* but many of them were not capable of being written down even approximately.

Even if Laura's vocal sounds are not classed as real words, a
distinction between the articulate sounds used by the deaf-and-
dumb for child, water, eating and drinking, etc., and the words
of ordinary language, could not easily be made, whether the deaf-
mutes invented these sounds or imitated them from the lips of
others. To go upon the broadest ground, the mere fact that teachers can take children who have no means of uttering their thoughts
but the gesture-language, and teach them to articulate words, to
recognise them by sight when uttered by others, to write them,
and to understand them as equivalents for their own gestures, is
sufficient to bridge over the gulf which lies between the gesture-
language and, at least, a rudimentary form of word-language.
These two kinds of utterance are capable of being translated with
more or less exactness into one another; and it seems more likely
than not that there may be a similarity between the process by
which the human mind first uttered itself in speech, and that by
which the same mind still utters itself in gestures.

To turn to another subject. We have no evidence of man ever
having lived in society without the use of spoken language; but
there are some myths of such races, and, moreover, statements
have been made by modern writers of eminence as to an intermediate state between gesture-language and word-language, which
deserve careful examination.

* * * *

In modern times we hear little of dumb races, at least from
authors worthy of credit; but we find a number of accounts of
people occupying as it were a half-way house between the mythic

dumb nations and ourselves, and having a speech so imperfect that even if talking of ordinary matters they have to eke it out by gestures. . . .

Describing the Puris and Coroados of Brazil, Spix and Martius, having remarked that different tribes converse in signs, and explained the difficulty they found in making them understand by signs the objects or ideas for which they wanted the native names, go on to say how imperfect and devoid of inflexion or construction these languages are. Signs with hand or mouth, they say, are required to make them intelligible. To say, "I will go into the wood," the Indian uses the words "wood-go," and points his mouth like a snout in the direction he means.[16] Madame Pfeiffer, too, visited the Puris, and says that for "to-day," "to-morrow," and "yesterday," they have only the word "day"; the rest they express by signs. For "to-day" they say "day," and touch themselves on the head, or point straight upward; for "to-morrow" they say also "day," pointing forward with the finger; and for "yesterday," again "day," pointing behind them.[17]

Mr. Mercer, describing the low condition of some of the Veddah tribes of Ceylon, stated that not only is their dialect incomprehensible to a Singhalese, but that even their communications with one another are made by signs, grimaces, and guttural sounds, which bear little or no resemblance to distinct words or systematized language.[18]

Dr. Milligan, speaking of the language of Tasmania, and the rapid variation of its dialects, says, "The habit of gesticulation, and the use of signs to eke out the meaning of monosyllabic expressions, and to give force, precision, and character to vocal sounds, exerted a further modifying effect, producing, as it did, carelessness and laxity of articulation, and in the application and pronunciation of words." "To defects in orthoepy the aborigines added short-comings in syntax, for they observed no settled order or arrangement of words in the construction of their sentences, but conveyed in a supplementary fashion by tone, manner, and

[16] Spix and Martius, 'Reise in Brasilien'; Munich, 1823, etc., vol. i. p. 385, etc.

[17] Ida Pfeiffer, 'Eine Frauenfahrt um die Erde'; Vienna, 1850, p. 102.

[18] Sir J. Emerson Tennent, 'Ceylon,' 3rd ed.; London, 1859, vol. ii. p. 441.

gesture those modifications of meaning, which we express by mood, tense, number, etc."[19]

We find a similar remark made about a tribe of North American Indians, by Captain Burton. "Those natives who, like the Arapahos, possess a very scanty vocabulary, pronounced in a quasi-unintelligible way, can hardly converse with one another in the dark; to make a stranger understand them they must always repair to the camp-fire for 'pow-wow.' "[20]

In South Africa, the same is said of the Bushmen:—"So imperfect, indeed, is the language of the Bosjesmans, that even those of the same horde often find a difficulty in understanding each other without the use of gesture; and at night, when a party of Bosjesmans are smoking, dancing, and talking, they are obliged to keep up a fire so as to be able by its light to see the explanatory gestures of their companions."[21]

The array of evidence in favour of the existence of tribes whose language is incomplete without the help of gesture-signs, even for things of ordinary import, is very remarkable. The matter is important ethnologically, for if it may be taken as proved that there are really people whose language does not suffice to speak of the common subjects of every-day life without the aid of gesture, the fact will either furnish about the strongest case of degeneration known in the history of the human race, or supply a telling argument in favour of the theory that the gesture-language is part of the original utterance of mankind which speech has more or less fully superseded among different tribes. Unfortunately, however, the evidence is in every case more or less defective. Spix and Martius make no claim to having mastered the Puri and Coroado languages. The Coroado words for "to-morrow" and "the day after to-morrow," viz., *herinanta* and *hinó herinanta,* make it unlikely that their neighbours the Puris, who are so nearly on the same level of civilization, have no such words. Mr. Mercer seems to have adopted the common view of foreigners about the Veddahs, but it has happened here, as in many other accounts of savage tribes, that closer acquaintance

[19] Milligan, in Papers and Proc. of Roy. Soc. of Tasmania, 1859; vol. iii. part ii.
[20] Burton, 'City of the Saints,' p. 151. See Schoolcraft, part i. p. 564.
[21] J. G. Wood, 'Nat. Hist. of Man'; vol. i. p. 266.

has shown them to have been wrongly accused. Mr. Bailey, who has had good opportunities of studying them, contradicts their supposed deficiency in language with the remark, "I never knew one of them at a loss for words sufficiently intelligible to convey his meaning, not to his fellows only, but to the Singhalese of the neighborhood, who are all, more or less, acquainted with the Veddah patois."[22] Dr. Milligan is, I believe, our best authority as to the Tasmanians and their language, but he probably had to trust in this matter to native information, which is far from being always safe.[23] Lastly, Captain Burton only paid a flying visit to the Western Indians, and his interpreters could hardly have given him scientific information on such a subject.

The point in question is one which it is not easy to bring to a perfectly distinct issue, seeing that all people, savage and civilised, do use signs more or less. As has been remarked already, many savage tribes accompany their talk with gestures to a great extent, and in conversation with foreigners, gestures and words are usually mixed to express what is to be said. It is extremely likely that Madame Pfeiffer's savages suffered the penalty of being set down as wanting in language, for no worse fault than using a combination of words and signs in order to make what they meant as clear as possible to her comprehension. But the existence of a language incomplete, even for ordinary purposes, without the aid of gesture-signs, could only be proved by the evidence of an educated man so familiar with the language in question, as to be able to say from absolute personal knowledge not only what it can, but what it cannot do, an amount of acquaintance to which I think none of the writers quoted would lay claim. In the case of languages spoken by very low races, like the Puris and the Tasmanians, the difficulty of deciding such a point must be very great. The strongest fact bearing upon the matter of which I am aware, is that savage tribes whose numeral words do

22 J. Bailey, in Tr. Eth. Soc.; London, 1863, p. 300.

23 The objection to trusting native information as to grammatical structure, may be seen in the difficulty, so constantly met with in investigating the languages of rude tribes, of getting a substantive from a native without a personal pronoun tacked to it. Thus in Dr. Milligan's vocabulary, the expressions *puggan neena, noonalmeena,* given for "husband" and "father," seem really to mean "your husband," "my father," or something of the kind.

not go beyond some low number, as five or ten, are well known to be able to reckon much farther on their fingers and toes, here distinctly using gesture-language where word-language fails.[24]

There is a point of some practical importance involved in the question, whether gestures or words are, so to speak, most natural. If signs form an easier means for the reception and expression of ideas than words, then idiots ought to learn to understand and use gestures more readily than speech. I have only been able to get a distinct answer to the question, whether they do so or not, from one competent judge in such a matter, Dr. Scott, of Exeter, who assures me that semi-idiotic children, to whom there is no hope of teaching more than the merest rudiments of speech, are yet capable of receiving a considerable amount of knowledge by means of signs, and of expressing themselves by them. It is well known that a certain class of children are dumb from deficiency of intellect, rather than from want of the sense of hearing, and it is to these that the observation applies.[25]

The idea of solving the problem of the origin of language by actual experiment, must have very often been started. There are several stories of such an experiment having been tried. One is Herodotus's well-known tale of Psammitichus, King of Egypt, who had the two children brought up by a silent keeper, and suckled by goats. The first word they said, *bekos,* meaning bread in the Phrygian language, of course proved that the Phrygians were the oldest race of mankind. It is a very trite remark that there is nothing absolutely incredible in the story, and that *bek, bek,* is a good imitative word for bleating, as in βληχάομαι, μηκάομαι, *blöken, meckern,* etc. But the very name of Psammitichus, who has served as a lay-figure for so many tales to be draped upon, is fatal to any claim to the historical credibility of such a story. He sounds the springs of the Nile with a cord thousands of fathoms long, and finds no bottom; he accomplishes the prediction of one oracle by pouring a libation out of a brazen helmet, and of another, concerning cocks, by leading an army of

---

[24] For further remarks on such mixed expression by gesture and word, as bearing on development of language, see the author's 'Primitive Culture,' chap. v and vii. [Note to 3rd Edition].

[25] See W. R. Scott, 'Remarks on the Education of Idiots'; London, 1847.

Carians, with crested helmets, against Tementhes, king of Egypt, and he figures in the Greek version of the story of Cinderella's slipper. Another account is related in the life of James IV of Scotland. "The King also caused tak ane dumb voman, and pat her in Inchkeith, and gave hir tuo bairnes with hir, and gart furnisch hir in all necessares thingis perteaning to thair nourischment, desiring heirby to knaw quhat languages they had when they cam to the aige of perfyte speach. Some sayes they spak guid Hebrew, but I knaw not by authoris rehearse," etc.[26] Another story is told of the great Mogul, Akbar Khan. It is mentioned by Purchas, only twenty years after Akbar's death, and told in detail by the Jesuit Father Catrou, as follows:—"Indeed it may be said that desire of knowledge was Akbar's ruling passion, and his curiosity induced him to try a very strange experiment. He wished to ascertain what language children would speak without teaching, as he had heard that Hebrew was the natural language of those who had been taught no other. To settle the question, he had twelve children at the breast shut up in a castle six leagues from Agra, and brought up by twelve dumb nurses. A porter, who was dumb also, was put in charge and forbidden on pain of death to open the castle door. When the children were twelve years old [there is a decided feeling for duodecimals in the story], he had them brought before him, and collected in his palace men skilled in all languages. A Jew who was at Agra was to judge whether the children spoke Hebrew. There was no difficulty in finding Arabs and Chaldeans in the capital. On the other hand the Indian philosophers asserted that the children would speak the Hanscrit [i.e. Sanskrit] language, which takes the place of Latin among them, and is only in use among the learned, and is learnt in order to understand the ancient Indian books of Philosophy and Theology. When however the children appeared before the Emperor, every one was astonished to find that they did not speak any language at all. They had learnt from their nurses to do without any, and they merely expressed their thoughts by gestures which answered the purpose of words. They

26 Herod. ii. c. 2. Lindsay of Pitscottie, 'Chronicles of Scotland,' vol. i. p. 249. For other European legends, see De Brosses, 'Traité des Langues,' vol. ii. p. 7; Farrar, 'Chapters on Language,' p. 13.

were so savage and so shy that it was a work of some trouble to tame them and to loosen their tongues, which they had scarcely used during their infancy."[27]

There may possibly be a foundation of fact for this story, which fits very well with what is known of Akbar's unscrupulous character, and his greediness for knowledge. Moreover it tells in its favour, that had a story-teller invented it, he would hardly have brought it to what must have seemed to him such a lame and impotent conclusion, as that the children spoke no language at all.

[27] 'Purchas, His Pilgrimes'; London, 1625–6, vol. v. (1626) p. 516. Catrou, 'Hist. Gén. de l'Empire du Mogol'; Paris, 1705, p. 259, etc. A Singhalese legend in Hardy, 'Eastern Monarchism,' p. 192.

CHAPTER V

PICTURE-WRITING
AND WORD-WRITING

The art of recording events, and sending messages, by means of pictures representing the things or actions in question, is called Picture-Writing.

The deaf-and-dumb man's remark, that the gesture-language is a picture-language, finds its counterpart in an observation of Wilhelm von Humboldt's, that "In fact, gesture, destitute of sound, is a species of writing." There is indeed a very close relation between these two ways of expressing and communicating thought. Gesture can set forth thought with far greater speed and fulness than picture-writing, but it is inferior to it in having to place the different elements of a sentence in succession, in single file, so to speak; while by a picture the whole of an event may be set in view at one glance, and that permanently, so as to serve as a message to a distant place or a record to a future time. But the imitation of visible qualities as a means of expressing ideas is common to both methods, and both belong to similar conditions of the human mind. Both are found in very distant countries and times, and spring up naturally under favourable circumstances, provided that a higher means of supplying the same wants has not already occupied the place which they can only fill very partially and rudely.

There being so great a likeness between the conditions which cause the use of the gesture-language and of picture-writing, it is not surprising to find the natives of North America as great proficients in the one as in the other. Their pictures, as drawn and interpreted by Schoolcraft and other writers, give the best information that is to be had of the lower development of the art.[1]

1 Figs. 2 to 7, and their interpretations, are from Schoolcraft, 'Indian Tribes,' part i. See also the 'Narrative of the Captivity and Adventures of John Tanner,' edited by Edwin James, 1830, from which many of Schoolcraft's pictures and interpretations seem taken.

Fig. 2 is an Indian record on a blazed pine-tree (to blaze a tree is to wound (*blesser*) its side with an axe, so as to mark it with a conspicuous white patch). On the right are two canoes (2 and 4), with a catfish (1) in one of them, and a fabulous animal, known as the copper-tailed bear (3), in the other. On the left are a bear and six catfish; and the sense of the picture is

FIG. 2

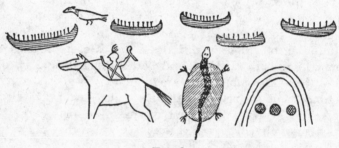

FIG. 3

simply that two hunters, whose names, or rather totems or clannames, were "Copper-tailed Bear" and "Catfish," went out on a hunting expedition in their canoes, and took a bear and six catfish.

Fig. 3 is a picture on the face of a rock on the shore of Lake Superior, and records an expedition across the lake, which was led by Myeengun, or "Wolf," a celebrated Indian chief. The canoes with the upright strokes in them represent the force of the party in men and boats, and Wolf's chief ally, Kishkemunasee, that is, "Kingfisher," goes in the first canoe. The arch with three circles below it shows that there were three suns under heaven, that is, that the voyage took three days. The tortoise seems to indicate their getting to land, while the representation of the chief himself on horseback shows that the expedition took place since the time when horses were introduced into Canada.

The Indian grave-posts, Fig. 4, tell their story in the same child-like manner. Upon one is a tortoise, the dead warrior's totem, and a figure beside it representing a headless man, which shows he is dead. Below are his three marks of honour. On the other post there is no separate sign for death, but the chief's totem, a crane, is reversed. Six marks of honour are awarded to him

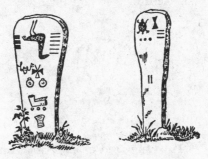

FIG. 4

on the right, and three on the left. The latter represent three important general treaties of peace which he had attended; the former would seem to stand for six war-parties or battles. The pipe and hatchet are symbols of influence in peace and war.

The great defect of this kind of record is that it can only be understood within a very limited circle. It does not tell the story at length, as is done in explaining it in words; but merely suggests some event, of which it only gives such details as are required to enable a practised observer to construct a complete picture. It may be compared in this respect to the elliptical forms of expression which are current in all societies whose attention is given specially to some narrow subject of interest, and where, as all men's minds have the same frame-work set up in them, it is not necessary to go into an elaborate description of the whole state of things; but one or two details are enough to enable the hearer to understand the whole. Such expressions as "new white at 48," "best selected at 92," though perfectly understood in the commercial circles where they are current, are as unintelligible to any one who is not familiar with the course of events in those circles, as an Indian record of a war-party would be to an ordinary Londoner.

Though, however, familiarity with the picture-writing of the Indians, as well as with their habits and peculiarities, might enable the student to make a pretty good guess at the meaning of such documents as the above, which are meant to be understood by strangers, there is another class of picture-writings, used principally by the magicians or medicine-men, which cannot be even

FIG. 5

thus interpreted. The songs and charms used among the Indians of North America are repeated or sung by memory, but, as an assistance to the singer, pictures are painted upon sticks, or pieces of birch-bark or other material, which serve to suggest to the mind the successive verses. Some of these documents, with the songs to which they refer, are given in Schoolcraft, and one or two examples will show sufficiently how they are used, and make it evident that they can only convey their full meaning to those who know by heart already the compositions they refer to. They are mere Samson's riddles, only to be guessed by those who have ploughed with his heifer. Thus, a drawing of a man with two marks on his breast and four on his legs (Fig. 5) is to remind the singer that at this place comes the following verse:—

> Two days must you sit fast, my friend,—
> Four days must you sit still.

Fig. 6 is the record of a love-song—(1) represents the lover; in (2) he is singing, and beating a magic drum; in (3) he surrounds himself with a secret lodge, denoting the effects of his necromancy; in (4) he and his mistress are shown joined by a single arm, to indicate the union of their affections; in (5) she is shown on an island; in (6) she is asleep, and his voice is shown, while his magical powers are reaching her heart; and the heart itself is shown in (7). To each of these figures a verse of the song corresponds.

1. It is my painting that makes me a god.
2. Hear the sounds of my voice, of my song; it is my voice.
3. I cover myself in sitting down by her.
4. I can make her blush, because I hear all she says of me.
5. Were she on a distant island, I could make her swim over.
6. Though she were far off, even on the other hemisphere.
7. I speak to your heart.

Fig. 7 is a war-song. The warrior is shown in (1); he is drawn with wings, to show that he is active and swift of foot. In (2)

FIG. 6

FIG. 7

he stands under the morning star; in (3) he is standing under the centre of heaven, with his war-club and rattle; in (4) the eagles of carnage are flying round the sky; in (5) he lies slain on the field of battle; and in (6) he appears as a spirit in the sky. The words are these:—

1. I wish to have the body of the swiftest bird.
2. Every day I look at you; the half of the day I sing my song.
3. I throw away my body.
4. The birds take a flight in the air.
5. Full happy am I to be numbered with the slain.
6. The spirits on high repeat my name.

Catlin tells how the chief of the Kickapoos, a man of great ability, generally known as the "Shawnee Prophet," having, as was said, learnt the doctrines of Christianity from a missionary, taught them to his tribe, pretending to have received a supernatural mission. He composed a prayer, which he wrote down on a flat stick, "in characters somewhat resembling Chinese letters." When Catlin visited the tribe, every man, woman, and child used to repeat this prayer morning and evening, placing the forefinger under the first character, repeating a sentence or two, and so going on to the next, till the prayer, which took some ten minutes to repeat, was finished.[2] I do not know whether any of these curious prayer-sticks are now to be seen, but they were probably made on the same principle as the suggestive pictures used for the native Indian songs.

Picture-writing is found among savage races in all quarters of the globe, and, so far as we can judge, its principle is the same everywhere. The pictures on the Lapland magic drums, of which we have interpretations, serve much the same purpose as the American writing. Savage paintings, or scratchings, or carvings on rocks, have a family likeness, whether we find them in North or South America, in Siberia or Australia. The interpretation of rock-pictures, which mostly consist of few figures, is in general a hopeless task, unless a key is to be had. Many are, no doubt, mere pictorial utterances, drawings of animals and things without any historical sense; some are names, as the totems carved by those who sprang upon the dangerous leaping-rock at the Red Pipe-

---

[2] Catlin, 'North American Indians,' 7th ed.; London, 1848, vol. ii. p. 98.

stone Quarry.[3] Dupaix noticed in Mexico a sculptured eagle, apparently on the boundary of Quauhnahuac, "the place *near the eagle*," now called Cuernavaca,[4] and the fact suggests that rock-sculptures may often be, like this, symbolic boundary marks. But there is seldom a key to be had to the reading of rock-sculptures, which the natives generally say were done by the people long ago. I have seen them in Mexico on cliffs where one can hardly imagine how the savage sculptors can have climbed. When Humboldt asked the Indians of the Oronoko who it was that sculptured the figures of animals and symbolic signs high up on the face of the crags along the river, they answered with a smile, as relating a fact of which only a stranger, a white man, could possibly be ignorant, "that at the time of the *great waters* their fathers went up to that height in their canoes."[5]

As the gesture-language is substantially the same among savage tribes all over the world, and also among children who cannot speak, so the picture-writings of savages are not only similar to one another, but are like what children make untaught even in civilized countries. Like the universal language of gestures, the art of picture-writing tends to prove that the mind of the uncultured man works in much the same way at all times and everywhere.

*   *   *   *

Map-making is a branch of picture-writing with which the savage is quite familiar, and he is often more skilful in it than the generality of civilized men. In Tahiti, for instance, the natives were able to make maps for the guidance of foreign visitors.[6] Maps made with raised lines are mentioned as in use in Peru before the Conquest,[7] and there is no doubt about the skill of

[3] Catlin, vol. ii. p. 170.

[4] Lord Kingsborough, 'Antiquities of Mexico'; London, 1830, etc., vol. iv. part i., no. 31, and vol. v. Expl.

[5] Humboldt and Bonpland, vol. ii. p. 239.

[6] Gustav Klemm, 'Allgemeine Cultur-Geschichte der Menschheit'; Leipzig, 1843–52, vol. iv. p. 396.

[7] Rivero and v. Tschudi, 'Antigüedades Peruanas'; Vienna, 1851, p. 124. Prescott, 'Peru'; vol. i. p. 116.

the North American Indians and Esquimaux in the art, as may be seen by a number of passages in Schoolcraft and elsewhere.[8] The oldest map known to be in existence is the map of the Ethiopian gold-mines, dating from the time of Sethos I., the father of Rameses II.,[9] long enough before the time of the bronze tablet of Aristagoras, on which was inscribed the circuit of the whole earth, and all the sea and all rivers.[10]

The highest development of the art of picture-writing is to be found among the ancient Mexicans. Their productions of this kind are far better known than those of the Red Indians, and are indeed much more artistic, as well as being more systematic and copious. Some of the most characteristic specimens have been drawn and described by Alexander von Humboldt, and Lord Kingsborough's great work contains a huge mass of them, which he published in facsimile in support of his views upon that philosopher's stone of ethnologists, the Lost Tribes of Israel.

The bulk of the Mexican paintings are mere pictures, directly representing migrations, wars, sacrifices, deities, arts, tributes, and such matters, in a way not differing in principle from that of the lowest savages. But in the historical records and calendars, the events are accompanied by a regular notation of years, and sometimes of divisions of years, which entitles them to be considered as regularly dated history. The art of dating events was indeed not unknown to the Northern Indians. A resident among the Kristinaux (generally called for shortness, Crees), who knew them before they were in their present half-civilized state, says that they had names for the moons which make up the year, calling them "whirlwind moon," "moon when the fowls go to the south," "moon when the leaves fall off from the trees," and so on. When a hunter left a record of his chase pictured on a piece of birch-bark, for the information of others who might pass that way, he would draw a picture which showed the name of the month, and make beside it a drawing of the shape of the moon at the time, so accurately, that an Indian could tell within

8 Schoolcraft, part i. pp. 334, 353; part iii. pp. 256, 485. Harmon, 'Journal'; Andover, 1820, p. 371. Klemm, C. G., vol. ii. pp. 189, 280.

9 Birch, in "Archæologia,' vol. xxxiv. p. 382.

10 Herod, v. 49.

twelve or twenty-four hours the month and the day of the month, when the record was set up.[11]

It is even related of the Indians of Virginia, that they recorded time by certain hieroglyphic wheels, which they called "Sagkokok Quiacosough," or "record of the gods." These wheels had sixty spokes, each for a year, as if to mark the ordinary age of man, and they were painted on skins kept by the principal priests in the temples. They marked on each spoke or division a hieroglyphic figure, to show the memorable events of the year. John Lederer saw one in a village called Pommacomek, on which the year of the first arrival of the Europeans was marked by a swan spouting fire and smoke from its mouth. The white plumage of the bird and its living on the water indicated the white faces of the Europeans and their coming by sea, while the fire and smoke coming from its mouth meant their firearms.[12] Thus the ancient Mexicans (as well as the civilized nations of Central America, who used a similar system) can only claim to have dated their records more generally and systematically than the ruder North American tribes.

The usual way of recording series of years among the Mexicans has been often described. It consists in the use of four symbols—tochtli, acatl, tecpatl, calli, i.e., *rabbit, cane, cutting-stone, house,* each symbol being numbered by dots from 1 to 13, making thus 52 distinct signs. Each year of a cycle of 52 has thus a distinct numbered symbol belonging to it alone, the numbering of course not going beyond 13. These numbered symbols are, however, not arranged in their reasonable order, but the signs change at the same time as the numbers, till all the 52 combinations are exhausted, the order being 1 rabbit, 2 cane, 3 knife, 4 house, 5 rabbit, 6 cane, and so on. I have pointed out elsewhere the singular coincidence of a Mexican cycle with an ordinary French or English pack of playing-cards, which, arranged on this plan, as for instance ace of hearts, 2 of spades, 3 of diamonds, 4 of clubs, 5 of hearts again, and so on, forms an exact counterpart

11 Harmon, p. 371.

12 'Journal des Sçavans,' 1681, p. 46. Sir W. Talbot, 'The Discoveries of John Lederer'; London, 1672, p. 4. Humboldt, 'Vues des Cordillères'; Paris, 1810–12, pl. xiii.

of an Aztec cycle of 52 years. The account of days was kept by series combined in a similar way, but in different numbers.[13]

The extraordinary analogy between the Mexican system of reckoning years in cycles, and that still in use over a great part of Asia, forms the strongest point of Humboldt's argument for the connexion of the Mexicans with Eastern Asia, and the remarkable character of the coincidence is greatly enforced by the fact, that this complex arrangement answers no useful purpose whatever, inasmuch as mere counting by numbers, or by signs numbered in regular succession, would have been a far better arrangement. It may perhaps have been introduced for some astrological purpose.

The historical picture-writings of the Mexicans seem for the most part very bare and dull to us, who know and care so little about their history. They consist of records of wars, famines, migrations, sacrifices, and so forth, names of persons and places being indicated by symbolic pictures attached to them, as King Itzcoatl, or "knife-snake," by a serpent with stone knives on its back; Tzompanco, or "the place of a skull," now Zumpango, by a picture of a skull skewered on a bar between two upright posts, as enemies' skulls used to be set up; Chapultepec, or "grasshopper hill," by a hill and a grasshopper, and so on, or by more properly phonetic characters, such as will be presently described. The positions of footprints, arrows, etc., serve as guides to the direction of marches and attacks, in very much the same way as may be seen in Catlin's drawing of the pictured robe of Ma-to-toh-pa, or "Four Bears." The mystical paintings which relate to religion and astrology are seldom capable of any independent interpretation, for the same reasons which make it impossible to read the pictured records of songs and charms used further north, namely, that they do not tell their stories in full, but only recall them to the minds of those who are already acquainted with them. The paintings which represent the methodically arranged life of the Aztecs from childhood to old age, have more human interest about them than all the rest put together. In judging the

13 Tylor, 'Mexico and the Mexicans'; London, 1861, p. 239.

Mexican picture-writings as a means of record, it should be borne in mind that though we can understand them to a considerable extent, we should have made very little progress in deciphering them, were it not that there are a number of interpretations, made in writing from the explanations given by Indians, so that the traditions of the art have never been wholly lost. Some few of the Mexican pictures now in existence may perhaps be original documents made before the arrival of the Spaniards, and a great part of those drawn since are certainly copied, wholly or in part, from such original pictures.

It is to M. Aubin, of Paris, a most zealous student of Mexican antiquities, that we owe our first clear knowledge of a phenomenon of great scientific interest in the history of writing. This is

Fig. 8

a well-defined system of phonetic characters, which Clavigero and Humboldt do not seem to have been aware of, as it does not appear in their descriptions of the art.[14] Humboldt indeed speaks of vestiges of phonetic hieroglyphics among the Aztecs, but the examples he gives are only names in which meaning, rather than mere sound, is represented, as in the pictures of a face and water for Axayacatl, or "Water-Face," five dots and a flower for Macuilxochitl, or "Five-Flowers." So Clavigero gives in his list the name of King Itzcoatl, or "Knife-Snake," as represented by a picture of a snake with stone knives upon its back, a more genuine drawing of which is given here (Fig. 8), from the Le Tellier Codex. This is mere picture-writing, but the way in which the same king's name is written in the Vergara Codex, as shown in Fig. 9, is something very different. Here the first syllable, *itz*, is indeed represented by a weapon armed with blades of obsidian,

[14] Clavigero, 'Storia Antica del Messico'; Cesena, 1780–1, vol. ii. pp. 191, etc., 248, etc. Humboldt, 'Vues des Cord.,' pl. xiii.

itz(tli); but the rest of the word, *coatl*, though it means snake, is written, not by a picture of a snake, but by an earthen pot, *co(mitl)*, and above it the sign of water, *a(tl)*. Here we have real phonetic writing, for the name is not to be read, according to sense, "knife-kettle-water," but only according to the sound of the Aztec words, Itz-co-atl. Again, in Fig. 10, in the name of Teocaltitlan, which means "the place of the god's house," the different syllables (with the exception of the *ti*, which is only put in for euphony) are written by (*b*) lips, (*c*) a path (with footmarks

FIG. 9

FIG. 10

on it), (*a*) a house, (*d*) teeth. What this combination of pictures means is only explained by knowing that lips, path, house, teeth, are called in Aztec, *ten(tli)*, *o(tli)*, *cal(li)*, *tlan(tli)*, and thus come to stand for the word Te-o-cal-(ti)-tlan. The device is perfectly familiar to us in what is called a "rebus," as where Prior Burton's name is sculptured in St. Saviour's Church as a cask with a thistle on it, "burr-tun." Indeed, the puzzles of this kind in children's books keep alive to our own day the great transition stage from picture-writing to word-writing, the highest intellectual effort of one period in our history coming down, as so often happens, to be the child's play of a later time.

M. Aubin may be considered as the discoverer of these phonetic signs in the Mexican pictures, or at least he is the first who has worked them out systematically and published a list of them.[15] But the ancient written interpretations have been standing for centuries to prove their existence. Thus, in the Mendoza Codex, the name of a place, pictured as in Fig. 11 by a fishing-net and teeth, is interpreted Matlatlan, that is "Net-Place." Now, *matla(tl)* means a net, and so far the name is a picture, but the teeth, *tlan(tli)*, are used, not pictorially but phonetically, for *tlan,* place. Other more complicated names, such as Acolma, Quauhpanoayan, etc., are written in like manner in phonetic symbols in the same document.[16]

There is no sufficient reason to make us doubt that this purely phonetic writing was of native Mexican origin, and after the Spanish Conquest they turned it to account in a new and curious

FIG. 11

way. The Spanish missionaries, when embarrassed by the difficulty of getting the converts to remember their Ave Marias and Paternosters, seeing that the words were of course mere nonsense to them, were helped out by the Indians themselves, who substituted Aztec words as near in sound as might be to the Latin, and wrote down the pictured equivalents for these words, which enabled them to remember the required formulas. Torquemada and Las Casas have recorded two instances of this device, that *Pater noster* was written by a flag (*pantli*) and a prickly pear (*nochtli*), while the sign of water, *a(tl)*, combined with that of aloe, *me(tl)*, made a compound word *ametl,* which would mean "water-aloe," but in sound made a very tolerable substitute for

15 Aubin, in 'Revue Orientale et Américaine,' vols. iii.–v. Brasseur, 'Hist. des Nat. Civ. du Mexique et de l'Amérique Centrale'; Paris, 1857–9, vol. i. An attempt to prove the existence of something more nearly approaching alphabetic signs (Rev., vol. iv, p. 276–7; Brasseur, p. lxviii.) requires much clearer evidence.

16 Kingsborough, vol. i., and Expl. in vol. vi.

Amen.[17] But M. Aubin has actually found the beginning of a Paternoster of this kind in the metropolitan library of Mexico (Fig. 12), made with a flag, *pan(tli)*, a stone, *te(tl)*, a prickly pear, *noch(tli)*, and again a stone, *te(tl)*, and which would read Pa-te noch-te, or perhaps Pa-tetl noch-tetl.[18]

After the conquest, when the Spaniards were hard at work introducing their own religion and civilization among the conquered Mexicans, they found it convenient to allow the old picture-writing still to be used, even in legal documents. It disappeared in time, of course, being superseded in the long-run by the alphabet; but it is to this transition-period that we owe many, perhaps most, of the picture-documents still preserved. Copies of old historical paintings were made and continued to dates after the arrival of Cortes, and the use of records written

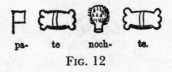

pa-   te   noch-   te.

FIG. 12

in pictures, or in a mixture of pictures and Spanish or Aztec words in ordinary writing, relating to lawsuits, the inheritance of property, genealogies, etc., were in constant use for many years later, and special officers were appointed under government to interpret such documents. To this transition-period, the writing whence the name of Teocaltitlan (Fig. 10) is taken, clearly belongs, as appears by the drawing of the house with its arched door.

A genealogical table of a native family in the Christy Museum is as good a record of this time of transition as could well be cited. The names in it are written, but are accompanied by male and female heads drawn in a style that is certainly Aztec. The names themselves tell the story of the change that was going on in the country. One branch of the family, among whom are to be read the names of Citlalmecatl, or "Star-Necklace," and

17 Brasseur, vol. i. p. xli.

18 Aubin, Rev. O. and A., vol. iii. p. 255.

Cohuacihuatl, or "Snake-Woman," ends in a lady with the Spanish name of Justa; while another branch, beginning with such names as Tlapalxilotzin and Xiuhcozcatzin, finishes with Juana and her children Andres and Francisco. The most thoroughly native thing in the whole is a figure referring to an ancestor of Justa's, and connected with his name by a line of footprints to show how the line is to be followed, in true Aztec fashion. The figure itself is a head drawn in native style, with the eye in full front, though the face is in profile, in much the same way as an Egyptian would have drawn it, and it is set in a house as a symbol of dignity, having written over against it the high title of Ompamozcaltitotzaqualtzinco, which, if I may trust the imperfect dictionary of Molina, and my own weak knowledge of Aztec, means "His excellency our twice skilful gaoler."

The importance of this Mexican phonetic system in the History of the Art of Writing may be perhaps made clearer by a comparison of the Aztec pictures with the Egyptian hieroglyphics.

Egyptian hieroglyphic inscriptions consist of figures of objects, animate and inanimate, men and animals, and parts of them, plants, the heaven bodies, and an immense number of different weapons, tools, and articles of the most miscellaneous character. These figures are arranged in upright columns or horizontal bands, and are to be read in succession, but they are not all intended to act upon the mind in the same way. When an ordinary inscription is taken to pieces, it is found that the figures composing it fall into two great classes. Part of them are to be read and understood as pictures, a drawing of a horse for "horse," a branch for "wood," etc., upon the same principle as in any savage picture-writing. The other part of the figures are phonetic. How they came to be so, seems plain from cases where we find the same picture sometimes used to stand for the object it represents, and sometimes for the sound of that object's name, after the manner just described of the rebus. Thus the picture of a star may represent a star, called in Egyptian *sba,* and the picture of a kid may stand for a kid, called in Egyptian *ab;* but these pictures may also be brought in to help in the spelling of the words *sba,* "door," and *ab,* "thirst," so that here they have passed into phonetic signs.[19] It is not always possible to distinguish whether a hieroglyph is used as a syllable or a letter. But it is clear that from an early period the Egyptians had chosen a number of hieroglyphs to be used as vowels and consonants to write words with, that is to say, they had invented alphabetic writing. Their use of hieroglyphs in all these stages, picture, syllable, letter, is of great interest in the history of writing, as giving the whole course of development by which a picture, of a mouth for instance, meant first simply mouth, then the name of mouth *ro*, and lastly dropped its vowel and became the letter *r*. Of these three steps, the Mexicans made the first two.

In Egyptian hieroglyphics, special figures are not always set apart for phonetic use. At least, a number of signs are used sometimes as letters, and sometimes as pictures, in which latter case they are often marked with a stroke. Thus the mouth, with a stroke to it, is usually (though not always) pictorial, as it were, "one mouth," while without the stroke it is *r* or *ro*, and so on. The words of a sentence are frequently written by a combination of these two methods, that is, by spelling the word first, and then adding a picture sign to remove all doubt as to its meaning. Thus the letters read as *futi* in an inscription, followed by a drawing of a worm, mean "worm" (Coptic, *fent*), and the letters *kk*, followed by the picture of a star hanging from heaven, mean "darkness" (Coptic, *kake*). There may even be words written in ancient hieroglyphics which are still alive in English. Thus *hbn*, followed by two signs, one of which is the determinative for wood, is *ebony*; and *tb*, followed by the drawing of a brick, is a sun-dried brick, Coptic *tôbe*, *tôbi*, which seems to have passed into the Arabic *tob*, or with the article, *attob*, thence into Spanish through the Moors, as *adobe*, in which form, and as *dobie*, it is current among the English-speaking population of America.

*   *   *   *

We thus see that the ancient Egyptians and the Aztecs made in much the same way the great step from picture-writing to word-writing. To have used the picture of an object to represent

[19] Renouf, 'Elementary Grammar of the Ancient Egyptian Language,' London, 1875.

the sound of the root or crude-form of its name, as the Mexicans did in drawing a hand, *ma(itl)*, to represent, not a hand, but the sound *ma;* and teeth, *tlan(tli)*, to represent, not teeth, but the sound *tlan,* though they do not seem to have applied to anything but the writing of proper names and foreign words, is sufficient to show that they had started on the road which led the Egyptians to a system of syllabic, and to some extent of alphabetic writing. There is even evidence that the Maya nation of Yucatan, the ruins of whose temples and palaces are so well known from the travels of Catherwood and Stephens, not only had a system of phonetic writing, but used it for writing ordinary words and sentences. A Spanish MS., "Relación de las Cosas de Yucatan," bearing the date of 1561, and the name of Diego de Landa, Bishop of Merida, has been published by the Abbé Brasseur,[20] and contains not only a set of chronological signs resembling the figures of the Central American sculptures and the Dresden Codex, but a list of over thirty characters, some alphabetic, as *a, i, m, n;* some syllabic, as *ku, ti;* and a sentence, *ma in kati,* "I will not," written with them. The genuineness of this information, and its bearing on the interpretation of the inscriptions on the monuments, are matters for future investigation.

Yet another people, the Chinese, made the advance from pictures to phonetic writing, and it was perhaps because of the peculiar character of their spoken language that they did it in so different a way. The whole history of their art of writing still lies open to us. They began by drawing the plainest outlines of sun, moon, tortoise, fish, boy, hatchet, tree, dog, and so forth, and thus forming characters which are still extant, and are known as the *Ku-wăn,* or "ancient pictures."[21] Such pictures, though so much altered that, were not their ancient forms still to be seen, it would hardly be safe to say that they had ever been pictures at all, are still used to some extent in Chinese writing, as in the characters for man, sun, moon, tree, etc. There are also combined pictorial signs, as water and eye for "tears," and other kinds of

---

[20] Brasseur, 'Relation des Choses de Yucatan de Diego de Landa,' etc.; Paris and London, 1864.

[21] J. M. Callery, 'Systema Phoneticum Scripturæ Sinicæ,' part i.; Macao, 1841, p. 29. Endlicher, Chin. Gramm., p. 3, etc.

purely symbolic characters. But the great mass of characters at present in use are double, consisting of two signs, one for sound, the other for sense. They are called *hing-shing*, that is, "pictures and sounds." In one of the two signs the transition from the picture of the object to the sound of its name has taken place; in the other it has not, but it is still a picture, and its use (something like that of the determinative in the Egyptian hieroglyphics) is to define which of the meanings belonging to the spoken word is to be taken. Thus a ship is called in Chinese *chow*, so a picture of a ship stands for the sound *chow*. But the word *chow* means several other things; and to show which is intended in any particular instance, a determinative sign or key is attached to it. Thus the ship joined with the sign of water stands for *chow*, "ripple," with that of speech for *chow*, "loquacity," with that of fire, for *chow*, "flickering of flame"; and so on for "waggon-pole," "fluff," and several other things, which have little in common but the name of *chow*. If we agreed that pictures of a knife, a tree, an 0, should be determinative signs of things which have to do with cutting, with plants, and with numbers, we might make a drawing of a pear to do duty, with the assistance of one of these determinative signs, for *pare, pear, pair*. . . .

Looking now at the history of purely alphabetical writing, it has been shown that there is one alphabet, that of the Egyptian hieroglyphics, the development of which (and of course of its derived forms) is clearly to be traced from the stage of pure pictures to that of pure letters. It was long ago noticed that some of the old Egyptian hieratic characters have been directly retained in use in Egypt. The Coptic Christians still keep up in their churches their sacred language, which is a direct descendant of the ancient Egyptian; and the Coptic alphabet, in which it is written and printed, was formed in early Christian times by adding to the Greek alphabet certain new characters to express articulations not properly belonging to the Greek. Among these additional letters, at least four are clearly seen to be taken from the old hieroglyphics, probably from their hieratic or cursive form, and thus to preserve an unbroken tradition at once from the period of picture-writing to that of the alphabet, and from times earlier than the building of the pyramids up to the present day.

It has long been known that the great family of alphabets to which the Roman letters belong with the Greek, the Gothic, the Northern Runes, etc., are to be traced back into connection with the Phœnician and Old Hebrew characters, the very word *alphabet* (alpha-bēta, aleph-beth) being an acknowledgment of the derivation from Semitic writing. But sufficient proof was wanting as to how these ancient Semitic letters came to be made. . . .

After the deciphering of the Egyptian hieroglyphs, it was seen to be probable that not only were the ancient Egyptians the first inventors of alphabetic writing, but that the Phœnician and Hebrew alphabet was itself borrowed from the Egyptian hieroglyph-alphabet. Mr. Samuel Sharpe made the attempt to bring together the Egypian hieroglyphs in their pictorial form with the square Hebrew characters. The Vicomte de Rougé's comparison left for years unpublished, of the Egyptian hieratic characters with the old Phœnician letters, confirms Mr. Sharpe's view as to the letters Vav and Shin (*f* and *sh*), and on the whole, though identifying several characters on the strength of too slight a resemblance, it lays what seems a solid foundation for the opinion that the main history of alphabetic writing is open to us, from its beginning in the Egyptian pictures to the use of these pictures to express sounds, which led to the formation of the Egyptian mixed pictorial, syllabic, and alphabetic writing, from which was derived the pure alphabet known to us in its early Phœnician, Moabite, and Hebrew stages, whence the Greek, Latin, and numerous other derived forms come down to modern times.[22]

It remains to point out the possibility of one people getting the art of writing from another, without taking the characters they used for particular letters. Two systems of letters, or rather of characters representing syllables, have been invented in modern times, by men who had got the idea of representing sound

22 Sharpe, 'Egyptian Hieroglyphics'; London, 1861, p. 17. Vte. Em. de Rougé, 'Mémoire sur l'Origine Egyptienne de l'Alphabet Phénicien,' Paris, 1874. In former editions of the present work, the Egyptian origin of the alphabet was only treated as a likely supposition. In consequence of the appearance of M. de Rougé's argument since, the text has been altered to embody the now more advanced position of the subject. [Note to 3rd Edition.]

by written characters from seeing the books of civilized men, and
applied it in their own way to their own languages. Some forty
years ago a halfbreed Cherokee Indian, named Sequoyah (otherwise George Guess), invented an ingenious system of writing his
language in syllabic signs, which were adopted by the missionaries, and came into common use. In the table given by Schoolcraft there are eighty-five such signs, in great part copied or
modified from those Sequoyah had learnt from print; but the
letter D is to be read *a;* the letter M, *lu;* the figure 4, *se;* and so
on through R, T, i, A, and a number more.[23] The syllabic system
invented by a West African negro, Momoru Doalu Bukere, was
found in use in the Vei country, about fifteen years since.[24]
When Europeans inquired into its origin, Doalu said that the
invention was revealed to him in a dream by a tall venerable

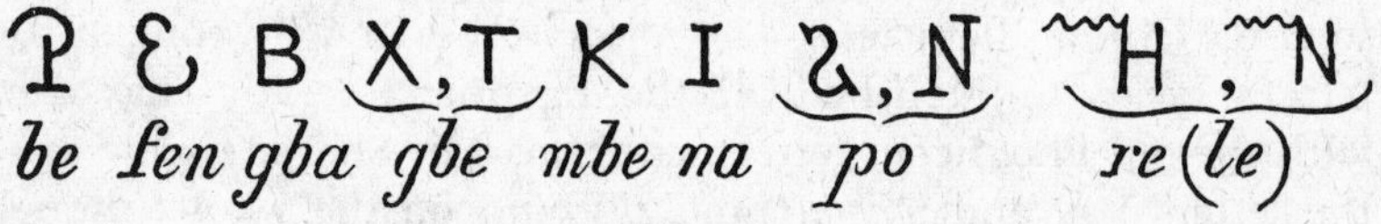

be ʃen gba gbe mbe na po re (le)

FIG. 13

white man in a long coat, who said he was sent by other white
men to bring him a book, and who taught him some characters
to write words with. Doalu awoke, but never learnt what the
book was about. So he called his friends together, and one of
them afterwards had another dream, in which a white man appeared to him, and told him that the book had come from God.
It appears that Doalu, when he was a boy, had really seen a white
missionary, and had learnt verses from the English Bible from
him, so that it is pretty clear that the sight of a printed book
gave him the original idea which he worked out into his very
complete and original phonetic system. It is evident from Fig. 13
that some part of the characters he adopted were taken, of course
without any reference to their sound, from the letters he had
seen in print. His system numbers 162 characters, representing

23 Schoolcraft, part ii. p. 228. Bastian, vol. i. p. 423.

24 Koelle, 'Grammar of the Vei Language'; London, 1854, p. 229, etc. J. L.
Wilson, 'Western Africa'; London, 1856, p. 95.

mostly syllables, as *a, be, bo, dso, fen, gba;* but sometimes longer articulations, as *seli, sediya, taro.* Though it is almost entirely and purely phonetic, it is interesting to observe that it includes three genuine picture-signs, o o *gba,* "money"; ₒ°ₒ *bu,* "gun," (represented by bullets), and ~~~~ *chi,* "water," this last sign being identical with that which stands for water in the Egyptian hieroglyphics.

It appears from these facts that the transmission of the art of writing does not necessarily involve a detailed transmission of the particular signs in use, and the difficulty in tracing the origin of some of the Semitic characters may result from their having been made in the same way as these American and African characters. If this be the case, there is an end of all hope of tracing them any further.

In conclusion, it may be observed that the art of picture-writing soon dwindles away in all countries when word-writing is introduced, yet there are a few isolated forms in which it holds its own, in spite of writing and printing, at this very day. The so-called Roman numerals are still in use, and I II III are as plain and indisputable picture-writing as any sign on an Indian scroll of birch-bark. Why V and X mean five and ten is not so clear, but there is some evidence in favour of the view that it may have come by counting fingers or strokes up to nine, and then making a stroke with another across to mark it, somewhat as the deaf-and-dumb Massieu tells us that, in his untaught state, his fingers taught him to count up to ten, and then he made a mark. Loskiel, the Moravian missionary, says of the Iroquois, "They count up to ten, and make a cross; then ten again, and so on, till they have finished; then they take the tens together, and make with them hundreds, thousands, and hundreds of thousands."[25] A more modern observer says of the distant tribe of the Creeks, that they reckon by tens, and that in recording on grave-posts the years of age of the deceased, the scalps he has taken, or the war-parties he has led, they make perpendicular strokes for units, and a cross for ten.[26] The Chinese character for ten is an upright

[25] Loskiel, Gesch. der Mission der evangelischen Brüder; Barby, 1789, p. 39.
[26] Schoolcraft, part i. p. 273.

cross; and in an old Chinese account of the life of Christ, it is said that "they made a very large and heavy machine of wood, resembling the character ten," which he carried, and to which he was nailed.[27] The Egyptians, in their hieroglyphic character, counted by upright strokes up to nine, and then made a special sign for ten, in this respect resembling the modern Creek Indians, and the fact that the Chinese only count I II III in strokes, and go on with an X for four, and then with various other symbols till they come to + or ten, does not interfere with the fact, that in three or four systems of numeration, so far as we know independent of one another, in Italy, China, and North America, more or less of the earlier numerals are indicated by counted strokes, and ten by a crossed stroke. Such an origin for the Roman X is quite consistent with a half X or V being used for five, to save making a number of strokes, which would be difficult to count at a glance.[28]

However this may be, the pictorial origin of I II III is beyond doubt. And in technical writing, such terms as T-square and S-hook, and phrases such as "⊙ before clock 4 min.," and " ☽ rises at 8h. 35m.," survive to show that even in the midst of the highest European civilization, the spirit of the earliest and rudest form of writing is not yet quite extinct.

[27] Davis, 'The Chinese'; London, 1851, vol. ii. p. 176.

[28] A dactylic origin of V, as being a rude figure of the open hand, with thumb stretched out, and fingers close together, succeeding the I II III IIII, made with the upright fingers, has been propounded by Grotefend, and has occurred to others. It is plausible, but wants actual evidence.

CHAPTER VI

IMAGES AND NAMES

* * * *

When a child plays with a doll or plaything, the toy is commonly made to represent in the child's mind some imaginary object which is more or less like it. Wooden soldiers, for instance, or the beasts in a Noah's ark, have a real resemblance which any one would recognise at once to soldiers and beasts, and all that the child has to do is to suppose them bigger, and alive, and to consider them as walking of themselves when they are pushed about. But an imaginative child will be content with much less real resemblance than this. It will bring in a larger subjective element, and make a dog do duty for a horse, or a soldier for a shepherd, till at last the objective resemblance almost disappears, and a bit of wood may be dragged about, representing a ship on the sea, or a coach on the road. Here the likeness of the bit of wood to a ship or a coach is very slight indeed; but it is a thing, and can be moved about in an appropriate manner, and placed in a suitable position with respect to other objects. Unlike as the toy may be to what it represents in the child's mind, it still answers a purpose, and is an evident assistance to the child in enabling it to arrange and develop its ideas, by working the objects and actions of stories it is acquainted with into a series of dramatic pictures. Of how much use the material object is in setting the mind to work, may be seen by taking it away and leaving the child with nothing to play with.

At an early age, children learn more from play than from teaching; and the use of toys is very great in developing their minds by giving them the means of, as it were, taking a scene or an event to pieces, and putting its parts together in new combinations, a process which immensely increases the definiteness of the children's ideas and their power of analysis. It is because the use of toys is principally in developing the subjective side of the mind, that the elaborate figures and models of which the toy-shops have been full of late years are of so little use. They are carefully worked out into the nicest details; but they are models or pictures, not playthings, and children, who know quite well what it is they want, tire of them in a few hours, unless, indeed, they can break them up and make real toys of the bits. What a child wants is not one picture, but the means of making a thousand. Objective knowledge, such as is to be gained from the elaborate doll's houses and grocer's shops with their appurtenances, may be got in plenty elsewhere by mere observation; but toys, to be of value in early education, should be separate, so as to allow of their being arranged in any variety of combination, and not too servile and detailed copies of objects, so that they may not be mere pictures, but symbols, which a child can make to stand for many objects with the aid of its imagination.

In later years, and among highly educated people, the mental process which goes on in a child playing with wooden soldiers and horses, though it never disappears, must be sought for in the midst of more complex phenomena. Perhaps nothing in after life more closely resembles the effect of a doll upon a child, than the effect of the illustrations of a tale upon a grown-up reader. Here the objective resemblance is very indefinite: two artists would make pictures of the same scene that were very unlike one another, the very persons and places depicted are imaginary, and yet what reality and definiteness is given to the scene by a good picture. But in this case the direct action of an image on the mind complicates itself with the deepest problems of painting and sculpture. . . .

Mr. Backhouse one day noticed in Van Diemen's Land a native woman arranging several stones that were flat, oval, and about two inches wide, and marked in various directions with black and red lines. These he learned represented absent friends, and one larger than the rest stood for a fat native woman on Flinders Island, known by the name of Mother Brown.[1] Similar practices are found among far higher races than the ill-fated Tasmanians. Among some North American tribes, a mother who has lost a

---

[1] Backhouse, 'Narrative of a Visit to the Australian Colonies'; London, 1843, p. 104.

child keeps its memory ever present to her by filling its cradle with black feathers and quills, and carrying it about with her for a year or more. When she stops anywhere, she sets up the cradle and talks to it as she goes about her work, just as she would have done if the dead baby had been still alive within it.[2] Here we have no image; but in Africa we find a rude doll, representing the child, kept as a memorial. It is well known that over a great part of Africa the practice prevails, that whenever twin children are born, one or both of them are immediately killed. Among the Wanyamwezi, one of the two is always killed; and, strange to say, "the universal custom amongst these tribes, is for the mother to wrap a gourd or calabash in skins, to place it to sleep with, and feed it like, the survivor."[3] Bastian saw Indian women in Peru, who had lost an infant, carrying about on their backs a wooden doll to represent it.[4] Among the Bechuanas, it is a custom for married women to carry a doll with them till they have a child, when the doll is discarded. There is one of these dolls in the London Missionary Museum, consisting simply of a long calabash, like a bottle, wound round with strings of beads. The Basuto women use clay dolls in the same way, giving them the names of tutelary deities, and treating them as children.[5] Among the Ostyaks of Eastern Siberia, there is found a still more instructive case, in which we see the transition from the image of the dead man to the actual idol. When a man dies, they set up a rude wooden image of him, which receives offerings and has honours paid to it, and the widow embraces and caresses it. As a general rule, these images are buried at the end of three years or so, but sometimes the image of a shaman[6] is set up permanently, and remains as a saint for ever.[7]

2 Catlin, vol. ii. p. 133.

3 Burton, 'Central Africa,' vol. ii. p. 23.

4 Bastian, vol. ii. p. 376.   5 Casalis, p. 251.

6 A *shaman* is a native sorcerer or medicine-man. His name is corrupted from Sanskrit çramana, a Buddhist ascetic, a term which is one of the many relics of Buddhism in Northern Asia, having been naturalized into the grovelling fetish-worship of the Ostyaks and Tunguzes. See Weber, 'Indische Skizzen,' p. 66.

7 Erman, 'Reise um die Erde'; Berlin, 1833–48, vol. ii. p. 677. 'Voyages au Nord,' vol. viii. p. 415.

The principal use of images to races in the lower stages of civilization is that to which their name of "the visible," εἴδωλον, idol, has come to be in great measure restricted in modern language. The idol answers to the savage in one province of thought the same purpose that its analogue the doll does to the child. It enables him to give a definite existence and a personality to the vague ideas of higher beings, which his mind can hardly grasp without some material aid. How these ideas came into the minds of even the lowest savages, need not be discussed here; it is sufficient to know that, so far as we have accurate information, they seem to be present everywhere in at least a rudimentary state.

It does not appear that idols accompany religious ideas down to the lowest levels of the human race, but rather that they belong to a period of transition and growth. At least this seems the only reasonable explanation of the fact, that in America, for instance, among the lowest races, the Fuegians and the Indians of the southern forests, we hear little or nothing of idols. Among the so-called Red Indians of the North, we sometimes find idols worshipped and sacrificed to, but not always, while in Mexico and Peru the whole apparatus of idols, temples, priests, and sacrifices is found in a most complex and elaborate form. It does not seem, indeed, that the growth of the use of images may be taken as any direct measure of the growth of religious ideas, which is complicated with a multitude of other things. Image-worship depends in considerable measure on the representation of ideal beings. In so far as this symbolical element is concerned, it seems that when man has got some way in developing the religious element in him, he begins to catch at the device of setting a puppet or a stone as the symbol and representative of the notions of a higher being which are floating in his mind. He sees in it, as a child does in a doll, a material form which his imagination can clothe with all the attributes of a being which he has never seen, but of whose existence and nature he judges by what he supposes to be its works. He can lodge it in the place of honour, cover it up in the most precious garments, propitiate it with offerings such as would be acceptable to himself. The Christian missionary goes among the heathen to teach the doctrines of a higher religion, and to substitute for the cruder theology of the savage a belief in a God so far beyond human comprehension, that no definition of the Deity is possible to man beyond vague predications, as of infinite power, duration, knowledge, and goodness. It is not perhaps to be wondered at, that the missionary should see nothing in idol-worship but hideous folly and wickedness, and should look upon an idol as a special invention of the devil. He is strengthened, moreover, in such a view by the fact that by the operation of a certain law of the human mind (of which more will be said presently), the idol, which once served a definite and important purpose in the education of the human race, has come to be confounded with the idea of which it was the symbol, and has thus become the parent of the grossest superstition and delusion. But the student who occupies himself in tracing the early stages of human civilization, can see in the rude image of the savage an important aid to early religious development, while it often happens that the missionary is as unable to appreciate the use and value of an idol, as the grown-up man is to realize the use of a doll to a child.

Man being the highest living creature that can be seen and imitated, it is natural that idols should mostly be imitations, more or less rude, of the human form. To show that the beings they represent are greater and more powerful than man, they are often huge in size, and sometimes, by a very natural expedient, several heads and pairs of arms and legs show that they have more wisdom, strength, and swiftness than man. The sun and moon, which in the physical system of the savage are often held to be living creatures of monstrous power, are represented by images. The lower animals, too, are often raised to the honour of personating supernatural powers, a practice which need not surprise us, when we consider that the savage does not set the lower animals at so great a depth below him as the civilized man does, but allows them the possession of language, and after his fashion, of souls, while we perhaps err in the opposite direction, by stretching the great gap which separates the lowest man from the highest animal, into an impassable gulf. Moreover, as animals have some powers which man only possesses in a less degree, or not at all, these powers may be attributed to a deity by personating him under the forms of the animals which possess them, or by giving to an image of human form parts of such animals; thus the feet of a stag, the head of a lion, or the wings of a bird, may serve to express the swiftness or ferocity of a god, or to show that he can fly into the upper regions of the air, or, like the goat's feet of Pan, they may be mere indications of his character and functions.

* * * *

The rudeness and shapelessness of some of the blocks and stones which serve as idols among many tribes, and those not always the lowest, is often surprising. There seems to be mostly, though not always, a limit to the shapelessness of an idol which is to represent the human form; this is the same which a child would unconsciously apply, namely, that its length, breadth, and thickness must bear a proportion not too far different from the proportions of the human body. A wooden brick or a cotton-reel, set up or lying down, will serve well enough for a child to represent a man or woman standing or lying, but a cube or a ball would not answer the purpose so well, and if put for a man, could hardly be supposed even by the imagination of a child to represent more than position and movement, or relative size when compared with larger or smaller objects. Much the same test is applied by the uncivilized man in a particular class of myths or legends, which come to be made in this wise. We all have more or less of the power of seeing forms of men and animals in inanimate objects, which sometimes have in fact a considerable likeness of outline to what they suggest, but which, in some instances, have scarcely any other resemblance to the things into which fancy shapes them than a rough similarity in the proportions of their longer and shorter diameters. Myths which have been applied to such fancied resemblances, or have grown up out of them, may be collected from all parts of the world, and from races high and low in the scale of culture.

Among the Riccaras, there was once a young Indian who was in love with a girl, but her parents refused their consent to the marriage, so the youth went out into the prairie, lamenting his fate, and the girl wandered out to the same place, and the faithful dog followed his master. There they wandered with nothing to live on but the wild grapes, and at last they were turned into stone, first their feet, and then gradually the upper part of their bodies, till at last nothing was left unchanged but a bunch of grapes, which the girl holds in her hand to this day. And all this story has grown out of the fancied likeness of three stones to two human figures and a dog. There are many grapes growing near, and the Riccaras venerate these figures, leaving little offerings for them when they pass by.[8] So the Seneca Indians affirm that the rounded head-like pebbles on the shore of Lake Canandaigua are the petrified skulls of the devoured tribe disgorged by the great snake in its death-agony.[9]

There was a Maori warrior named Hau, and his wife Wairaka deserted him. So he followed her, going from one river to the next, and at last he came to one where he looked out slyly from the corner of his eye to see if he could discover her. He breathed hard when he reached the place where Wairaka was sitting with her paramour. He said to her, "Wairaka, I am thirsty, fetch me some water." She got up and walked down to the sea with a calabash in each hand. He made her go on until the waves flowed over her shoulders, when he repeated a charm, which converted her into a rock that still bears her name. Then he went joyfully on his way.[10]

So the figure of the weeping Niobe turned into a rock, might be seen on Mount Sipylus.[11] The groups of upright stones, set up by old inhabitants in Africa and India, are now giants, men, flocks and herds changed into stone; the avenues of monoliths at Karnak are petrified battalions; the stone-circles on English downs have suggested other fanciful legends, as where for instance the story has shaped itself that such a ring was a party of girls who were turned into stone for dancing carols on a Sunday.[12] There is a tradition, probably still current in Palestine, of

8 Lewis and Clarke, Expedition; Philadelphia, 1814, p. 107.

9 Schoolcraft, part iii. p. 323.

10 W. B. Baker, On Maori Popular Poetry, Trans. Eth. Soc.; London, 1861, p. 49.

11 Pausanias, i. 21.

12 See Forbes-Leslie, 'Early Races of Scotland'; Edinburgh, 1866, vol. i. p. 191. William of Malmesbury, ii. 174; see Liebrecht in Heidelberger Jahrbücher, 1868, p. 328.

a city between Petra and Hebron, whose inhabitants were turned into stone for their wickedness. Seetzen, the traveller, visited the spot where the remains of the petrified inhabitants of the wicked city are still to be seen, and, just as in the American tale, he found their heads a number of stony concretions, lying scattered on the ground.[13] The imagination which could work on these rude objects could naturally discover in stone statues the result of such a transformation. Statues sculptured by a higher Peruvian race at Tiahuanaco, seemed to the ruder Indians petrified men,[14] and the clumsy stone busts on Asiatic steppes are, to the rude Turanians who worship them, as it were fossilized deities.[15] Especially the Jewish and Moslem iconoclastic mind thinks ancient statues men transformed by enchantment or judgment, and here we have the source of the Arabian Nights' tale of the infidel city, found with its inhabitants turned to lifelike counterfeits in stone.[16]

The myths of footprints stamped into the rock by gods or mighty men are not the least curious of this class, not only from the power of imagination required to see footprints in mere round or long cavities, but also from the unanimity with which Egyptians, Greeks, Brahmans, Buddhists, Christians, and Moslems have adopted them as relics, each from their own point of view. The typical case is the sacred footprint of Ceylon, which is a cavity in the rock, 5 feet long by 2.5 feet wide, at the top of Adam's Peak, made into something like a huge footstep by mortar divisions for the toes. Brahmans, Buddhists, and Moslems still climb the mountain to do reverence to it; but to the Brahman it is the footstep of Siva, to the Buddhist of the great founder of his religion, Gautama Buddha, and to the Moslem it is the spot where Adam stood when he was driven from Paradise; while the Gnostics have held it to be the footprint of Ieû, and Christians have been divided between the conflicting claims of St. Thomas

13 Kenrick, 'Essay on Primaeval History'; London, 1846, p. 41.

14 Cieza de Leon, Travels (tr. and ed. by Markham), Hakluyt Soc. 1864, p. 378.

15 Latham, 'Descriptive Ethnology'; vol. i. p. 360.

16 Lane, 'Thousand and One Nights,' vol. iii. p. 141. M. A. Walker, 'Macedonia,' London, 1864, p. 48.

and the Eunuch of Candace, Queen of Ethiopia.[17] The followers of these different faiths have found holy footprints in many countries of the Old World, and the Christians have carried the idea into various parts of Europe, where saints have left their footmarks; while, even in America, St. Thomas left his footsteps on the shores of Bahia, as a record of his mythic journey.[18]

For all we know, the whole mass of the Old World footprint-myths may have had but a single origin, and have travelled from one people to another. The story is found, too, in the Pacific Islands, for in Samoa two hollow places, near six feet long, in a rock, are shown as the footprints of Tiitii, where he stood when he pushed the heavens up from the earth.[19] But there are reasons which may make us hesitate to consider the whole Polynesian mythology as independent of Asiatic influence. In North America, at the edge of the Great Pipestone Quarry, where the Great Spirit stood when the blood of the buffalos he was devouring ran down upon the stone and turned it red, there his footsteps are to be seen deeply marked in the rock, in the form of the track of a great bird;[20] while Mexican eyes could discern in the solid rock at Tlanepantla the mark of hand and foot left by the mighty Quetzalcoatl.[21]

There are three kinds of prints in the rock which may have served as a foundation for such tales as these. In many parts of the world there are fossil footprints of birds and beasts, many of huge size. The North American Indians also, whose attention is specially alive to the footprints of men and animals, very often carve them on rocks, sometimes with figures of the animals to which they belong. These footprints are sometimes so naturally done as to be mistaken for real ones. The rock of which Andersson heard in South Africa, "in which the tracks of all the different animals indigenous to the country are distinctly vis-

[17] Tennent, 'Ceylon'; vol. ii. p. 132. Scherzer, Voy. of the Novara, E. Tr.; London, 1861, etc., vol. i. p. 413.

[18] Southey, 'History of Brazil'; London, 1822, vol. i.; Sup. p. xx.

[19] Rev. G. Turner, 'Nineteen Years in Polynesia'; London, 1861, p. 245.

[20] Catlin, vol. ii. p. 165, etc.

[21] J. G. Müller, 'Amerikanische Urreligionen'; Basle, 1855, p. 578, see 272.

ible,"[22] is probably such a sculptured rock. Thirdly, there are such mere shapeless holes as those to which most or all of the Old World myths seem to be attached. Now the difficulty in working out the problem of the origin of these myths is this, that if the prints are real fossil ones, or good sculptures, stories of the beings that made them might grow up independently anywhere; but one can hardly fancy men in many different places coming separately upon the quaint notion of mere hollows, six feet long, being monstrous footprints, unless the notion of monstrous footprints being found elsewhere were already current. At the foot of the page are references to some passages relating to the subject.[23]

It has just been remarked that there is a certain process of the human mind through which, among men at a low level of education, the use of images leads to gross superstition and delusion. No one will deny that there is an evident connexion between an object, and an image or picture of it; but we civilized men know well that this connexion is only *subjective*, that is, in the mind of the observer, while there is no *objective* connexion between them. By an objective connexion, I mean such a connexion as there is between the bucket in the well and the hand that draws it up—when the hand stops, the bucket stops too; or between a man and his shadow—when the man moves, the shadow moves too; or between an electro-magnet and the iron filings near it— when the current passes through the coil, a change takes place in the condition of the iron filings. These are, of course, crude examples; but if more nicety is necessary, it might be said that the connexion is in some degree what a mathematician expresses in saying that y is a function of x, when, if x changes, y changes too. The connexion between a man and his portrait is not objective, for what is done to the man has no effect upon the portrait, and vice versâ.

To an educated European nowadays this sounds like a mere

22 C. J. Andersson, Lake Ngami, etc., p. 327.

23 Lyell, Second Visit to U.S.; London, 1850, vol. ii. p. 313. C. Hamilton Smith, Nat. Hist. of Human Species; Edinburgh, 1848, p. 35. Schoolcraft, part iii. p. 74. Burton, 'Central Africa'; vol. i. p. 288. Squier and Davis, Anct. Mon. of Mssi. Valley, vol. i. of Smithsonian Contr.; Washington, 1848, p. 293. Rawlinson, Herodotus; book ii. 91. iv. 82.

truism, so self-evident that it is not necessary to make a formal statement of it; but it may nevertheless be shown that this is one of the cases in which the accumulated experience and the long course of education of the civilized races have brought them not only to reverse the opinion of the savage, but commonly to think that their own views are the only ones that could naturally arise in the mind of any rational human being. It needs no very large acquaintance with the life and ways of thought of the savage, to prove that there is to be found all over the world, especially among races at a low mental level, a view as to this matter which is very different from that which a more advanced education has impressed upon us. Man, in a low stage of culture, very common-ly believes that between the object and the image of it there is a real connexion, which does not arise from a mere subjective process in the mind of the observer, and that it is accordingly possible to communicate an impression to the original through the copy. We may follow this erroneous belief up into periods of high civilization, its traces becoming fainter as education ad-vances, and not only is this confusion of subjective and objective relations connected with many of the delusions of idolatry, but even so seemingly obscure a subject as magic and sorcery may be brought in great measure into clear daylight, by looking at it as evolved from this process of the mind.

It is related by an early observer of the natives of Australia, that in one of their imitative dances they made use of a grass-figure of a kangaroo, and the ceremony was held to give them power over the real kangaroos in the bush.[24] In North America, when an Algonquin wizard wishes to kill a particular animal, he makes a grass or cloth image of it, and hangs it up in his wigwam. Then he repeats several times the incantation, "See how I shoot," and lets fly an arrow at the image. If he drives it in, it is a sign that the animal will be killed next day. Again, while an arrow touched by the magical wedáwin, and afterwards fired into the track of an animal, is believed to arrest his course, or otherwise affect him, till the hunter can come up, a similar virtue is be-lieved to be exerted, if but the figure of the animal sought be drawn on wood or bark, and afterwards submitted to the influ-

24 Collins, 'New South Wales'; London, 1798, vol. i. p. 569.

ences of the magic medicine and incantation. In their picture-writings, a man or beast is shown to be under magic influence by drawing a line from the mouth to the heart, as in the annexed figure, which represents a wolf under the charm of the magician, and corresponds to the incantation sung by the medicine-man, "Run, wolf, your body's mine."[25] Writing in the last century, Charlevoix remarks that the Illinois and some other tribes make little marmouzets or puppets to represent those whose lives they wish to shorten, and pierce these images to the heart.[26]

We find thus among the Indians of North America one of the commonest arts of magic practiced in Europe in ancient and mediæval times. The art of making an image and melting it away, drying it up, shooting at it, sticking pins or thorns into it,

FIG. 14

that some like injury may befall the person it is to represent, is too well known to need detailed description here,[27] and it is still to be found existing in various parts of the world. Thus the Peruvian sorcerers are said still to make rag dolls and stick cactus-thorns into them, and to hide them in secret holes in houses, or in the wool of beds or cushions, thereby to cripple people, or turn them sick or mad.[28] In Borneo the familiar European practice still exists, of making a wax figure of the enemy to be be-

[25] Schoolcraft, part i. pp. 372, 380–382, part ii. p. 180. See 'Narrative of John Tanner,' part ii.

[26] Charlevoix, vol. vi. p. 88. See Waitz, 'Anthropologie,' vol. iii. p. 214.

[27] Jacob Grimm, 'Deutsche Mythologie,' Göttingen, 3rd Edit.; 1854, p. 1045, etc. Brand, 'Popular Antiquities,' Bohn's Series; London, 1855, vol. iii. pp. 10, 52, 141.

[28] Rivero and Tschudi, p. 181.

witched, whose body is to waste away as the image is gradually melted,[29] as in the story of Margery Jordane's waxen image of Henry VI. The old Roman law punished by the extreme penalty the slaying of an absent person by means of a wax figure. The Hindoo arts are thus described by the Abbé Dubois:—"They knead earth taken from the sixty-four most unclean places, with hair, clippings of hair, bits of leather, etc., and with this they make little figures, on the breasts of which they write the name of the enemy; over these they pronounce magical words and mantrams, and consecrate them by sacrifices. No sooner is this done, than the *grahas*, or planets, seize the hated person, and inflict on him a thousand ills. They sometimes pierce these figures right through with an awl, or cripple them in different ways, with the intention of killing or crippling in reality the object of their vengeance."[30] Again, the Karens of Burmah model an image of a person from the earth of his footprints, and stick it over with cotton seeds, intending thereby to strike the person represented with dumbness.[31] Here we have the making of the figure combined with the ancient practice in Germany known as the "earth-cutting" (erdschnitt), cutting out the earth or turf where the man who is to be destroyed has stood, and hanging it in the chimney, that he may perish as his footprint dries and shrivels.[32]

In these cases the object in view is to hurt the original through the image, but it is also possible to make an image, transfer to it the evil spirit of the disease which has attacked the person it is to represent, and then send it out like a scapegoat into the wilderness. They conjure devils into puppets in West Africa;[33] in Siam the doctor makes an image of clay, sends his patient's disease into it, and then takes it away to the woods and buries it;[34]

29 St. John, vol. ii. p. 260.

30 Dubois, 'Mœurs, etc., des Peuples de l'Inde'; Paris, 1825, vol. ii. p. 63.

31 Mrs. Mason, 'Civilizing Mountain Men'; London, 1862, p. 121. See Mason in Journ. As. Soc. Bengal, part ii. 1865, p. 224.

32 Grimm, D. M., p. 1047. Wuttke, 'Deutsche Volksaberglaube'; Hamburg, 1860, pp. 102, 120.

33 Hutchinson, in Tr. Eth. Soc.; London, 1861, p. 336.

34 Bowring, 'Siam'; London, 1857, vol. i. p. 139.

while the Tunguz cures his leg or his heart by wearing a carved model of the part affected about him.[35]

The transfer of life or the qualities of a living being to an image may be made by giving it a name, or by the performance of a ceremony over it. Thus, at the festival of the Durga Pûja, the officiating Brahman touches the cheeks, eyes, breast, and forehead of each of the images that have been prepared, and says, "Let the soul of Durga long continue in happiness in this image." Till life is thus given to them, they may not be worshipped.[36] But the mere making of the image of a living creature is very commonly sufficient to set up at once its connexion with life, among races who have not thoroughly passed out of the state of mind to which these practices belong. Looking at the matter from a very different point of view, and yet with the same feeling of a necessary connexion between life and the image of the living creature, the Moslem holds that he who makes an image in this world will have it set before him on the day of judgment, and will be called upon to give it life, but he will fail to finish the work he has thus left half done, and will be sent to expiate his offence in hell.

With such illustrations to show how widely spread and deeply rooted is the belief that there is a real connexion between a being and its image, we can see how almost inevitable it is, that man at a low stage of education should come to confound the image with that which it was made to represent. The strong craving of the human mind for a material support to the religious sentiment has produced idols and fetishes over most parts of the world, and at most periods in its history; and while the more intelligent, even among many low tribes, have often clearly enough taken the images as mere symbols of superhuman beings, the vulgar have commonly believed that the idols themselves had life and supernatural powers. Missionaries have remarked this difference in the views of more and less intelligent members of the same tribe; and it is emphatically true of a large part of Christendom, that the images and pictures, which, to the more instructed, serve merely as a help to realise religious ideas and to

[35] Ravenstein, 'The Russians on the Amur'; London, 1861, p. 351.
[36] Coleman, 'The Mythology of the Hindus'; London, 1832, p. 83.

suggest devotional thoughts, are looked upon by the uneducated and superstitious crowd as beings endowed not only with a sort of life, but with miraculous influences.[37]

The line between the cases in which the connexion between object and figure is supposed to be real, and those in which it is known to be imaginary, is often very difficult to draw. Thus idols and figures of saints are beaten and abused for not granting the prayers of their worshippers, which may be a mere expression of spite towards their originals, but then two rival gods may be knocked together when their oracles disagree, that the one which breaks first may be discarded, and here a material connexion must certainly be supposed to exist. To the most difficult class belong the symbolic sacrifices of models of men and animals in Italy and Greece, and the economical paper-offerings of Eastern Asia. The Chinese perform the rite of burning money and clothes for the use of the dead; but the real things are too valuable to be wasted by a thrifty people, so paper figures do duty for them. Thus they set burning junks adrift as sacrifices to get a favourable wind, but they are only paper ones. Perhaps the neatest illustration of this kind of offerings, and of the state of mind in which the offerer makes them, is to be found in Huc and Gabet's story of the Tibetan lamas, who sent horses flying from the mountain-top in a gale of wind, for the relief of worn-out pilgrims who could get no further on their way. The horses were bits of paper, with a horse printed on each, saddled, bridled, and galloping at full speed.[38]

Hanging and burning in effigy is a proceeding which, in civilized countries at any rate, at last comes fairly out into pure symbolism. The idea that the burning of the straw and rag body should act upon the body of the original, perhaps hardly comes into the mind of any one who assists at such a performance. But it is not easy to determine how far this is the case with the New Zealanders, whose minds are full of confusion between object and

[37] For discussion of image-worship or idolatry, where the image is considered to be actually animated by a human soul or divine spirit which has taken up its abode in it as a body, see Tylor, 'Primitive Culture,' chap. xiv. [Note to 3rd Edition.]

[38] Huc and Gabet, 'Voy. dans la Tartarie, etc.'; Paris, 1850, vol. ii. p. 136.

image, as we may see by their witchcraft, and who also hold strong views about their effigies, and ferociously revenge an insult to them. One very curious practice has come out of their train of thought about this matter. They were very fond of wearing round their necks little hideous figures of green jade, with their heads very much on one side, which are called *tiki,* and are often to be seen in museums. It seems likely that they are merely images of Tiki, creator of man and god of the dead. They are carried as memorials of dead friends, and are sometimes taken off and wept and sung over by a circle of natives; but a *tiki* commonly belongs, not to the memory of a single individual, but of a succession of deceased persons who have worn it in their time, so that it cannot be considered as having in it much of the nature of a portrait.[39] Some New Zealanders, however, who were lately in London, were asked why these *tikis* usually, if not always, have but three fingers on their hands, and they replied that if an image is made of a man, and any one should insult it, the affront would have to be revenged, and to avoid such a contingency the *tikis* were made with only three fingers, so that, not being any one's image, no one was bound to notice what happened to them.

In medicine, the notion of the real connexion between object and image has manifested itself widely in both ancient and modern times. Pliny speaks of the folly of the magicians in using the catanance ($\kappa\alpha\tau\alpha\nu\acute{\alpha}\gamma\kappa\eta$, compulsion) for love-potions, because it shrinks in drying into the shape of the claws of a dead kite (and so, of course, holds the patient fast); but it does not strike him that the virtues of the lithospermum or "stone-seed" in curing calculus were no doubt deduced in just the same way.[40] In more modern times, such notions as these were elaborated into the old medical theory known as the "Doctrine of Signatures," which supposed that plants and minerals indicated by their external characters the diseases for which nature had intended them as remedies. Thus the Euphrasia or eyebright was, and is, supposed to be good for the eyes, on the strength of a black pupil-

---

[39] Hale, in U.S. Exploring Exp.; Philadelphia, vol. vi., 1846, p. 23. W. Yate, 'Account of New Zealand'; London, 1835, p. 151; R. Taylor, 'New Zealand and Its Inhabitants,' 2nd ed., London, 1870, chap. vi.

[40] Plin. xxvii. 35, 74.

like spot in its corolla, the yellow turmeric was thought good for jaundice, and the blood-stone is probably used to this day for stopping blood.[41] By virtue of a similar association of ideas, the ginseng, which is still largely used in China, was also employed by the Indians of North America, and in both countries its virtues were deduced from the shape of the root, which is supposed to resemble the human body. Its Iroquois name, *abesoutchenza,* means "a child," while in China it is called *jin-seng,* that is to say, "resemblance of man."[42]

Such cases as these bring clearly into view the belief in a real and material connexion existing between an object and its image. By virtue of their resemblance, the two are associated in thought, and being thus brought into connexion in the mind, it comes to be believed that they are also in connexion in the outside world. Now the association of an object with its name is made in a very different way, but it nevertheless produces a series of very similar results. Except in imitative words, the objective resemblance between thing and word, if it ever existed, is not discernible now. A word cannot be compared to an image or a picture, which, as everybody can see, is like what it stands for; but it is enough that idea and word come together by habit in the mind, to make men think that there is some real bond of connexion between the thing, and the name which belongs to it in their mother-tongue. Professor Lazarus, in his "Life of the Soul," tells a good story of a German who went to the Paris Exhibition, and remarked to his companion what an extraordinary people the French were, "For bread, they say *du pain!*" "Yes," said the other, "and we say *bread.*" "To be sure," replied the first, *"but it is bread, you know."*[43]

As, then, men confuse the word and the idea, in much the same way as they confuse the image with that which it represents, there springs up a set of practices and beliefs concerning names, much like those relating to images. Thus it is thought that the

41 Paris, 'Pharmacologia'; London, 1843, p. 47.

42 Charlevoix, vol. vi. p. 24. For a similar case, see the 'Penny Cyclopædia,' art. "Atropa Mandragora" (mandrake).

43 Lazarus, 'Leben der Seele'; Berlin, 1856–7, vol. ii. p. 77.

utterance of a word ten miles off has a direct effect on the object which that word stands for. A man may be cursed or bewitched through his name, as well as through his image. You may lay a smock-frock on the door-sill, and pronounce over it the name of the man you have a spite against, and then when you beat that smock, your enemy will feel every blow as well as if he were inside it in the flesh.[44] Thus, too, when the root of the dead-nettle was plucked to be worn as a charm against intermittent fevers, it was necessary to say for what purpose, and for whom, and for whose son it was pulled up, and other magical plants required also a mention of the patient's name to make them work.[45]

How the name is held to be part of the very being of the man who bears it, so that by it his personality may be carried away, and, so to speak, grafted elsewhere, appears in the way in which the sorcerer uses it as a means of putting the life of his victim into the image upon which he practises. Thus King James in his 'Dæmonology,' says that "the devil teacheth how to make pictures of wax or clay, that by roasting thereof, the persons that they bear the name of may be continually melted or dried away by continual sickness."[46] A mediæval sermon speaks of baptizing a "wax" to bewitch with; and in the eleventh century, certain Jews, it was believed, made a waxen image of Bishop Eberhard, set about with tapers, bribed a clerk to baptize it, and set fire to it on that sabbath, the which image burning away at the middle, the bishop fell grievously sick and died.[47]

A similar train of thought shows itself in the belief, that the utterance of the name of a deity gives to man a means of direct communication with the being who owns it, or even places in his hands the supernatural power of that being, to be used at his will. The Moslems hold that the "great name" of God (not Allah, which is a mere epithet), is known only to prophets and apostles, who, by pronouncing it, can transport themselves from place to place at will, can kill the living, raise the dead, and do any other miracle.[48]

[44] Kuhn, 'Die Herabkunft des Feuers und des Göttertranks'; Berlin, 1859, p. 227. Wuttke, pp. 16, 67.

[45] Plin., xxii. 16, 24; xxiii. 54.   [47] Grimm, D. M., p. 1047.

[46] Brand, vol. iii. p. 10.   [48] Lane, Mod. Eg., vol. i. p. 361.

The concealment of the name of the tutelary deity of Rome, for divulging which Valerius Soranus is said to have paid the penalty of death, is a case in point. As to the reason of its being kept a secret, Pliny says that Verrius Flaccus quotes authors whom he thinks trustworthy, to the effect that when the Romans laid siege to a town, the first step was for the priests to summon the god under whose guardianship the place was, and to offer him the same or a greater place of worship among the Romans. This practice, Pliny adds, still remains in the pontifical discipline, and it is certainly for this reason that it has been kept secret under the protection of what god Rome itself has been, lest its enemies should use a like proceeding.[49]

Moreover, as man puts himself into communication with spirits through their names, so they know him through his name. In Borneo, they will change the name of a sickly child to deceive the evil spirits that have been tormenting it.[50] In South America, among the Abipones and Lenguas, when a man died, his family and neighbours would change their own names[51] to cheat Death when he should come to look for them. As examples of beliefs connected with personal names among more civilized races, may be mentioned the custom in Tonquin of giving young children horrid names to frighten the demons from them,[52] the Jewish superstition that a man's destiny may be changed by changing his name, and the Abyssinian concealment of the child's real name, lest the Budas should bewitch him through it.[53]

It is perhaps a falling off from these extreme instances of the intimacy with which name and object have grown together in the savage mind, to cite the practice of exchanging names, which was found in the West Indies at the time of Columbus,[54] and in the South Seas by Captain Cook, who was called Oree, while his

49 Plin., xxviii. 4. Plut., Q. R. Macrob., Sat., iii. 9. See Bayle, art. "Soranus."

50 St. John, 'Borneo,' vol. i. p. 197.

51 Dobrizhoffer, 'The Abipones,' E. Tr.; London, 1822, vol. ii. p. 273. Southey, 'History of Brazil'; London, 1819, vol. iii. p. 394.

52 Richard, 'Tonquin,' in Pinkerton, vol. ix. p. 734.

53 Eisenmenger, part i. p. 489. Parkyns, 'Abyssinia,' vol. ii. p. 146.

54 'Letters of Columbus' (Hakluyt Soc.); London, 1847, p. 217. Rochefort, 'Iles Antilles'; Rotterdam, 1658, p. 458.

friend Oree went by the name of Cookee.[55] But Cadwallader Colden's account of his new name is admirable evidence of what there is in a name in the mind of the savage. "The first Time I was among the *Mohawks,* I had this Compliment from one of their old *Sachems,* which he did, by giving me his own Name, *Cayenderongue.* He had been a notable Warrior; and he told me, that now I had a Right to assume to myself all the Acts of Valour he had performed, and that now my Name would echo from Hill to Hill over all the *Five Nations.*" When Colden went back into the same part ten or twelve years later, he found that he was still known by the name he had thus received, and that the old chief had taken another.[56]

Taking a still wider stretch, the power of association grasps not only the spoken word, but its written representative. It has been seen how the Hindoo sorcerers wrote the name of their victim on the breast of the image made to personate him. A Chinese physician, if he has not got the drug he requires for his patient, will write the prescription on a piece of paper, and let the sick man swallow its ashes, or an infusion of the writing, in water.[57] This practice is no doubt very old, and may even descend from the time when the picture-element in Chinese writing, now almost effaced, was still clearly distinguishable, so that the patient would at least have the satisfaction of eating a picture, not a mere written word. Whether the Moslems got the idea from them or not, I do not know, but among them a verse of the Koran washed off into water and drunk, or even water from a cup in which it is engraved, is an efficacious remedy.[58] Here the connexion between the two ends of the chain is very remote indeed. The arbitrary characters, which represent the sound of the word, which represents the idea, have to do duty for the idea itself. The example is

[55] Cook, First Voy. II., vol. ii. p. 251. Second Voyage; London, 2nd edit., 1777, vol. i. p. 167. See Dumont d'Urville, 'Voy. de l'Astrolabe,' vol. i. p. 189 (Australia).

[56] Colden, 'Hist. of the Five Indian Nations of Canada'; London, 1747, part i. p. 10.

[57] Davis, vol. ii. p. 215.

[58] Lane, Mod. Eg., vol. i. p. 347–8. Petherick, Egypt, etc.; Edinburgh, 1861, p. 221.

a striking one, and will serve to measure the strength of the tendency of the uneducated mind to give an outward material reality to its own inward processes.

This confusion of objective with subjective connexion, which shows itself so uniform in principle, though so various in details, in the practices upon images and names done with a view of acting through them on their originals or their owners, may be applied to explain one branch after another of the arts of the sorcerer and diviner, till it almost seems as though we were coming near the end of his list, and might set down practices not based on this mental process as exceptions to a general rule.

When a lock of hair is cut off as a memorial, the subjective connexion between it and its former owner, is not severed. In the mind of the friend who treasures it up, it recalls thoughts of his presence, it is still something belonging to him. We know, however, that the objective connexion was cut by the scissors, and that what is done to that hair afterwards, is not felt by the head on which it grew. But this is exactly what the savage has not come to know. He feels that the subjective bond is unbroken in his own mind, and he believes that the objective bond, which his mind never gets clearly separate from it, is unbroken too. Therefore, in the remotest parts of the world, the sorcerer gets clippings of the hair of his enemy, parings of his nails, leavings of his food, and practises upon them, that their former possessor may fall sick and die. This is why South Sea Island chiefs had servants always following them with spittoons, that the spittle might be buried in some secret place, where no sorcerer could find it, and why even brothers and sisters had their food in separate baskets. In the island of Tanna, in the New Hebrides, there was a colony of disease-makers who lived by their art. They collected any *nahak* or rubbish that had belonged to any one, such as the skin of a banana he had eaten, wrapped it in a leaf like a cigar, and burnt it slowly at one end. As it burnt, the owner got worse and worse, and if it was burnt to the end, he died. When a man fell ill, he knew that some sorcerer was burning his rubbish, and shell-trumpets, which could be heard for miles, were blown to signal to the sorcerers to stop, and wait for the presents which would be sent next morning. Night after night, Mr. Turner used to hear the melancholy too-tooing of the shells, entreating the wizards to stop plaguing their victims. And when a disease-maker fell sick himself, he believed that some one was burning his rubbish, and had his shells too blown for mercy.[59] It is not needful to give another description after this, the process is so perfectly the same in principle wherever it is found, all over Polynesia,[60] in Africa,[61] in India,[62] in North and South America,[63] in Australia.[64] Superstitions of this kind as to hair and nails belong to Zoroastrian, Jewish, and Moslem lore. They are alive to this day in Europe, where, for instance, the German who walks over nails hurts their former owner, and the Italian does not like to trust a lock of his hair in the hands of any one, lest he should be bewitched or enamoured against his will.[65]

One of the best accounts we have of the art of procuring death by sorcery, is given in Sir James Emerson Tennent's work on Ceylon. It is not that there is much that is peculiar in the processes it describes, but just the contrary; its importance lies in its presenting, among a somewhat isolated race, a system of sorcery, which is quite a little museum of the arts practised among the most dissimilar tribes in the remotest regions of the world. The account is as follows: "The vidahu stated to the magistrate that a general belief existed among the Tamils [of Ceylon] in the fatal effects of a ceremony, performed with the skull of a child, with the design of producing the death of an individual against whom the incantation is directed. The skull of a male child, and particularly of a first-born, is preferred, and the effects are regarded as

59 Turner, 'Polynesia,' pp. 18, 89, 424.

60 Polack, 'Manners and Customs of the New Zealanders'; London, 1840, vol. i. p. 282, Ellis, vol. ii. p. 228. Williams, 'Fiji,' vol. i. p. 249. Purchas, vol. ii. p. 1652, etc.

61 Casalis, p. 276. J. L. Wilson, p. 215. D. & C. Livingstone, 'Exp. to Zambesi'; London, 1865, p. 46.

62 Roberts, Or. Illustr., p. 470.

63 Klemm, C. G., vol. ii. p. 168. Fitz Roy, in Tr. Eth. Soc.; London, 1861, p. 5. Forbes in Journ. Eth. Soc. vol. ii. p. 236.

64 Stanbridge, id. p. 299.

65 See Lipschütz, 'De Communi Humani Generis Origine'; Hamburg, 1864, p. 59, etc.; Lane, Thousand and One N., vol. ii. p. 215; Story, Roba di Roma, vol. ii. p. 342.

more certain if it be killed expressly for the occasion; but for ordinary purposes, the head of one who had died a natural death is presumed to be sufficient. The form of the ceremony is to draw certain figures and cabalistic signs upon the skull, after it has been scraped and denuded of the flesh; adding the name of the individual upon whom the charm is to take effect. A paste is then prepared, composed of sand from the footprints of the intended victim, and a portion of his hair moistened with his saliva, and this, being spread upon a leaden plate, is taken, together with the skull, to the graveyard of the village, where for forty nights the evil spirits are invoked to destroy the person so denounced. The universal belief of the natives is, that as the ceremony proceeds, and the paste dries up on the leaden plate, the sufferer will waste away and decline, and that death, as an inevitable consequence, must follow."[66] Here we have at once the name, the earth-cutting, the hair and saliva, the cursing, and the drying up. The use of the skull lies in its association with death, and we shall presently find it used in the same way in a very different place.

Even the spirits of the dead may be acted on through the remains of their bodies. Though the savage commonly holds that after death the soul goes its own way, for the most part independently of the body to which it once belonged, yet in his mind the soul and the body of his enemy or his friend are inseparably associated, and thus he comes to hold, in his inconsistent way, that a bond of connexion must after all survive between them. Therefore, the African fastens the jaw of his slain enemy to a tabor or a horn, and his skull to the big drum, that every crash and blast may send a thrill of agony through the ghost of their dead owner.[67]

The connexion between a cut lock of hair and its former owner is, in the mind at least, much closer than is necessary for these purposes. As has been seen, the remains of a person's food are sufficient to bewitch him by. In a witchcraft case in the seventeenth century, the supposed sorceress confessed that "there was a glove of the said Lord Henry buried in the ground, and as that glove did rot and waste, so did the liver of the said lord rot

66 Tennent, 'Ceylon,' vol. ii. p. 545.
67 Römer, 'Guinea,' p. 112. Klemm, C. G., vol. iii. p. 352.

and waste."[68] Indeed, any association of ideas in a man's mind, the vaguest similarity of form or position, even a mere coincidence in time, is sufficient to enable the magician to work from association in his own mind, to association in the material world. Nor is there any essential difference in the process, whether his art is that of the diviner or of the sorcerer, that is, whether his object is merely to foretell something that will happen to a person, or actually to make that something happen; or if he is only concerned with the searching out of the hidden past, the process remains much the same, the intention only is different.

*   *   *   *

On this principle of association, it is easy to understand how, in the Old World, the names of the heavenly bodies, and their position at the time of a man's birth, should have to do with his character and fate; while, in the astrology of the Aztecs, the astronomical signs have a similar connexion with the parts of the human body, so that the sign of the Skull has to do with the head, and the sign of the Flint with the teeth.[69] Why fish may be caught in most plenty when the Sun is in the sign of Pisces, is as clear as the reason why trees are to be felled, or vegetables gathered, or manure used, while the moon is on the wane, for these things have to fall, or be consumed, or rot; while, on the other hand, grafts are to be set while the moon is waxing;[70] and it is only lucky to begin an undertaking when the moon is on the increase, as has been held even in modern times. It is as clear why the Chinese doctor should administer the heads, middles, and roots of plants, as medicine for the heads, bodies, and legs of his patients respectively, and why passages in books looked at while some thought is in the reader's mind, should be taken as omens, from Western Europe to Eastern Asia, in old times and new. When it is borne in mind that the Tahitians ascribe their internal pains to demons who are inside them, tying their intestines in knots, it becomes easy to understand why the Laplanders, under certain circumstances, object to knots being tied in clothes,

---

68 Brand, vol. iii. p. 29.

69 Kingsborough, Vatican MS., vol. ii. pl. 75; vols. v. and vi. Expl.

70 Plin., ix. 35; xviii. 75; xvii. 24.

and how it comes to pass that in Germany witches are still believed to tie magic knots, which bring about a corresponding knotting inside their victims' bodies. And so on from one phase to another of witchcraft and superstition.

It would be quite intelligible on this principle, that the sorcerer should think it possible to impress his own mind upon the outer world, even without any external link of communication. The mere presence of the thought in his mind might be enough to cause, as it were by reflection, a corresponding reality. He is usually found, however, working his will by some material means, or at least by an utterance of it into the world. This seems to be the case with the rainmaker, or weather-changer, wherever he is met with, that is to say, among most races of man below the highest culture. Sometimes he works by clear association of ideas, as the Samoan rainmakers with their sacred stone, which they wet when they want rain, and put to the fire to dry when they want to dry the weather,[71] or the Lapland wizards, with the winds they used to sell to our seacaptains in a knotted cord, to be let out by untying it knot by knot. In the notable practice of killing an enemy by prophesying that he will die, or by uttering a wish that he may, the outward act of speech comes between the thought and the reality, but perhaps a mere unspoken wish may be held sufficient. This kind of bewitching is found over almost as wide a range as the practices of the rainmaker, and extends like them into the upper regions of our race.

> There dwalt a weaver in Moffat toun,
> That said the minister wad dee sune;
> The minister dee'd; and the fouk o' the toun,
> They brant the weaver wi' the wudd o' his lume,
> And ca'd it weel-wared on the warlock loon.[72]

As has been so often said, these two arts are encouraged by the unfailing test of success, if they have but time enough, and the latter justifies itself by killing the patient through his own imagination. When he hears that he has been "wished," he goes home and takes to his bed at once. It is impossible to realize the state of mind into which the continual terror of witchcraft brings

71 Turner, p. 347, and see p. 428.

72 R. Chambers, 'Popular Rhymes of Scotland'; Edinburgh, 1826, p. 23.

the savage. It is held by many tribes to be the necessary cause of death. Over great parts of Africa, in South America and Polynesia, when a man dies, the question is at once, "who killed him?" and the soothsayer is resorted to, to find the murderer, that the dead man may be avenged. The Abipones held that there was no such thing as natural death, and that if it were not for the magicians and the Spaniards, no man would die unless he were killed. The notion that, after all, a man might perhaps die of himself, comes out curiously in the address of an old Australian to the corpse at a funeral, "If thou comest to the other black fellows and they ask thee who killed thee, answer, 'No one, but I died.' "[73]

There are of course branches of the savage wizard's art that are not connected with the mental process to which so many of his practices may be referred. He is often a doctor with some skill in surgery and medicine, and an expert juggler; and often, though knavery is not the basis of his profession, a cunning knave. One of the most notable superstitions of the human race, high and low, is the belief in the Evil Eye. Knowing, as we all do, the strange power which one mind has of working upon another through the eye, a power which is not the less certain for being wholly unexplained, it seems not unreasonable to suppose that the belief in the mysterious influences of the Evil Eye flows from the knowledge of what the eye can do as an instrument of the will, while experience has not yet set such limits as we recognize to the range of its action. The horror which savages so often have of being looked full in the face, is quite consistent with this feeling. You may look at him or his, but you must not stare, and above all, you must not look him full in the face, that is to say, you must not do just what the stronger mind does when it uses the eye as an instrument to force its will upon the weaker.

* * * *

The question whether there is any historical connexion among the superstitious practices of the lower races, is distinct from that of their development from the human mind. On the whole, the similarity that runs through the sorcerer's art in the most remote countries, not only in principle, but so often in details, as for

[73] Lang, 'Queensland'; London, 1861, p. 360.

instance in the wide prevalance of the practice of bewitching by locks of hair and rubbish which once belonged to the victim, often favours the view that these coincidences are not independent growths from the same principle, but practices which have spread from one geographical source. . . . The value of this belief to the ethnologist depends much on its being difficult to explain it, and therefore also difficult to look upon it as having often arisen independently in the human mind. But from the intelligible, and to a particular state of mind one might even say reasonable, beliefs and practices which have been described in the present chapter, it seems hardly prudent to draw inferences as to the descent and communication of the races among whom they are found, at least while the ethnological argument from beliefs and customs is still in its infancy.

To turn now to a different subject, the same state of mind which has had so large a share in the development of sorcery, has also manifested itself in a very remarkable series of observances regarding spoken words, prohibiting the mention of the names of people, or even sometimes of animals and things. A man will not utter his own name; husband and wife will not utter one another's names; the son or daughter-in-law will not mention the name of the father or mother-in-law, and *vice versâ;* the names of chiefs may not be uttered, nor the names of certain other persons, nor of superhuman beings, nor of animals and things to which supernatural powers are ascribed. These various prohibitions are not found all together, but one tribe may hold to several of them. A few details will suffice to give an idea of the extent and variety of this series of superstitions.

The intense aversion which savages have from uttering their own names, has often been noticed by travellers. Thus Captain Mayne says of the Indians of British Columbia, that "one of their strangest prejudices, which appears to pervade all tribes alike, is a dislike to telling their names—thus you never get a man's right name from himself; but they will tell each other's names without hesitation."[74] So Dobrizhoffer says that the Abipones of South America think it a sin to utter their own names, and when a man was asked his name, he would nudge his neighbour to answer for

[74] Mayne, 'British Columbia,' etc.; London, 1862, p. 278.

him,[75] and in like manner, the Fijians and the Sumatrans are described as looking to a friend to help them out of the difficulty, when this indiscreet question is put to them.[76]

Nor does the dislike to mentioning ordinary personal names always stop at this limit. Among the Algonquin tribes, children are generally named by the old woman of the family, usually with reference to some dream, but this real name is kept mysteriously secret, and what usually passes for the name is a mere nickname, such as "Little Fox," or "Red-Head." The real name is hardly ever revealed even by the grave-post, but the totem or symbol of the clan is held sufficient. The true name of La Belle Sauvage was not Pocahontas, "her true name was Matokes, which they concealed from the English, in a superstitious fear of hurt by the English, if her name was known."[77] "It is next to impossible to induce an Indian to utter personal names; the utmost he will do, if a person implicated is present, is to move his lips, without speaking, in the direction of the person." Schoolcraft saw an Indian in a court of justice pressed to identify a man who was there, but all they could get him to do was to push his lips towards him.[78] So Mr. Backhouse describes how a native woman of Van Diemen's Land threw sticks at a friendly Englishman, who in his ignorance of native manners, mentioned her son, who was at school at Newtown.[79]

In various parts of the world, a variety of remarkable customs are observed between men and women, and their fathers- and mothers-in-law. These will be noticed elsewhere, but it is necessary to mention here, that among the Dayaks of Borneo, a man must not pronounce the name of his father-in-law;[80] among the Omahas of North America, the father- and mother-in-law do not

[75] Dobrizhoffer, vol. ii. p. 444. See also Cullen, 'Darien Indians,' in Tr. Eth. Soc. vol. iv. p. 265.

[76] Seemann, 'Viti'; London, 1862, p. 190. Marsden, Hist. of Sumatra; London, 1811, p. 286.

[77] Schoolcraft, part ii. p. 65.

[78] Id. p. 433. See also Burton, 'City of the Saints,' p. 141.

[79] Backhouse, 'Australia,' p. 93.

[80] St. John, vol. i. p. 51.

speak to their son-in-law, or mention his name,[81] nor do they call him or he them by name among the Dacotahs.[82] Again, the wife is in some places prohibited from mentioning her husband's name. "A Hindoo wife is never, under any circumstances, to mention the name of her husband. 'He,' 'The Master,' 'Swamy,' etc., are titles she uses when speaking of, or to her lord. In no way can one of the sex annoy another more intensely and bitterly, than by charging her with having mentioned her husband's name. It is a crime not easily forgiven."[83] In East Africa, among the Barea, the wife never utters the name of her husband, or eats in his presence, and even among the Beni Amer, where the women have extensive privileges and great social power, the wife is still not allowed to eat in the husband's presence, and only mentions his name before strangers.[84] The Kafir custom prohibits wives from speaking the names of relatives of their husbands and fathers-in-law. In Australia, among the names which in some tribes must not be spoken, are those of a father- or mother-in-law, of a son-in-law, and of persons in some kind of connexion by marriage. Another of the Australian prohibitions is not only very curious, but is curious as having apparently no analogue elsewhere. Among certain tribes in the Murray River district, the youths undergo, instead of circumcision, an operation called *wharepin*, and afterwards, the natives who have officiated, and those who have been operated upon, though they may meet and talk, must never mention one another's names, nor must the name of one even be spoken by a third person in the presence of the other.[85]

It is especially in Eastern Asia and Polynesia, that we find the names of kings and chiefs held as sacred, and not to be lightly spoken. In Siam, the king must be spoken of by some epithet;[86] In India and Burmah, the royal name is avoided as something sacred and mysterious; and in Polynesia, the prohibition to men-

81 Long's Exp., vol. i. p. 253.

82 Schoolcraft, part ii. p. 196.

83 F. de W. Ward, 'India and the Hindoos'; London, 1853, p. 189.

84 Munzinger, 'Ostafrikanische Studien'; Schaffhausen, 1864, pp. 325, 526.

85 Eyre, vol. ii. pp. 336–9. The wharepin is a ceremonial depilation.

86 Bowring, p. 38.

tion chiefs' names has even impressed itself deeply in the language of the islands where it prevails.[87]

But it is among the most distant and various races that we find one class of names avoided with mysterious horror, the names of the dead. In North America, the dead is to be alluded to, not mentioned by name, especially in the presence of a relative.[88] In South America, he must be mentioned among the Abipones as "the man who does not now exist," or some such periphrasis;[89] and the Fuegians have a horror of any kind of allusion to their dead friends, and when a child asks for its dead father or mother, they will say, "Silence! don't speak bad words."[90] The Samoied only speaks of the dead by allusion, for it would disquiet them to utter their names.[91] The Australians, like the North Americans, will set up the pictured crest or symbol of the dead man's clan, but his name is not to be spoken. Dr. Lang tried to get from an Australian the name of a native who had been killed. "He told me who the lad's father was, who was his brother, what he was like, how he walked when he was alive, how he held the tomahawk in his left hand instead of his right (for he had been left-handed), and with whom he usually associated; but the dreaded name never escaped his lips; and I believe no promises or threats could have induced him to utter it."[92] The Papuans of the Eastern Archipelago avoid speaking the names of the dead, and in Africa, a like prejudice is found among the Masai.[93] In the Old World, Pliny says of the Roman custom, "Why, when we mention the dead, do we declare that we do not vex their memory?"[94] and indeed, the superstition is still to be found in modern Europe, and better marked than in ancient Rome; perhaps nowhere more

[87] Polack, vol. i. p. 38.

[88] Simpson, Journey, vol. i. p. 130. Schoolcraft, part iii. p. 234.

[89] Dobrizhoffer, vol. ii. p. 273.

[90] Despard, 'Fireland' ('Sunday at Home,' Oct. 31, 1863).

[91] Klemm, C. G., vol. ii. p. 226.

[92] Lang, 'Queensland,' pp. 367, 387. Eyre, l. c.

[93] Bastian, vol. ii. p. 276, etc. See also Fontana, 'Nicobar Is.' in As. Res., vol. iii. p. 154. Callaway, 'Religion of Amazulu,' p. 169.

[94] Plin., xxviii. 5.

notably than in Shetland, where it is all but impossible to get a widow, at any distance of time, to mention the name of her dead husband, though she will talk about him by the hour. No dead person must be mentioned, for his ghost will come to him who speaks his name.[95]

To conclude the list, the dislike to mentioning the names of spiritual or superhuman beings, and everything to which supernatural powers are ascribed, is, as every one knows, very general. The Dayak will not speak of the small-pox by name, but will call it "the chief" or "jungle leaves," or say "Has he left you?"[96] The euphemism of calling the Furies the Eumenides, or 'gracious ones,' is the stock illustration of this feeling, and the euphemisms for fairies and for the devil are too familiar to quote. The Yezidis, who worship Satan, have a horror of his name being mentioned. The Laplanders will call the bear "the old man with the fur coat," but they do not like to mention his name; and East Prussian peasants still say that in midwinter you must speak of the wolf as "the vermin," not call him by name, lest werewolves tear you.[97] In Asia, the same dislike to speak of the tiger is found in Siberia, among the Tunguz;[98] and in Annam, where he is called "Grandfather" or "Lord,"[99] while in Sumatra, they are spoken of as the "wild animals" or "ancestors."[100] The name of Brahma is a sacred thing in India, as that of Jehovah is to the Jews, not to be uttered but on solemn occasions. The Moslem, it is true, has the name of Allah for ever on his lips, but this, as has been mentioned, is only an epithet, not the "great name."

Among this series of prohibitions, several cases seem, like the burning in effigy among the practices with images, to fall into mere association of ideas, devoid of any superstitious thought. The names of husbands, of chiefs, of supernatural beings, or of the dead, may be avoided from an objection to liberties being

[95] Mrs. Edmondston, 'Shetland Islands'; Edin. 1856, p. 20.

[96] St. John, vol. i. p. 62.

[97] Wuttke, p. 118. See also Grimm, D. M., p. 633, 1213.

[98] Ravenstein, p. 382.

[99] Mouhot, 'Travels in Indo-China,' etc.; London, 1864, vol. i. p. 263.

[100] Marsden, p. 292.

taken with the property of a superior, from a dislike to associate names of what is sacred with common life, or to revive hateful thoughts of death and sorrow. But in other instances, the notion comes out with great clearness, that the mere speaking of a name acts upon its owner, whether that owner be man, beast, or spirit, whether near or far off. Sometimes it may be explained by considering supernatural creatures as having the power of hearing their names wherever they are uttered, and as sometimes coming to trouble the living when they are thus disturbed. Where this is an accepted belief, such sayings as "Talk of the Devil and you see his horns," "Parlez du Loup," etc., have a far more serious meaning than they bear to us now. Thus an aged Indian of Lake Michigan explained why the native wonder-tales must only be told in the winter, for then the deep snow lies on the ground, and the thick ice covers up the waters, and so the spirits that dwell there cannot hear the laughter of the crowd listening to their stories round the fire in the winter lodge. But in spring the spirit-world is all alive, and the hunter never alludes to the spirits but in a sedate, reverent way, careful lest the slightest word should give offence.[101] In other cases, however, the effect of the utterance of the name on the name's owner would seem to be different from this. The explanation does not hold in the case of a man refusing to speak his own name, nor would he be likely to think that his mother-in-law could hear whenever he mentioned hers.

Some of these prohibitions of names have caused a very curious phenomenon in language. When the prohibited name is a word in use, and often when it is only something like such a word, that word has to be dropped and a new one found to take its place. Several languages are known to have been specially affected by this proceeding, and it is to be remarked that in them the causes of prohibition have been different. In the South Sea Islands, words have been tabued, from connexion with the names of chiefs; in Australia, Van Diemen's Land, and among the Abipones of South America, from connexion with the names of the dead; while in South Africa, the avoidance of the names of certain relatives by marriage has led to a result in some degree similar.

101 Schoolcraft, part iii. pp. 314, 492.

Captain Cook noticed in Tahiti that when a chief came to the royal dignity, any words resembling his name were changed. Even to call a horse or a dog "Prince" or "Princess," was disgusting to the native mind.[102] Polack says that from a New Zealand chief being called "Wai," which means "water," a new name had to be given to water. A chief was called "Maripi," or "knife"; and knives were called, in consequence, by another name, "nekra."[103] Hale, the philologist to the U.S. Exploring Expedition, gives an account of the similar Tahitian practice known as *te pi*, by virtue of which, for instance, the syllable *tu* was changed even in indifferent words, because there was a king whose name was Tu. Thus *fetu* (star) was changed to *fetia*, *tui* (to strike) became *tiai*, and so on.[104]

Mentioning the Australian prohibition of uttering the names of the dead, Mr. Eyre says:—"In cases where the name of a native has been that of some bird or animal of almost daily recurrence, a new name is given to the object, and adopted in the language of the tribe. Thus at Moorunde, a favourite son of the native Tenberry was called Torpool, or the Teal; upon the child's death the appellation of tilquaitch was given to the teal, and that of torpool altogether dropped among the Moorunde tribe."[105] The change of language in Tasmania, which has resulted from dropping the names of the dead, is thus described by Mr. Milligan:— "The elision and absolute rejection and disuse of words from time to time has been noticed as a source of change in the Aboriginal dialects. It happened thus:—The names of men and women were taken from natural objects and occurrences around, as, for instance, a kangaroo, a gum-tree, snow, hail, thunder, the wind, the sea, the Waratah—or Blandifordia or Boronia when in blossom, etc., but it was a settled custom in every tribe, upon the death of any individual, most scrupulously to abstain ever after from mentioning the name of the deceased,—a rule, the infraction

102 Cook, Third Voyage, vol. ii. p. 170.

103 Polack, vol. i. p. 38 (mikara?); vol. ii. p. 126.

104 Hale, in U.S. Exp., vol. vi. p. 288. Max Müller, 'Lectures,' 2nd series; London, 1864, pp. 34–41. Tyerman and Bennet, vol. ii. p. 520.

105 Eyre, vol. ii. p. 354.

of which would, they considered, be followed by some dire calamities: they therefore used great circumlocution in referring to a dead person, so as to avoid pronunciation of the name,—if, for instance, William and Mary, man and wife, were both deceased, and Lucy, the deceased sister of William, had been married to Isaac, also dead, whose son Jemmy still survived, and they wished to speak of Mary, they would say 'the wife of the brother of Jemmy's father's wife,' and so on. Such a practice must, it is clear, have contributed materially to reduce the number of their substantive appellations, and to create a necessity for new phonetic symbols to represent old ideas, which new vocables would in all probability differ on each occasion, and in every separate tribe; the only chance of fusion of words between tribes arising out of the capture of females for wives from hostile and alien people,—a custom generally prevalent, and doubtless as beneficial to the race in its effects as it was savage in its mode of execution."[106]

Martin Dobrizhoffer, the Jesuit missionary, gives the following account of the way in which this change was going on in the language of the Abipones in his time. "The Abiponian language is involved in new difficulties by a ridiculous custom which the savages have of continually abolishing words common to the whole nation, and substituting new ones in their stead. Funeral rites are the origin of this custom. The Abipones do not like that anything should remain to remind them of the dead. Hence appellative words bearing any affinity with the names of the deceased are presently abolished. During the first years that I spent amongst the Abipones, it was usual to say *Hegmalkam kahamátek?* 'When will there be a slaughtering of oxen?' On account of the death of some Abipone, the word *kahamátek* was interdicted, and, in its stead, they were all commanded, by the voice of a crier, to say, *Hegmalkam négerkata?* The word *nihirenak,* a tiger, was exchanged for *apañigehak; peúe,* a crocodile, for *kaeprhak,* and *kadma,* Spaniards, for *Rikil,* because these words bore some resemblance to the names of Abipones lately deceased. Hence it is that our vocabularies are so full of blots, occasioned by our hav-

106 Milligan, in Papers, etc., of Roy. Soc. of Tasmania, vol. iii. part ii. 1859, p. 281.

ing such frequent occasion to obliterate interdicted words, and insert new ones."[107]

In South Africa, it appears that some Kafir tribes drop from their language words resembling the names of their former chiefs. Thus the Ama-Mbalu do not call the sun by its ordinary Zulu name *i-langa,* but their first chief's name having been Ulanga, they use the word *i-sota* instead. It is also among the Kafirs that the peculiar custom of *uku-hlonipa* is found, which is remarked upon by Professor Max Müller in his second course of lectures.[108] The following account of it is from another source, the Rev. J. L. Döhne, who thus speaks of it under the verb *hlonipa,* which means to be bashful, to keep at a distance through timidity, to shun approach, to avoid mentioning one's name, to be respectful. "This word describes a custom between the nearest relations, and is exclusively applied to the female sex, who, when married, are not allowed to call the names of the relatives of their husbands nor of their fathers-in-law. They must keep at a distance from the latter. Hence they have the habit of inventing new names for the members of the family, which is always resorted to when those names happen to be either derived from, or are equivalent to some other word of the common language, as, for instance, if the father or brother-in-law is called Umehlo, which is derived from amehlo, eyes, the isifazi [female sex] will no longer use amehlo but substitute amakangelo (lookings), etc., and hence, the izwi lezifazi, i.e.: women-word or language, has originated."[109]

Other instances of change of language by interdicting words are to be found. The Yezidis, who worship the devil, not only refuse to speak the name of *Sheitan,* but they have dropped the word *shat,* "river," as too much like it, and use the word *nahr* instead. Nor will they utter the word *keitan,* "thread," or "fringe," and even *naal,* "horse-shoe," and *naal-band,* "farrier," are forbidden words, because they approach to *laan,* "curse," and *maloun,* "accursed."[110] It is curious to observe that a "disease of

[107] Dobrizhoffer, vol. ii. p. 203.

[108] Max Müller, l. c.

[109] Döhne, 'Zulu-Kafir Dictionary'; Cape Town, 1857, s. v. *hlonipa.* See Bastian, 'Rechtsverhältnisse,' p. 352 (name of King of Wadai).

[110] Layard, 'Nineveh'; London, 1849, vol. i. p. 297.

language" belonging to the same family has shown itself in English speaking countries and in modern times. In America especially, a number of very harmless words have been "tabooed" of late years, not for any offence of their own, but for having a resemblance in sound to words looked upon as indelicate, or even because slang has adopted them to express ideas ignored by a somewhat over-fastidious propriety. We in England are not wholly clear from this offence against good taste, but we have been fortunate in seeing it developed into its full ugliness abroad, and may hope that it is checked once for all among ourselves.

It may be said in concluding the subject of Images and Names, that the effect of an inability to separate, so clearly as we do, the external object from the mere thought or idea of it in the mind, shows itself very fully and clearly in the superstitious beliefs and practices of the untaught man, but its results are by no means confined to such matters. It is not too much to say that nothing short of a history of Philosophy and Religion would be required to follow them out. The accumulated experience of so many ages has indeed brought to us far clearer views in these matters than the savage has, though after all we soon come to the point where our knowledge stops, and the opinions which ordinary educated men hold, or at least act upon, as to the relation between ideas and things, may come in time to be superseded by others taken from a higher level. But between our clearness of separation of what is in the mind from what is out of it, and the mental confusion of the lowest savages of our own day, there is a vast interval. Moreover, as has just been said, the appearance even in the system of savage superstition, of things which seem to have outlived the recollection of their original meaning, may perhaps lead us back to a still earlier condition of the human mind. Especially we may see, in the superstitions connected with language, the vast difference between what a name is to the savage and what it is to us, to whom "words are the counters of wise men and the money of fools." Lower down in the history of culture, the word and the idea are found sticking together with a tenacity very different from their weak adhesion in our minds, and there is to be seen a tendency to grasp at the word as though it were the object it stands for, and to hold that to be able to speak of a thing gives a sort of possession of it, in a way that we can scarcely realize. Perhaps this state of mind was hardly ever so clearly brought into view as in a story told by Dr. Lieber. "I was looking lately at a negro who was occupied in feeding young mocking-birds by the hand. 'Would they eat worms?' I asked. The negro replied, 'Surely not, they are too young, they would not know what to call them.' "[111]

[111] Lieber, 'Laura Bridgman'; Smithsonian C., 1851, p. 9.

CHAPTER VII

GROWTH AND DECLINE
OF CULTURE

Direct record is the mainstay of History, and where this fails us in remote places and times, it becomes much more difficult to make out where civilization has gone forward, and where it has fallen back. As to progress in the first place; when any important movement has been made in modern times, there have usually been well-informed contemporary writers, only too glad to come before the public with something to say that the world cared to hear. But in going down to the lower levels of traditional history, this state of things changes. It is not only that real information becomes more and more scarce, but that the same curiosity that we feel about the origin and growth of civilization, unfortunately combined with a disposition to take any semblance of an answer rather than live in face of mere blank conscious ignorance, has favoured the growth of the crowd of mythic inventors and civilizers, who have their place in the legends of so many distant ages and countries. Their stories often give us names, dates, and places, even the causes which led to change,—just the information wanted, if only it were true. And, indeed, recollections of real men and their inventions may sometimes have come to be included among the tales of these gods, heroes, and sages; and sometimes a mythic garb may clothe real history, as when Cadmus, קדם, "The East," brings the Phœnician letters to Greece. But, as a rule, not history, but mythology fallen cold and dead, or even etymology, allusion, fancy, are their only basis, from Sol the son of Oceanus, who found out how to mine and melt the brilliant sun-like gold, and Pyrodes, the "Fiery," who discovered how to get fire from flint, and the merchants who invented the art of glass-making (known in Egypt in such remote antiquity) by making fires on the sandy Phœnician coast, with their kettles set to boil over them on lumps of natron, brought for this likely purpose from their ship,—across the world to Kahukura, who got the fairies' fishing-net from which the New Zealanders learnt the art of netting, and the Chinese pair, Hoei and Y-meu, of whom the one invented the bow, and the other the arrow.

As the gods Ceres and Bacchus become the givers of corn and wine to mortals, so across the Atlantic there has grown out of a simple mythic conception of nature, the story of the great enlightener and civilizer of Mexico. When the key which Professor Müller and Mr. Cox have used with such success in unlocking the Indo-European mythology is put to the mass of traditions of the Mexican Quetzalcohuatl, callected by the Abbé Brasseur,[1] the real nature of this personage shows out at once.

He was the son of Camaxtli, the great Toltec conqueror who reigned over the land of Anahuac. His mother died at his birth, and in his childhood he was cared for by the virgin priestesses who kept up the sacred fire, emblem of the sun. While yet a boy he was bold in war, and followed his father on his marches. But while he was far away, a band of enemies rose against his father, and with them joined the Mixcohuas, the "Cloud-Snakes," and they fell upon the aged king and choked him, and buried his body in the temple of Mixcoatepetl, the "Mountain of the Cloud-Snakes." Time passed on, and Quetzalcohuatl knew not what had happened, but at last the Eagle came to him and told him that his father was slain and had gone down into the tomb. Then Quetzalcohuatl rose and went with his followers to attack the temple of the Cloud-Snakes' Mountain, where the murderers had fortified themselves, mocking him from their battlements. But he mined in a way from below, and rushed into the temple among them with his Tigers. Many he slew outright, but the bodies of the guiltiest he hewed and hacked, and throwing red pepper on their wounds, left them to die.

After this there comes another story. Quetzalcohuatl appeared at Panuco, up a river on the Eastern Coast. He had landed there from his ship, coming no man knew from whence. He was tall, of white complexion, pleasant to look upon, with fair hair and bushy beard, dressed in long flowing robes. Received everywhere

[1] Brasseur, 'Hist. du Mexique,' vol. i. books ii. and iii. See vol. iii. book xii. chapter iii.

as a messenger from heaven, he travelled inland across the hot countries of the coast to the temperate regions of the interior, and there he became a priest, a lawgiver, and a king. The beautiful land of the Toltecs teemed with fruit and flowers, and his reign was their Golden Age. Poverty was unknown, and the people revelled in every joy of riches and well-being. The Toltecs themselves were not like the small dark Aztecs of later times; they were large of stature and fair almost as Europeans, and (sun-like) they could run unresting all the long day. Quetzalcohuatl brought with him builders, painters, astronomers, and artists in many other crafts. He made roads for travel, and favoured the wayfaring merchants from distant lands. He was the founder of history, the lawgiver, the inventor of the calendar of days and years, the composer of the Tonalamatl, the "Sun-Book," where the Tonapouhqui, "he who counts by the sun," read the destinies of men in astrological predictions, and he regulated the times of the solemn ceremonies, the festival of the new year and of the fifty-two years' cycle. But after a reign of years of peace and prosperity, trouble came upon him too. His enemies banded themselves against him, and their head was a chief who bore a name of the Sun, Tetzcatlipoca, the "Smoking mirror," a splendid youth, a kinsman of Quetzalcohuatl, but his bitter enemy. They rose against Quetzalcohuatl, and he departed. The kingdom, he said, was no longer under his charge, he had a mission elsewhere; for the master of distant lands had sent to seek him, and this master was the Sun. He went to Cholullan, "the place of the fugitive," and founded there another empire, but his enemy followed him with his armies, and Quetzalcohuatl said he must be gone to the land of Tlapallan, for Heaven willed that he should visit other countries, to spread there the light of his doctrine; but when his mission was done, he would return and spend his old age with them. So he departed and went down a river on his ship to the sea, and there he disappeared. The sunlight glows on the snow-covered peak of Orizaba long after the lands below are wrapped in darkness, and there, some said, his body was carried, and rose to heaven in the smoke of the funeral pile, and when he vanished, the sun for a time refused to show himself again.

How dim the meaning of these tales had grown among the

Mexicans, when Montezuma thought he saw in Cortes and the Spanish ships the return of the great ruler and his age of gold. Quetzalcohuatl had come back already many a time, to bring light, and joy, and work, upon the earth, for he was the Sun.[2] We may even find him identified with the Sun by name, and his history is perhaps a more compact and perfect series of solar myths than hangs to the name of any single personage in our own Aryan mythology. His mother, the Dawn or the Night, gives birth to him, and dies. His father Camaxtli is the Sun, and was worshipped with Solar rites in Mexico, but he is the old Sun of yesterday. The clouds, personified in the mythic race of the Mixcohuas, or "Cloud-Snakes" (the Nibelungs of the western hemisphere), bear down the old Sun and choke him and bury him in their mountain. But the young Quetzalcohuatl, the Sun of to-day, rushes up into the midst of them from below, and some he slays at the first onset, and some he leaves, rift with red wounds, to die. We have the Sun-boat of Helios of the Egyptian Ra, of the Polynesian Maui. Quetzalcohuatl, his bright career drawing towards its close is chased into far lands by his kinsmen Tetzcatlipoca, the young Sun of to-morrow. He, too, is well-known as a Sun-god in the Mexican theology. Wonderfully fitting with all this, one incident after another in the life of Quetzalcohuatl falls into its place. The guardians of the sacred fire tend him, his funeral pile is on the top of Orizaba, he is the helper of travellers, the maker of the calendar, the source of astrology, the beginner of history, the bringer of wealth and happiness. He is the patron of the craftsman, whom he lights to his labour; as it is written in an ancient Sanskrit hymn, "He steps forth, the splendour of the sky, the wide-seeing, the far-aiming, the shining wanderer; surely, enlivened by the sun, do men go to their tasks and do their work."[3] Even his people the Toltecs catch from him solar qualities. Will it be even possible to grant to this famous race, in whose story the legend of Quetzalcohuatl is the leading incident, anything more than a mythic existence?

[2] The author, after ten years' more experience, would now rather say more cautiously not that Quetzalcohuatl is the Sun personified, but that his story contains episodes seemingly drawn from sun-myth. [Note to 3rd edition.]

[3] Müller, 'Lectures,' 2nd series, p. 497.

The student, then, may well look suspiciously on statements professing to be direct history of the early growth of civilization, and may even find it best to err on the safe side and not admit them at all, unless they are shown to be probable by other evidence, or unless the tradition is of such a character that it could hardly have arisen but on a basis of fact. For instance, both these tests seem to be satisfied by the Chinese legend concerning quipus. In the times of Yung-ching-che, it is related, people used little cords marked by different knots, which, by their numbers and distances, served them instead of writing. The invention is ascribed to the Emperor Suy-jin, the Prometheus of China.[4] Putting names and dates out of the question, this story embodies the assertion that in old times the Chinese used quipus for records, till they were superseded by the art of writing. Now in the first place, it is not easy to imagine how such a story could come into existence, unless it were founded on fact; and in the second place, an examination of what is known of this curious art in other countries, shows that just what the Chinese say once happened to them, is known to have happened to other races in various parts of the world.

The quipu is a near relation of the rosary and the wampum-string. It consists of a cord with knots tied in it for the purpose of recalling or suggesting something to the mind. When a farmer's daughter ties a knot in her handkerchief to remember a commission at market by, she makes a rudimentary quipu. Darius made one when he took a thong and tied sixty knots in it, and gave it to the chiefs of the Ionians, that they might untie a knot each day, till, if the knots were all undone, and he had not returned, they might go back to their own land.[5] Such was the string on which Le Boo tied a knot for each ship he met on his voyage, to keep in mind its name and country, and that one on which his father, Abba Thulle, tied first thirty knots, and then six more, to remember that Captain Wilson was to come back in thirty moons, or at least in six beyond.[6]

4 Goguet, vol. iii. p. 322. De Mailla, 'Histoire Gén. de la Chine'; Paris, 1777, vol. i. p. 4.

5 Herod., iv. 98. See Plin., x. 34. Bastian, vol. i. p. 415.

6 Keate, 'Pelew Islands'; London, 1788, pp. 367, 392.

This is so simple a device that it may, for all we know, have been invented again and again, and its appearance in several countries does not necessarily prove it to have been transmitted from one country to another. It has been found in Asia,[7] in Africa,[8] in Mexico, among the North American Indians;[9] but its greatest development was in South America.[10] The word *quipu*, that is, "knot," belongs to the language of Peru, and quipus served there as the regular means of record and communication for a highly organized society. Von Tschudi describes them as consisting of a thick main cord, with thinner cords tied on to it at certain distances, in which the knots are tied. The length of the quipus varies much, the main trunk being often many ells long, sometimes only a single foot, the branches seldom more than two feet, and usually much less. He has dug up a quipu, he says, towards eight pounds in weight, a portion of which is represented in the woodcut from which the accompanying (Fig. 15) is taken. The cords are often of various colours, each with its own proper meaning; red for soldiers, yellow for gold, white for silver, green for corn, and so on. This knot-writing was especially suited for reckonings and statistical tables; a single knot meant ten, a double one a hundred, a triple one a thousand, two singles side by side twenty, two doubles two hundred. The distances of the knots from the main cord were of great importance, as was the sequence of the branches, for the principal objects were placed on the first branches and near the trunk, and so in decreasing order. This art of reckoning, continues Von Tschudi, is still in use among the herdsmen of the Puna (the high mountain plateau of Peru), and he had it explained to him by them, so that with a little trouble he could read any of their quipus. On the first branch they usually register the bulls, on the second the cows, these again they divide into milch-cows and those that

7 Erman (E. Tr.); London, 1848, vol. i. p. 492. Macpherson, 'Memorials of India,' p. 359. As. Res. vol. iv. p. 64, vol. v. p. 127. Journ. Ind. Archip. vol. i. pp. 260, 330.

8 Goguet, vol. i. pp. 161, 212. Klemm, C. G., vol. i. p. 3. Bastian, vol. i. p. 412.

9 Charlevoix, vol. vi. p. 151. Long's Exp., vol. i. p. 235 (a passage which suggests a reason for Lucina being the patroness of child-birth). Talbot, Disc. of Lederer, p. 4.

10 Humboldt and Bonpland, vol. iii. p. 20. Rochefort, p. 412.

are dry; the next branches contain the calves, according to age and sex, then the sheep in several subdivisions, the number of foxes killed, the quantity of salt used, and, lastly, the particulars of the cattle that have died. On other quipus is set down the produce of the herd in milk, cheese, wool, etc. Each heading is indicated by a special colour or a differently twined knot.

It was in the same way that in old times the army registers were kept; on one cord the slingers were set down, on another the spearmen, on a third those with clubs, etc., with their officers; and thus also the accounts of battles were drawn up. In each town were special functionaries, whose duty was to tie and inter-

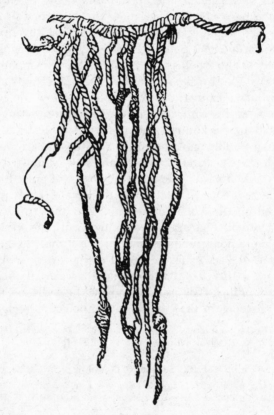

Fig. 15

pret the quipus; they were called Quipucamayocuna, Knot-officers. Insufficient as this kind of writing was, the official historians had attained, during the flourishing of the kingdom of the Incas, to great facility in its interpretation. Nevertheless, they were seldom able to read a quipu without the aid of an oral commentary; when one came from a distant province, it was necessary to give notice with it whether it referred to census, tribute, war, and so forth. In order to indicate matters belonging to their own immediate district, they made at the beginning of the main cord certain signs only intelligible to themselves, and they also carefully kept the quipus in their proper departments, so as not for instance to mistake a tribute cord for one relating to the census. By constant practice, they so far perfected the system as to be able to register with their knots the most important events of the kingdom, and to set down the laws and ordinances. In modern times, all the attempts made to read the ancient quipus have been in vain. The difficulty in deciphering them is very great, since every knot indicates an idea, and a number of intermediate notions are left out. But the principal impediment is the want of the oral information as to their subject-matter, which was needful even to the most learned decipherers. However, should we even succeed in finding the key to their interpretation, the results would be of little value; for what would come to light would be mostly census-records of towns or provinces; taxation-lists, and accounts of the property of deceased persons. There are still some Indians, in the southern provinces of Peru, who are perfectly familiar with the contents of certain historical quipus preserved from ancient times; but they keep their knowledge a profound secret, especially from the white men.[11]

Coming nearer to China, quipus are found in the Eastern Archipelago and in Polynesia proper,[12] and they were in use in Hawaii forty years ago, in a form seemingly not inferior to the most elaborate Peruvian examples. "The tax-gatherers, though they can neither read nor write, keep very exact accounts of all the articles, of all kinds, collected from the inhabitants through-

[11] J. J. v. Tschudi, 'Peru'; St. Gall, 1846, vol. ii. p. 383. See Markham, 'Gr. & Dic. of Quichua,' p. 11.

[12] Marsden, p. 192. Keate, *loc. cit.* Klemm, C. G., vol. iv. p. 396.

out the island. This is done principally by one man, and the register is nothing more than a line of cordage from four to five hundred fathoms in length. Distinct portions of this are allotted to the various districts, which are known from one another by knots, loops and tufts, of different shapes, sizes, and colours. Each taxpayer in the district has his part in this string, and the number of dollars, hogs, dogs, pieces of sandalwood, quantity of taro, etc., at which he is rated, is well defined by means of marks of the above kinds, most ingeniously diversified."[13]

The fate of the quipu has been everywhere to be superseded, more or less entirely, by the art of writing. Even the picture-writing of the ancient Mexicans appears to have been strong enough to supplant it. Whether its use in Mexico is mentioned by any old chronicler or not, I do not know; but Boturini placed the fact beyond doubt by not only finding some specimens in Tlascala, but also recording their Mexican name, *nepohualtzitzin*,[14] a word derived from the verb *tlapohua*, to count. When, therefore, the Chinese tell us that they once upon a time used this contrivance, and that the art of writing superseded it, the analogy of what has taken place in other countries makes it extremely probable that the tradition is a true one, and this probability is reinforced by the unlikeliness of such a story having been produced by mere fancy.

Moreover, the historical value of early tradition does not lie exclusively in the fragments of real history it may preserve. Even the myths which it carries down to later times may become important indirect evidence in the hands of the ethnologist. And ancient compositions handed down by memory from generation to generation, especially if a poetic form helps to keep them in their original shape, often give us, if not a sound record of real events, at least a picture of the state of civilization in which the compositions themselves had their origin. Perhaps no branch of indirect evidence, bearing on the history of culture, has been so well worked as the memorials of earlier states of society, which have thus been unintentionally preserved, for instance, in the Homeric poems. . . .

13 Tyerman and Bennet, Journal; London, 1831, vol. i. p. 455.
14 Boturini, 'Idea de una nueva Historia,' etc.; Madrid, 1746, p. 85.

It happens unfortunately that but little evidence as to the early history of civilization is to be got by direct observation, that is, by contrasting the condition of a low race at different times, so as to see whether its culture has altered in the meanwhile. The contact requisite for such an inspection of a savage tribe by civilized men, has usually had much the same effect as the experiment which an inquisitive child tries upon the root it put in the ground the day before, by digging it up to see whether it has grown. It is a general rule that original and independent progress is not found among a people of low civilization in presence of a higher race. It is natural enough that this should be the case, and it does not in the least affect the question whether the lower race was stationary or progressing before the arrival of the more cultivated foreigners. Even when the contact has been but slight and temporary, it either becomes doubtful whether progress made soon afterwards is original, or certain that it is not so. It has been asserted, for instance, that the Andaman Islanders had no boats in the ninth century, and that the canoe with an outrigger has only lately appeared among them.[15] If these statements should prove correct, we cannot assume, upon the strength of them, that the islanders made these inventions themselves, seeing that they could easily have copied them from foreigners. Moreover, the fact that they now use bits of glass bottles, and iron from wrecks, in making their tools and weapons, proves that slight as their intercourse has been with foreigners, and bitter as is their hostility to them, their condition has, nevertheless, been materially changed by foreign influence.

Though direct evidence thus generally fails us in tracing the history of the lower culture of mankind, there are many ways of bringing indirect evidence to bear on the problem. The early Culture History of Mankind is capable of being treated as an Inductive Science, by collecting and grouping facts. It is true that very little has as yet been done in this way, as regards the lower races at least; but the evidence has only to a very slight extent been got into a state to give definite results, and the whole argument is extremely uncertain and difficult: a fact which sufficiently

[15] Mouat, 'Andaman Islanders,' pp. 7, 11, 315.

accounts for writers on the Origin of Civilization being able to tell us all about it, with that beautiful ease and confidence which belong to the speculative philosopher, whose course is but little obstructed by facts.

*   *   *   *

Far more profitable work than the construction of speculative theories, may be done by collecting facts or groups of facts leading to direct inferences. When both fact and inference are sound, every such argument is a step gained, while if either be unsound, a distinct statement of fact and issue is the best means of getting them corrected, or, if needful, discarded altogether. A principal object of the present chapter is to bring forward a variety of instances drawn from sources where indirect evidence bearing on our early history is to be sought.

As examples of evidence from language, a few cases may be given. The word *calculation,* indicating the primitive art of reckoning by pebbles, or *calculi,* has passed on with the growth of science to designate the working of problems far beyond the reach of the abacus. So, though the Mexicans, when they were discovered, had a high numerical system and were good reckoners, the word *tetl,* "stone," remained as an integral part of one of their sets of numerals for counting animals and things; *centetl* "one stone," *ontetl* "two stone," *etetl* "three stone," etc., meaning nothing more than one, two, three. Nor is Mexico the only country where this curious phenomenon occurs. The Malays say for "one" not only *sa,* but also *sawatu,* that is literally "one stone," and the Javans say not only *sa* but *sawiji,* that is, "one corn, or seed," and in like manner the Nias language calls one and two *sambua* and *dumbua,* that is, apparently, "one fruit," "two fruits."[16]

Still more notable is the Aztec term for an eclipse. The idea that the sun and moon are swallowed or bitten by dragons, or great dogs, or other creatures, is not only very common in the Old World, but it is even found in North and South America

[16] Crawfurd, Gr. and Dic. of Malay Language; London, 1852, vol. i. pp. lvi. lviii. lxvii. and see ccxviii.

and Polynesia.[17] But there is evidence that the ancient Mexicans understood the real cause of eclipses. They are represented in the picture-writings by a figure of the moon's disc covering part of the sun's, and this symbol, Humboldt remarks, "proves exact notions as to the cause of eclipses; it reminds us of the allegorical dance of the Mexican priests, which represented the moon devouring the sun."[18] Yet the Mexicans preserved the memory of an earlier state of astronomical knowledge, by calling eclipses of the sun and moon *tonatiuh qualo, metztli qualo,* that is, "the sun's being eaten," "the moon's being eaten," just as the Finns say, *kuu syödää,* "the moon is eaten," and the Tahitians, that she is *natua,* that is "bitten" or "pinched."[19] In the Mexican celebration of the *Netonatiuh-qualo,* or eclipse of the sun, two of the captives sacrificed appeared as likenesses of the sun and moon.[20]

When a thing or an art is named in one country by a word belonging to the language of another, as *maize, hammock, algebra,* and the like, it is often good evidence that the thing or art itself came from thence, bringing its name with it. This kind of evidence, bearing upon the progress of civilization, has been much and successfully worked, but it has to be used with great caution when the foreign language is an important medium of instruction, or spoken by a race dominant or powerful in the country. As instances of words good or bad as historical evidence, may be taken the Arabic words in Spanish. While *alquimia* (alchemy), *albornóz* (bornoos), *acequia* (irrigating channel), *albaricoque* (apricot), and many more, may really carry with them historical information of more or less value, it must be borne in mind that the influence of the Arabic language in Spain was so great, that is has often given words for what was there long before Moorish times, *alacran* (scorpion), *alboroto* (uproar), *alcor* (hill), and so on; not satisfied with their own

17 Jacob Grimm, 'Deutsche Mythologie,' pp. 224–5, 668. Schoolcraft, part i. p. 271. Dobrizhoffer, vol. ii. p. 84. Du Tertre, 'Hist. Gén. des Antilles,' etc.; Paris, 1667, vol. ii. p. 371. Turner, 'Polynesia,' p. 531.

18 Humboldt, Vues, pl. 56.

19 Castrén, 'Finnische Mythologie,' pp. 63–5. Grimm, D. M. p. 669. Ellis, Polyn. Res. vol. ii. p. 415.

20 Nieremberg, Hist. Nat.; Antwerp, 1635, p. 143. Humboldt, Vues, pl. 23.

word for head, to express a head of cattle, the Spaniards must needs call it *res,* Arabic *ras,* head. So the New Zealanders' use of *buka-buka* for book is good evidence as to who taught them to read. But the name that the Tahitians nobles are now commonly adopting, instead of the native term *arii,* is bad evidence as to the origin of caste among them; they like the title of *tavana,* which is a native attempt at *governor.*

Even the etymology of a word may sometimes throw light upon the transmission of art and knowledge from one country to another, as where we may see how the Roman made *substantia* by translating ὑπόστασις, and the German, making himself a word for "superstition," *aberglaube,* Flemish *overgeloof,* that is "over belief," had the *super* of *superstitio* before him when he introduced into his language a notion which it had perhaps hardly realized before. To take a more speculative case of a very different kind, the tea-urns used in Russia are well known, but where did the Russians get the invention from? They get their tea from China, where tea-urns much resembling our own have long been in use. But the apparatus is no new thing in Europe, and the specimen in the Naples Museum, if it were coloured with the conventional chocolate colour, and had a tap put in to replace the original one which is lost, would perhaps be only remarked upon at an English tea-table as being beautiful but old-fashioned. It was kept hot by charcoal burning in a tube in the middle, like the Russian urns. Now the name of a vessel just answering this description has been preserved, *authepsa* (αὐθέψης, "self-boiler"), and of this term the Russian name for their urns, *samovar,* "self-boiler," is an exact translation. The coincidence suggests that they may have received both the thing and its name through Constantinople. Moreover, there is reason to think that the Western element in Chinese art is far more important than is popularly supposed, and the tea-urn is so peculiar an apparatus, and so strikingly alike in ancient Italy and in China, that it is scarcely possible that the two should be the results of separate invention. The Russians actually supply Bokhara with *samovars,*[21] so that on the whole

21 Vambéry, 'Travels in Central Asia'; London, 1864, p. 173.

there seems fair ground for the view that the hot-water urn originated very early in Europe, and travelled east as far as China.

It often happens that an old art or custom, which has been superseded for general purposes by some more convenient arrangement, is kept up long afterwards in solemn ceremonies and other matters under the control of priests and officials, who are commonly averse to change; as inventions have often to wait long after they have come into general use before they are officially recognized. Wooden tallies were given for receipts by our Exchequer up to the time of William IV, as if to keep up, as long as might be, the remembrance of the time when "our forefathers had no other books but the score and the tally." It is true that the notched Exchequer tally had long had a Latin inscription on it, and at last there was given into the bargain a fair English receipt, written on a separate paper. The tally survives still, not only in the broken sixpence, and in the bargains of peasants in outlying districts,[22] but in the counterfoil of the banker's cheque. . . .

Such helps as these in working out the problem of the Origin and Progress of Culture grow scarcer as we descend among the lower races, and those of which we have little or no historical knowledge. Mere observation of arts in use, and of objects belonging to tribes living or dead, forms at present the bulk of the evidence of the history of their culture accessible to us. Of these records an immense mass has been collected, but they are very hard to read.

Sometimes, indeed, an object carries its history written in its form, as some of the Esquimaux knives brought to England, which are carved out of a single piece of bone, in imitation of European knives with handles, and show that the maker was acquainted with those higher instruments, though he had not the iron to make a blade of, or even a few scraps to fix along the edge of the bone blade, as they so often do.

The keeping up in stone architecture of designs belonging to wooden buildings, furnishes conclusive proofs of the growth, in several countries, of the art of building in stone from the art of

22 Pictet, 'Origines,' part ii. p. 425.

building in wood,—an argument which is used with extraordinary clearness and power in Mr. Fergusson's Handbook. In Central America and Asia Minor there are still to be seen stone buildings more or less entirely copied from wooden constructions, while in Egypt a like phenomenon may be traced in structures belonging to the remote age of the pyramids. The student may see, almost as if he had been standing by when they were built, how the architect, while adopting the new material, began by copying from the wooden structures to which he had been accustomed. Speaking of the Lycian tombs which still remain with their beams, planks, and panels, as it were turned from wood into stone, Mr. Fergusson remarks upon the value of such monuments as records of the beginning of stone architecture among the people who built them. " . . . wherever the process can be detected, it is in vain to look for earlier buildings. It is only in the infancy of stone architecture that men adhere to wooden forms, and as soon as habit gives them familiarity with the new material, they abandon the incongruities of the style, and we lose all trace of the original form, which never reappears at an after age."[23]

There could hardly be a better illustration of an ethnological argument derived from the mere presence of an art, than in Marsden's remark about the iron-smelters of Madagascar. It is well known that the Madagascans are connected by language with the great Malayo-Polynesian family which extends half round the globe; but the art of smelting iron has only been found in the islands of this vast district near Eastern Asia, and in Madagascar itself. Even in New Zealand, where there is good iron ore, there was no knowledge of iron. Now at the time of our becoming acquainted with the races of Africa, in central latitudes and far down into the south, they were iron-smelters, and had been so for we know not how long, and Africa is only three or four hundred miles from Madagascar, whereas Sumatra is three or four thousand. Nevertheless, Marsden's observation connects the art in Madagascar with the distant Eastern Archipelago, rather than with the neighboring African

---

[23] Fergusson, 'Illustrated Handbook of Architecture'; London, 1855, vol. i. pp. 148, 208, 220, etc.

continent. The process of smelting in small furnaces or pits is much the same in these two districts, but the bellows are different. The usual African bellows consists of two skins with valves worked alternately by hand, so as to give a continuous draught, much the same as those of Modern India. These were not only in use among the ancient Greeks and Romans, but are still to be found in Southern Europe; I saw a wandering tinker at work at Pæstum with a pair of goatskins with the hair on, which he compressed alternately to drive a current of air into his fire, opening and shutting with his hands the slits which served as valves. Several of these skin-bellows are often used at once in Africa, and there are to be found improved forms which approach more nearly to our bellows with boards, but the principle is the same.[24] But the Malay blowing apparatus is something very different; it is a double-barreled air forcing-pump. It consists of two bamboos, four inches in diameter and five feet long, which are set upright, forming the cylinders, which are open above, and closed below except by two small bamboo tubes which converge and meet at the fire. Each piston consists of a bunch of feathers or other soft substance, which expands and fits tightly in the cylinder while it is being forcibly driven down, and collapses to let the air pass as it is drawn up; and a boy perched on a high seat or stand works the two pistons alternately by the piston-rods, which are sticks. (It is likely that each cylinder may have a valve to prevent the return draught.) Similar contrivances have been described elsewhere in the Eastern Archipelago, in Java, Mindanao, Borneo, and New Guinea, and in Siam, the cylinders being sometimes bamboos and sometimes hollowed trunks of trees. Marsden called attention to the fact that the apparatus used in Madagascar is similar to that of Sumatra. There is a description and drawing in Ellis's 'Madagascar,' which need not be quoted in detail, as it does not differ in principle from that of the Eastern Archipelago. A single cylinder is sometimes used in Madagascar, and perhaps also in Borneo, but as a rule the far more advan-

24 Petherick, pp. 293, 395. Andersson, p. 304. Backhouse, Narr. of a Visit to the Mauritius and S. Africa; London, 1844, p. 377. Du Chaillu, 'Equatorial Africa,' p. 91, etc. etc. It appears, however, that a bellows on the Malagasy principle is known in West African districts. See Waitz, vol. ii. p. 378.

tageous plan of working two or several at once is adopted. The Chinese tinkers, who practise the art, quite unknown in Europe, of patching a cast-iron vessel with a clot of melted iron, perform this extraordinary feat with an air forcing-pump, which has indeed but a single trunk and a piston backed with feathers, but is improved by valves and a passage which give it what is known as a "double action," so that the single barrel does the work of two in the ruder construction of the islands.[25]

It seems from the appearance of this remarkable apparatus in Madagascar and in the Eastern Archipelago, that the art of iron-smelting in these distant districts has had a common origin. Very likely the art may have gone from Sumatra or Java to Madagascar, but if so, this must have happened when they were in the Iron Age, to which we have no reason to suppose they had come in the time of their connexon with the ironless Maoris and Tahitians. Language throws no light on the matter; iron is called in Malay, *bâsi*, and in Malagasy, *vi*.

It is but seldom that the transmission of an art to distant regions can be traced, except among comparatively high races, by such a beautiful piece of evidence as this. The state of things among the lower tribes which presents itself to the student, is a substantial similarity in knowledge, arts and customs, running through the whole world. Not that the whole culture of all tribes is alike,—far from it; but if any art or custom belonging to a low tribe is selected at random, it is twenty to one that something substantially like it may be found in at least one place thousands of miles off, though it very frequently happens that there are large portions of the earth's surface lying between, where it has not been observed. Indeed, there are few things in cookery, clothing, arms, vessels, boats, ornaments, found in one place, that cannot be matched more or less nearly somewhere else, unless we go into small details, or rise to the level of the Peruvians and Mexicans, or at least of the highest South Sea Islanders. A few illustrations may serve

25 Marsden, p. 181. Raffles, Hist. of Java, vol. i. pp. 168, 173. Dampier, 'Voyages'; London, 1703–9, 5th ed. vol. i. p. 332. Bishop of Labuan, in Tr. Eth. Soc.; London, 1863, p. 29. G. W. Earl, 'Papuans'; London, 1853, p. 76. Mouhot, 'Travels in Indo-China,' etc.; London, 1864, vol. ii. p. 133. Ellis, 'Madagascar,' vol. i. p. 307. Percy, 'Metallurgy'; London, 1864, pp. 255, 273–8, 746.

to give an idea of the kind of similarity which prevails so largely among the simpler arts of mankind.

The most rudimentary bird-trap is that in which the hunter is his own trap, as in Australia, where Collins thus describes it:— "A native will stretch himself upon a rock as if asleep in the sun, holding a piece of fish in his open hand; the bird, be it hawk or crow, seeing the prey and not observing any motion in the native, pounces on the fish, and, in the instant of seizing it, is caught by the native, who soon throws him on the fire and makes a meal of him." Ward, the missionary, declares that a tame monkey in India, whose food the crows used to plunder while he sat on the top of his pole, did something very near this, by shamming dead within reach of the food, and seizing the first crow that came close enough. When he had caught it, the story says, he put it between his knees, deliberately plucked it, and threw it up into the air. The other crows set upon their disabled companion and pecked it to death, but they let the monkey's store alone ever after. The Esquimaux so far improves upon the Australian form of the art as to build himself a little snow-hut to sit in, with a hole large enough for him to put his hand through to clutch the bird that comes down upon the bait.[26]

There is a curious little art, practised in various countries, that of climbing trees by the aid of hoops, fetters, or ropes. Father Gilij thus describes it among the Indians of South America:—"They are all extremely active in climbing trees, and even the weaker women may be not uncommonly seen plucking the fruit at their tops. If the bark is so smooth and slippery that they cannot go up by clinging, they use another means. They make a hoop of wild vines, and putting their feet inside, they use it as a support in climbing."[27] This is what the toddy-drawer of Ceylon uses to climb the palm with,[28] but the negro of the West Coast of Africa makes a larger hoop round the tree and

26 Collins, vol. i. p. 548. Ward, 'Hindoos,' p. 43. Klemm, C. G., vol. i. p. 314; vol. ii. p. 292.

27 Gilij, 'Saggio di Storia Americana'; Rome, 1780–4, vol. ii. p. 40. See Bates, 'The Naturalist on the R. Amazons'; London, 1863, vol. ii. p. 196.

28 Tennent, 'Ceylon,' vol. ii. p. 523. See Plin., xiii. 7.

gets inside it, resting the lower part of his back against it, and jerks it up the trunk with his hands, a little at a time, drawing his legs up after it.[29] Ellis describes the Tahitian boys tying their feet together, four or five inches apart, with a piece of palm-bark, and with the aid of this fetter going up the cocoa-palms to gather the nuts;[30] and Backhouse mentions a different plan in use in opossum-catching in Van Diemen's Land. The native women who climbed the tall, smooth gum-trees did not cut notches after the Australian plan, except where the bark was rough and loose near the ground. Having got over this part by the notches, they threw round the tree a rope twice as long as was necessary to encompass it, put their hatchets on their bare, cropped heads, and placing their feet against the tree and grasping the rope with their hands, they hitched it up by jerks, and pulled themselves up the enormous trunk almost as fast as a man would mount a ladder.[31]

The ancient Mexicans' art of turning the waters of their lakes to account by constructing floating gardens upon them, has been abandoned, apparently on account of the sinking of the waters, which are now shallow enough to allow the mud gardens to rest upon the bottom. At the time of Humboldt's visit to Mexico, however, there were still some to be seen, though their number was fast decreasing. The floating gardens, or *chinampas,* which the Spaniards found in great numbers, and several of which still existed in his time on the lake of Chalco, were rafts formed of reeds, roots, and branches of underwood. The Indians laid on the tangled mass quantities of the black mould, which is naturally impregnated with salt, but by washing with lake water is made more fertile. "The chinampas," he continues, "sometimes even carry the hut of the Indian who serves as guard for a group of floating gardens, They are towed, or propelled with long poles, to move them at will from shore to shore."[32] Though floating gardens are no longer to be met with in Mexico, they are still in full use in the shallow waters of Cashmere. They are made of mould

29 Klemm, C. G., vol. iii. p. 236. Adanson in Pinkerton, vol. xvi. p. 642.

30 Ellis, vol. i. p. 371.

31 Backhouse, 'Australia,' p. 172.

32 Humboldt, 'Essai Politique'; Paris, 1811, vol. ii. p. 185, etc.

heaped on masses of the stalks of aquatic plants, and will mostly bear a man's weight, though the fruit is generally picked from the banks. They differ from the ancient Mexican chinampas in not being towed from one place to another, but impaled on fixed stakes, which keep them to their moorings, but allow them to rise and fall with the level of the water.[33]

The floating islands of the Chinese lakes are far more artificial structures than those of Mexico or Cashmere. The missionary Huc thus describes those he saw on the lake of Pinghou:—"We passed beside several *floating islands,* quaint and ingenious productions of Chinese industry which have perhaps occurred to no other people. These floating islands are enormous rafts, constructed generally of large bamboos, which long resist the dissolving action of water. Upon these rafts there is placed a tolerably thick bed of good vegetable mould, and thanks to the patient labour of some families of aquatic agriculturists, the astonished eye sees rising from the surface of the waters smiling habitations, fields, gardens, and plantations of great variety. The peasants on these farms seem to live in happy abundance. During the moments of rest left them from the tillage of the rice plots, fishing is at once their lucrative and agreeable pastime. Often when they have gathered in their crop upon the lake, they throw their net and draw it on board their island loaded with fish. . . . Many birds, especially pigeons and sparrows, stay by their own choice in these floating fields to share the peaceable and solitary happiness of these poetical islanders. Towards the middle of the lake, we met with one of these farms attempting a voyage. It moved with extreme slowness, though it had the wind aft. Not that sails were wanting; there was a very large one above the house, and several others at the corners of the island; moreover, all the islanders, men, women, and children, provided with long sweeps, were working with might and main, though without putting much speed into their farm. But it is likely that the fear of delay does not much trouble these agricultural mariners, who are always sure to arrive in time to sleep on land. They are often seen to move from place to place without a motive, like the Mongols in the midst of their vast prairies; though, happier than those wan-

[33] Torrens, 'Travels in Ladâk,' etc.; London, 1862, p. 271.

derers, they have learned to make for themselves as it were a desert in the midst of civilization, and to ally the charms and pleasures of a nomade with the advantages of a sedentary life."[34]

Such coincidences as these, when found in distant regions between whose inhabitants no intercourse is known to have taken place, are not to be lightly used as historical evidence of connexion. It is safest to ascribe them to independent invention, unless the coincidence passes the limits of ordinary probability. Ancient as the art of putting in false teeth is in the Old World, it would scarcely be thought to affect the originality of the same practice in Quito, where a skeleton has been found with false teeth secured to the cheek-bone by a gold wire,[35] nor does the discovery in Egypt of mummies with teeth stopped with gold, appear to have any historical connexion with the same contrivance among ourselves.[36] Thus, too, the Australians were in the habit of cooking fish and pieces of meat in hot sand, each tied up in a sheet of bark, and this is called *yudarn dookoon,* or "tying-up cooking,"[37] but it does not follow that they had learnt from Europe the art of dressing fish *en papillote.*

Perhaps the occurrence of that very civilized instrument, the fork for eating meat with, in the Fiji Islands, is to be accounted for by considering it to have been independently invented there. The Greeks and Romans do not appear to have used forks in eating, and they are said not to have been introduced in England from the South of Europe, till the beginning of the seventeenth century.[38] At any rate, Hakluyt thus translates, in 1598, a remark made by Galeotto Perera, concerning the use of chopsticks in China;—"they feede with two sticks, refraining from touching their meate with their hands, even as we do with forkes;" but he finds it necessary to put a note in the margin, "We, that is the Italians and Spaniards."[39] How long forks had been used in the

---

34 Huc, 'L'Empire Chinois'; Paris, 1854, 2nd ed. p. 114.

35 Bollaert, Res. in New Granada, etc.; London, 1860, p. 83.

36 Wilkinson, Pop. Acc., vol. ii. p. 350.

37 Grey, Journals, vol. ii. p. 276.

38 Wright, 'Domestic Manners,' p. 457.

39 Hakluyt, 'The Principal Navigations, Voyages,' etc.; London, 1598, vol. ii. part ii. p. 68.

South of Europe, and where they originally came from, does not seem clear, but there is a remark to the purpose in William of Ruysbruck's description of the manners of the Tatars, through whose country he travelled about 1253. "They cut up (the meat) into little bits in a dish with salt and water, for they make no other sauce, and then with the point of a knife or with a little fork (*furciculâ*), which they make for the purpose, like those we use for eating pears and apples stewed in wine, they give each of the guests standing round one mouthful or two, according to their numbers."[40]

The circumstances under which the fork makes its appearance in the Fiji Islands, are remarkable. If it is known elsewhere in Polynesia (except of course as distinctly adopted with other European fashions), it is certainly not commonly so, and its use appears to be connected with the extraordinary development of the art of cooking there, as contrasted with most of the Pacific islands, where, generally speaking, there were no vessels in which liquid was boiled over the fire, and boiling, if done at all, was done by a ruder process. But the Fijians were accomplished potters, and continued to use their earthen vessels for the preparation of their various soups and stews, for fishing the hot morsels out of which the forks are used, perhaps exclusively. Those we hear of particularly are the "cannibal forks" for eating man's flesh, which are of wood, artistically shaped and sometimes ornamented, and were handed down as family heirlooms. Each had its individual name; for instance, one which belonged to a chief celebrated for his enormous cannibalism was called *undroundro,* "a word used to denote a small person or thing carrying a great burden."[41] It would be a remarkable point if, as Dr. Seemann thinks, the fork were only used for this purpose,[42] and we might be inclined to theorize on its invention as connected with the tabu, so common in Polynesia, which restricts the tabued person from touching his food with his hands, and compels him to be fed by some one else, or in default, to grovel on the ground and take up his food with

---

[40] Gul. de Rubruquis, in Hakluyt, vol. i. p. 75. See Ayton, in Purchas, vol. iii. p. 242.

[41] Williams, 'Fiji,' vol. i. pp. 212–3.

[42] Seemann, 'Viti,' p. 179.

his mouth. But a description by Williams of the furniture of a Fijian household, seems to imply its use for ordinary purposes as well. "On the hearth, each set on three stones, are several pots, capable of holding from a quart to five gallons. Near these are a cord for binding fuel, a skewer for trying cooked food, and, in the better houses, a wooden fork—a luxury which, probably, the Fijian enjoyed when our worthy ancestors were wont to take hot food in their practised fingers."[43] But whether the use of the fork in eating came about in Fiji as a consequence of the common use of stewed food, or from some more occult cause, it seems probable that their use of it and ours may spring from two independent inventions. That they got the art of pottery from Asia is indeed likely enough, but there seems very little ground for thinking that the eating-fork came to them from Asia, or from anywhere else.

If an art can be found existing in one limited district of the world, and nowhere else, there seems to be ground for assuming that it was invented by the people among whom it is found, with much greater confidence than if it appears in several distant places. Any one, however, who thinks this an unfair inference, may console himself with the knowledge that ethnologists seldom get a chance of using it at present, except for very trifling arts or for unimportant modifications. Indeed, any one who claims a particular place as the source of even the smallest art, from the mere fact of finding it there, must feel that he may be using his own ignorance as evidence, as though it were knowledge. It is certainly playing against the bank, for a student to set up a claim to isolation for any art or custom, not knowing what evidence there may be against him, buried in the ground, hidden among remote tribes, or contained even in ordinary books, to say nothing of the thousands of volumes of forgotten histories and travels.

Among the inventions which it seems possible to trace to their original districts, is the hammock, which is found, as it were, native in a great part of South America and the West Indies, and is known to have spread thence far and wide over the world, carrying with it its Haitian name, *hamac*.

The boomerang is a peculiar weapon, and moreover there are found beside it in its country, Australia, intermediate forms be-

43 Williams, vol. i. p. 138.

tween it and the battle-axe or pick; so that there is ground for considering it a native invention developed through such stages into its most perfect form. Various Old World missiles have indeed been claimed as boomerangs; a curved weapon shown on the Assyrian bas-reliefs, the throwing-cudgel of the Egyptian fowler, the African *lissán* or curved club, the iron *hungamunga* of the Tibbûs, but without proof being brought forward that these weapons, or the boomerang-like iron projectiles of the Niam-Nam, have either of the great peculiarities of the boomerang, the sudden swerving from the apparent line of flight, or the returning to the thrower. The accounts given by Colonel Lane Fox in his instructive lectures (1868-9) at the United Service Institution,[44] of the missiles of the indigenous tribes of India, whirled in the manner of boomerangs to bring down game, seem to me to furnish evidence similar to that from Australia, of the local and gradual invention of weapons. Sir Walter Elliot describes the rudest kind in the South Mahratta district as mere crooked sticks, and hence we trace the instrument up to the *katuria* of the Kulis of Gujerat, a weapon resembling the boomerang in shape, and in being an edged flat missile, preserving its plane of rotation, but differing from it in being too thick and heavy to swerve or return. While admitting the propriety of Colonel Lane Fox's classification of the Indian and Australian weapons together, I think we may regard their specific difference as showing independent though partly similar development in the two districts. Mr. Samuel Ferguson has written a very learned and curious paper[45] on supposed European analogues of the boomerang, in concluding which he remarks, not untruly, that "many of the foregoing inferences will, doubtless, appear in a high degree speculative." As might be expected, he makes the most of the obscure description of the *cateia,* set down about the beginning of the seventh century by Bishop Isidore of Seville.[46] But what is far

---

44 Lane Fox, 'Primitive Warfare,' in Journ. Royal United Service Inst.

45 S. Ferguson, in Trans. R. I. A.; Dublin, 1843, vol. xix.

46 "Est enim genus Gallici teli ex materia quàm maximè lenta, quæ jacta quidem non longe propter gravitatem evolat: sed quò pervenit, vi nimia perfringit: quòd si ab artifice mittatur: rursum redit ad cum, qui misit," etc. (Isid. Origg. xviii. 7.)

more to the purpose, Mr. Ferguson seems to have made trial of a carved club of ancient shape, and some hammer- and cross-shaped weapons, such as may have been used in Europe, and to have made them fly with something of the returning flight of the boomerang. On the whole, it would be rash to assert that the principle of the boomerang was quite unknown in the Old World. Another remarkable weapon, the *bolas*, seemed to be isolated in the particular region of South America where it was found in use, and was therefore very likely invented there; but its principle is known also among the Esquimaux, whose thin thongs, weighted with bunches of ivory knobs, are arranged to wind themselves round the bird they are thrown at, in much the same way as the much stouter cords, weighted at the ends with two or three heavy stone balls, which form the *bolas* of the Southern continent.

A few more instances may be given, rather for their quaintness than for their importance. The Australians practise an ingenious art in bee-hunting, which I have not met with anywhere else. The hunter catches a bee, and gums a piece of down to it, so that it can fly but slowly, and he can easily follow it home to the hive, and get the honey. The North American bee-hunters do not use this contrivance, but they put a bait of honey on a flat stone and surround it with a ring of thick white paint, across which the bee crawls to take flight from the edge of the stone, and at once clogs and marks itself.[47] Again, there is the curious art of changing the colour of a live macaw's feathers from blue or green to brilliant orange or yellow, by plucking them and rubbing some liquid into the skin (it is said the milky secretion from a small frog or toad), which causes the new feathers to grow with a changed colour.[48] This is done in South America, but, so far as I know, not elsewhere; and it seems reasonable to suppose that it was invented there. Travellers in the Malay Peninsula and Sumatra describe the thrilling effect of the tones, as of flutes and organs, that seem to grow out of the air as they approach

[47] Lang, p. 328. Backhouse, Austr., p. 380. J. G. Wood, in 'Boy's Own Mag.' vol. v. p. 526.

[48] Wallace, 'Travels on the Amazon and Rio Negro'; London, 1853, p. 294. De la Condamine, in Pinkerton, vol. xiv. p. 248. Dobrizhoffer, vol. i. p. 327.

some hamlet, sometimes single and interrupted notes rising, swelling into a burst of harmony, and dying away. These sounds are produced by bamboos fixed up in the trees, slit between the joints so that each bamboo becomes an Æolian flute of many tones.[49] This beautiful habit may well be of native origin. But it is curious to compare it with an early South American description from the province of Picara, now in Columbia. There, at the entrances of the caciques' houses, were platforms surrounded with stout canes, on which (in the fashion of the Dayaks) were set up heads of enemies, "looking fierce with long hair, and their faces painted in such sort as to appear like those of devils. In the lower part of the canes there are holes through which the wind can pass, and when it blows, there is a noise which sounds like the music of devils."[50]

When an art is practised upon some material which belongs exclusively, or in a large degree, to the place where the art is found, the probability that it was invented on the spot becomes almost a certainty. No one would dispute the claim of the Peruvians or Chilians to have discovered the use, for manure, of the *huanu,* or, as we call it, "guano," which their exceptionally rainless climate has allowed to accumulate on their coasts, nor the claim of the dwellers in the hot regions near the Gulf of Mexico to have found out how to make their *chocollatl* from a native plant.

On the other hand, when tribes are found living among the very materials which are turned to account by simple arts elsewhere, and yet are ignorant of those arts, we have good ethnological evidence as to their condition when they first settled in the place where we become acquainted with them. In investigating the difficult problem of Polynesian civilization, this state of things often presents itself, not uniformly, but in a partial, various way, that gives us a glimpse here and there of the trains of events that must have taken place, in different times and places, to produce the complex result we have before us. It is

<hr />

[49] Logan, in 'Journ. Ind. Archip.,' vol. iii. p. 35. Cameron, 'Malayan India,' p. 120.

[50] Cieza de Leon, 'Travels' (Tr. and Ed. by Markham), Hakluyt Soc. 1864, p. 81.

clear that a Malayo-Polynesian culture, proved by the combined evidence of language, mythology, arts, and customs, has spread itself over a great part of the Southern Islands, from the Philippines down to New Zealand, and from Easter Island to Madagascar, though the pure Malayo-Polynesian race only forms a part of the population of the district in which its language and civilization more or less predominate. The original condition of the Malayo-Polynesian family, as determined by the state of its lower members, presents us with few arts not found at least in a rudimentary state in Australia, though these arts were developed with immensely greater skill and industry. In most of the South Sea Islands there was no knowledge of pottery, nor of the art of boiling food in vessels over a fire. Great part of the race was strictly in the stone age, knowing nothing of metals. The sugar-cane grew in Tahiti, but the natives only chewed it, knowing nothing of the art of sugar-making;[51] nor did they make any use of the cotton plant, though it grew there.[52] The art of weaving was unknown in most of the islands away from Asia. Though the coco-nut palm was common, they did not tap it for toddy; and Dr. Seemann taught the Fijians the art of extracting sago from their native sago-palms.[53]

In other districts, however, a very different state of things was found. In Sumatra and other islands near Asia, and in Madagascar, iron was smelted and worked with much skill. The simplest kind of loom had appeared in the Eastern Archipelago, only, as the evidence seems to show, to be supplanted by a higher kind.[54] Pottery was made there, and even far into Polynesia, as in the Fiji Islands. All these things were probably introduced from Asia, to which country so very large a part of the present Malay culture is due, but there are local arts found cropping up in different groups of islands, which may be considered as native inventions peculiar to Polynesia. Thus, in some of the islands, it was customary to keep bread-fruit by fermenting it into a sour paste, in which state it could be stored away for use out of season,

---

[51] Cook, First Voy. H., vol. ii. p. 186. So the Birmese, Bastian, 'Oestl. Asien.,' vol. ii. p. 99; see also W. G. Palgrave, 'Central and Eastern Arabia,' vol. ii. p. 156.

[52] J. R. Forster, Observations (Cook's Second Voy.); London, 1778, p. 384.

[53] Seemann, pp. 291, 329.   [54] Marsden, p. 183,

an art of considerable value. This paste was called *mahi* in Tahiti, where Captain Cook first saw it prepared, but it would seem to have been invented at a period since the part of the race which went to the Sandwich Islands were separated from the Tahitians, for the Sandwich Islanders knew nothing of it till the English brought it to them from Tahiti.[55] The use of intoxicating liquor known as *ava, kava,* or *yangona,* appears to be peculiar to Polynesia, and therefore probably to have been invented there. It is true that the usual, though not universal practice of preparing it by chewing, gives it some resemblance to liquors so prepared on the American continent, but these latter are of an entirely different character, being fermented liquors of the nature of beer, made from vegetables rich in starch, while the *ava* is not fermented at all, the juice of the plant it is made from being intoxicating in its fresh state.[56]

The miscellaneous pieces of evidence given in this chapter have been selected less as giving grounds for arguments safe from attack, than as examples of the sort of material with which the ethnologist has to deal. The uncertainty of many of the inferences he makes must be counterbalanced by their number, and

[55] Cook's First Voy. H., vol. ii. p. 198; Third Voy., vol. iii. p. 141.

[56] The etymology of *kava* or *ava* is of interest. Its original meaning may have been that of bitterness or pungency; *kawa,* N. Z. = pungent, bitter, strong (as spirits, etc.); *'ava,* Tah. = a bitter, disagreeable taste; *kava,* Rar. Mang. Nuk., *'a'ava,* Sam., *awa awa,* Haw. = sour, bitter, pungent. Thence the name may have been given, not only to the plant of which the intoxicating drink is made, the *Macropiper methysticum kava,* Tong. Rar. Nuk.; *'ava,* Sam. Tah. Haw.; but also in N. Z. to the *Macropiper excelsum,* or *kawa kawa,* and in Tahiti to tobacco, *'ava 'ava.* Lastly, the drink is named in Tahiti and in other islands from the plant it is expressed from. But Mariner's Tongan vocabulary seems to go the other way; *cava* = the pepper plant; also the root of this plant, of which is made a peculiar kind of beverage, etc.; *cawna* = bitter, brackish, also intoxicated with cava, or anything else. This looks as though the name of the plant gave a name to the quality of bitterness, as we say "peppery" in the sense of hot. (See the Vocabularies of Mariner, Hale, Buschmann, and the Church Miss. Soc., N. Z.) Southey (Hist. of Brazil, vol. i. p. 245) compares the word *kava* with the South American word *caou-in* or *kaawy,* a liquor made from maize or the mandioc root by chewing, boiling with water, and fermenting; but the idea of bitterness or pungency is unsuitable to this liquor. Dias (Dic. da Lingua Tupy) gives perhaps a more accurate form, *cauím* = vinho, a derivative perhaps from *caú* = beber (vinho). To show how easily such accidental coincidences as that of *kava* and *cauím* may be found, a German root may be pointed out for both, looking as suitable as though it were a real one, *kauen,* to chew.

by the concurrence of independent lines of reasoning in favour of the same view. But in the arguments given here in illustration of the general method, only one side of history has been kept in view, and the facts have been treated generally as evidence of movement only in a forward direction, or (to define more closely what is here treated as Progress) of the appearance and growth of new arts and new knowledge, whether of a profitable or hurtful nature, developed at home or imported from abroad. Yet we know by what has taken place within the range of history, that Decline as well as Progress in art and knowledge really goes on in the world. Is there not then evidence forthcoming to prove that degradation as well as development has happened to the lower races beyond the range of direct history? The known facts bearing on this subject are scanty and obscure, but by examining some direct evidence of Decline, it may be perhaps possible to form an opinion as to what indirect evidence there may probably be, and how it is to be treated; though actually to find this and use it, is a very different matter.

There are developments of Culture which belong to a particular climate or a particular state of society, which require a despotic government, a democratic government, an agricultural life, a life in cities, a state of continued peace or of continued war, an accumulation of wealth which exceeds what is wanted for necessaries and is accordingly devoted to luxury and refinement, and so forth. Such things are all more or less local and unstable. The Chinese do not make now the magnificent cloisonné enamels and the high-class porcelain of their ancestors; we do not build churches, or even cast church-bells, as our forefathers did. In Egypt the extraordinary development of masonry, goldsmiths' work, weaving, and other arts which rose to such a pitch of excellence there thousands of years ago, have died out under the influence of foreign civilizations which contented themselves with a lower level of excellence in these things, and there seems to be hardly a characteristic native art of any importance practised there, unless it be the artificial hatching of eggs, and even this is found in China. As Sir Thomas Browne writes in his 'Fragment on Mummies,' "Egypt itself is now become the land of obliviousness and doteth. Her ancient civility is gone, and her glory hath vanished as a phantasma. Her youthful days are over, and her face hath become wrinkled and tetrick. She poreth not upon the heavens, astronomy is dead unto her, and knowledge maketh other cycles."

The history of Central America presents a case somewhat like that of Egypt. The not uncommon idea that the deserted cities, Copan, Palenque, and the rest, are the work of an extinct and quite unknown race, does not agree with the published evidence, which proves that the descendants of the old builders are living there now, speaking the old languages that were spoken before the Spanish Conquest. The ancient cities, with their wonders of masonry and sculpture, are deserted, the special native culture has in great measure disappeared, and the people have been brought to a sort of low European civilization; but a mass of records, corroborated in other ways, show us the Central Americans before the Conquest, building their great cities and living in them, cultivating, warring, sacrificing, much like their neighbours of Mexico, with whose civilization their own was intimately allied. An epitome of the fate of the ruined cities may be given in the words which conclude a remarkable native document published in Quiché and French by the Abbé Brasseur,—"Ainsi donc c'en est fait de tous ceux du Quiché, qui s'appelle *Santa-Cruz*." The ruins of the great city of Quiché are still to be seen; Santa Cruz, its successor, is a poor village of two thousand souls, a league or so away.[57]

Among the lower races, degeneration is seen to take place as a result of war, of oppression by other tribes, of expulsion into less favourable situations, and of various other causes. But arts which belong to the daily life of the man or the family and cannot be entirely suppressed by violent interference, do not readily disappear unless superseded by some better contrivance, or made unnecessary or very difficult by a change of life and manners. When the use of metals, of pottery, of the flint and steel, of higher tools and weapons, once fairly establishes itself, a falling back appears to be uncommon. The Metal Age does not degenerate into the Stone Age except under very peculiar circumstances. The history of a higher weapon is generally that it supplants

57 Brasseur, 'Popol Vuh'; pp. 345–7. See also Diego de Landa, Rel.

those that are less serviceable, to be itself supplanted by something better. We read of the Indian orator who exhorted his brethren to cast away the flint and steel of the white man, and to return to the fire-sticks of their ancestors, and of the Chinese sage desiring to discard the art of writing and return to the ancestral method of record by knotted cords, but such things are rather talked of than done. .

Cases of savage arts being superseded by a higher state of civilization are common enough. An African guide, or an Australian, will know a man by his footmark, while we hardly know what a footmark is like; at least, nine Englishmen out of ten of the shoe-wearing classes will not know that the footprints in the

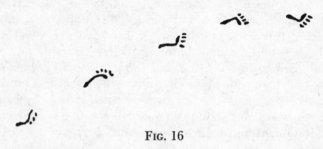

FIG. 16

Mexican picture-writings, as copied in Fig. 16, are true to nature, till they have looked at the print of a wet foot on a board or a flagstone. Captain Burton remarked, on his road to the great Salt Lake, that bones and skulls of cattle were left lying scattered about,[58] though travellers are often put to great straits for fuel. The Gauchos of South America know better, for when they kill a beast on a journey, they use the bones as fuel to cook the flesh,[59] as the Scythians did in the time of Herodotus; living in a country wanting wood, they made a fire of the bones of the beasts sacrificed, and boiled the flesh over it in a kettle, or if that were not forthcoming, in the paunch of the animal itself, "and thus the ox boils himself, and the other victims each the like."[60]

[58] Burton, 'City of the Saints,' p. 60.

[59] Darwin, Journal, p. 194.

[60] Herod., iv. 61. See Ezekiel, xxiv. 5 in LXX. Klemm, C. G., vol. ii. p. 229 (bones rubbed with fat burnt by Esquimaux).

It sometimes happens that degeneration is caused by conquest, when the conquering race is in anything at a lower level than the conquered. There is one art whose history gives some extraordinary cases of this kind of decline, the art of irrigation by watercourses. Within a few years one people, the Spaniards, conquered two nations, the Moors and the Peruvians, who were skilful irrigators, and had constructed great works to bring water from a distance to fertilize the land. These works were for the most part allowed to go to rack and ruin, and in Peru, as in Andalusia, great tracts of land which had been fruitful gardens fell back into parched deserts; while in Mexico the ruins of the great native aqueduct of Tetzcotzinco tell the same tale. Here, as in the irrigation of British India under our own rule, the results of higher culture in the conquered race declined in the face of a lower culture of the conquerors, but the sequel is still more curious. The Spaniards in America became themselves great builders of watercourses, and their works of this kind in Mexico are very extensive, and of great benefit to the drier regions where they have been constructed. But when a portion of territory that had been under Spanish rule was transferred to the United States, what the Spaniards had done to the irrigating works of the Moors and Peruvians, the new settlers did to theirs. In Froebel's time they were letting the old works go to ruin; thus history repeats itself.[61]

The disappearance of savage arts in presence of a higher civilization is however mostly caused by their being superseded by something higher, and this can hardly be called a decline of culture, which must not be confounded with the physical and moral decline of so many tribes under the oppression and temptation of civilized men. Real decline often takes place when a rude but strong race overcomes a cultivated but weak race, and of this we have good information; but neither this change, nor that which takes place in the savage in presence of the civilized invader, gives the student of the low races all the information he needs. What he wants besides is to put the high races out of the question altogether, and to find out how far a low race can lose its comparatively simple arts and knowledge, without these being

[61] Tylor, 'Mexico,' pp. 157–161.

superseded by something higher; in fact, how far such a race can suffer pure decline in culture. This information is, however, very hard to get.

Livingstone's remarks on the Bakalahari of South Africa show us a race which has fallen in civilization, but this fall has happened, partly or wholly, through causes acting from without. The great Kalahari desert is inhabited by two races, the Bushmen, who were perhaps the first human inhabitants of the country, and who never cultivate the soil, or rear any domestic animals but dogs, and the Ba-Kalahari, who are degraded Bechuanas. These latter are traditionally reported to have once possessed herds of cattle like the other Bechuanas, and though their hard fate has forced them to live a life much like that of the Bushmen, they have never forgotten their old ways. They hoe their gardens annually, though often all they can hope for is a supply of melons and pumpkins. And they carefully rear small herds of goats, though Livingstone has seen them obliged to lift water for them out of small wells with a bit of ostrich egg-shell, or by spoonfuls.[62] This remarkable account brings out strongly the manful struggle of a race which has been brought down by adverse circumstances, to keep up their former civilization, while the Bushmen, who, for all we know, may never have been in a higher condition than they are now, make no such effort. If we may judge these two races by the same standard, the Bushmen are either no lower than they have ever been, or if they have come down from a condition approaching that of the Bechuanas, the process of degradation must indeed have been a long one.

Tribes who are known to have once been higher in the scale of culture than they are now, are to be met with in Asia. Some of the coast Tunguz live by fishing, though they are still called Orochi, which is equivalent to the term "Reindeer Tunguz." No doubt the tradition is true of the Goldi that, though they have no reindeer now, they once had, like the Tunguz tribes north of the Amur.[63] There are Calmucks north of the Caspian who have lost their herds of cattle and degenerated into fishermen. The richest of them has still a couple of cows. They look upon horses, camels, and sheep as strange and wondrous crea-

---

[62] Livingstone, p. 49.   [63] Ravenstein, p. 318.

tures when foreigners bring them into their country. They listen with wonder to their old men's stories of life in the steppes, of the great herds and the ceaseless wanderings over the vast plains, while they themselves dwell in huts of reeds, and carry their household goods on their backs when they have to move to a new fishing place.[64] The miserable "Digger Indians" of North America are in part Shoshonees or Snake Indians, who were brought down to their present state by their enemies the Blackfeet, who got guns from the Hudson's Bay Company, and thus conquered the Snakes, and took away their hunting grounds. They lead a wandering life, lurking among hills and crags, slinking from the sight of whites and Indians, and subsisting chiefly on wild roots and fish, and such game as so helpless a race is able to get. They are lean and abject-looking creatures, deserving the name of *gens de pitié* given them by the French trappers, and they have been driven to abandon arts which they possessed in their more fortunate days, such as riding, and apparently even hut-building; but how far their degradation has brought with it decline in other parts of their former culture, it is not easy to say.[65]

Here, then, we have cases of material evidence which, as we happen to have other means of knowing, ought to be treated as recording decline. The sculptures and temples of Central America are the work of the ancestors of the present Indians, though if history, tradition, and transitional work had all perished, it would hardly be thought so. The gardening of the Bakalahari, if the account of their origin is to be received, is a proof, not of an art gained, but of a higher level of civilization for the most part lost.

It thus appears that, in the abstract, when there is found among a low tribe an art or a piece of knowledge which seems above their average level, three ways are open by which its occurrence may be explained. It may have been invented at home, it may have been imported from abroad, or it may be a relic of a higher condition which has mostly suffered degradation, like the column of earth which the excavator leaves to measure the depth of the ground he has cleared away.

[64] Klemm, C. G., vol. iii. p. 4.

[65] Buschmann, 'Spuren der Aztekischen Sprache im nördlichen Mexico,' etc., etc. (Abh. der K. A. v. W., 1854); Berlin, 1859, p. 633, etc.

Ethnologists have sometimes taken arts which appeared to them too advanced to fit with the general condition of their possessors, and have treated them as belonging to this latter class. But where such arguments have had no aid from direct history, but have gone on mere inspection of the arts of the lower races, all that I can call to mind, at least, seem open to grave exception.

Thus the boomerang has been adduced as proof that the Australians were once in a far higher state of civilization.[66] It is true that the author who argued thus confounded the boomerang with the throwing-cudgel, or, as a Hampshire man would call it, the *squoyle,* of the Egyptian fowler, so that he had at least an imaginary high civilization in view, of which the boomerang was an element. But, as has been mentioned, intermediate forms between the boomerang and the war-club or pick, are known in Australia, a state of things which fits rather with growth than with degeneration.[67]

In South America, Humboldt was so struck with the cylinders of very hard stone, perforated and sculptured into the forms of animals and fruits, that he founded upon them the argument that they were relics of an ancient civilization from which their possessors had fallen. "But it is not," he says, "the Indians of our own day, the dwellers on the Oronoko and the Amazons whom we see in the last degree of brutalization, who have perforated substances of such hardness, giving them the shapes of animals and fruits. Such pieces of work, like the pierced and sculptured emeralds found in the Cordilleras of New Granada and Quito, indicate a previous civilization. At present the inhabitants of these districts, especially of the hot regions, have so little idea of the possibility of cutting hard stones (emerald, jade, compact felspar, and rock crystal), that they have imagined the green stone to be naturally soft when taken out of the ground, and to harden after it has been fashioned by hand."[68] But while mentioning Humboldt's argument, it must also be said that he had not had

66 W. Cooke Taylor, The Nat. Hist. of Society; London, 1840, vol. i. p. 205.

67 See Eyre, vol. ii. p. 308; Klemm, C. G., vol. i. p. 316, pl. vii. Lane Fox, l. c.

68 Humboldt & Bonpland, vol. ii. p. 481, etc. It is a fact that some stone is more easily worked when fresh from the ground, than after its water has evaporated.

an opportunity of learning how these ornaments were made. Mr. Wallace has since found that at least plain cylinders of imperfect rock crystal, four to eight inches long, and one inch in diameter, are made and perforated by very low tribes on the Rio Negro. They are not, as Humboldt seems to have supposed, the result of high mechanical skill, but merely of the most simple and savage processes, carried on with that utter disregard of time that lets the Indian spend a month in making an arrow. They are merely ground down into shape by rubbing, and the perforating of the cylinders, crosswise or even lengthwise, is said to be done thus:—a pointed flexible leaf-shoot of wild plantain is twirled with the hands against the hard stone, till, with the aid of fine sand and water, it bores into and through it, and this is said to take years to do. Such cylinders as the chiefs wear are said sometimes to take two men's lives to perforate.[69] The stone is brought from a great distance up the river, and is very highly valued. It is, of course, not necessary to suppose that these rude Indians came of themselves to making such ornaments; they may have imitated things made by races in a higher state of culture; but the evidence, as it now stands, does not go for much in proving that the tribes of the Rio Negro have themselves fallen from a higher level.

On the other hand, it is much easier to go on pointing out arts practised by the less civilized races, which seem to have their fitting place rather in a history of progress than of degeneration. This remark applies to the case just mentioned, of the intermediate forms between the boomerang and the war-club being found in Australia, as though to mark the stages through which the perfect instrument had been developed. Several such cases occur among the arts of fire-making and cooking described in the following chapters. To glance for a moment at the history of Textile Fabrics (into which I hope to go more fully at a future time), it may be noticed that the spindle for twisting thread has been found in use in Asia, Africa, and North and South America, among people whose ruder neighbours had no better means of making their finest thread or cord than by twisting it with the hand, by rolling the fibres with the palm, on the thigh or some

---

[69] Wallace, p. 278. See Rau, 'Drilling in Stone without Metal,' in Smithsonian Report, 1868.

other parts of the body. Again, though every known tribe appears to twist cord, and to make matting or wicker-work, the combination of these two arts, weaving, which consists in matting twisted threads, is very far from being general among the lower races. The step seems from our point of view a very simple one, but a large proportion of mankind had never made it. Now there is a curious art, which is neither matting nor weaving, found among tribes to whom real weaving was unknown. It consists in laying bundles of fibres, not twisted into real cord, side by side, and tying or fastening them together with transverse cords or bands; varieties of fabrics made in this way are well known in New Zealand and among the Indians of North-Western America; and Mr. Henry Christy pointed out to me a sack-like basket made in this way, which he found in use in 1856 among an Indian tribe N. W. of Lake Huron, a very good example of this interesting transition-work. Nor do we look in vain for such a fabric in Europe; it is found in the Lake Habitations of Switzerland. M. Troyon's work shows a specimen from Wangen, which belongs to the Stone Age.[70] Mr. John Evans has three specimens of fabrics from the Swiss Lakes, which form a series of great interest. The first (Fig. 17) is also from Wangen, and, to use the description accompanying the sketches he has kindly given me, "the warp consists of strands of un-twisted fibre (hemp?) bound together at intervals of about an inch apart by nearly similar strands 'wattled in' among them." The next specimen (Fig. 18), from Nieder-Wyl, shows a great advance, for "the warp consists of twisted string, and the woof of a finer thread also twisted." The third specimen is a piece of ordinary plain weaving. Now all these things, European, Polynesian, and American, seem to be in their natural and reasonable places in a progress upward, but it is hard to imagine a people, under any combination of circumstances, dropping down from the art of weaving, to adopt a more tedious and less profitable way of working up the fibre which it had cost them so much trouble to prepare; knowing the better art, and deliberately devoting their material and time to practising the worse. So it is a very reasonable and natural thing, that tribes who had been used

[70] Troyon, 'Habitations Lacustres'; Lausanne, 1860, pl. vii. fig. 24, pp. 43, 429, 465.

FIG. 17

FIG. 18

to twist their thread by hand, should sometimes overcome their dislike to change, and adopt the spindle when they saw it in use; or such a tribe might be supposed capable of inventing it; but the going back from the spindle to hand-twisting is a thing scarcely conceivable. A spindle is made too easily by anyone who has once caught the idea of it; a stick and a bit of something heavy for a whorl is the whole machine. Not many months ago, an old lady was seen in the isle of Islay, comfortably spinning her flax with a spindle, which spindle was simply a bit of stick with a potato stuck on the end of it.

To conclude, the want of evidence leaves us as yet much in the dark as to the share which decline in civilization may have had in bringing the lower races into the state in which we find them. But perhaps this difficulty rather affects the history of particular tribes, than the history of Culture as a whole. To judge from experience, it would seem that the world, when it has once got a firm grasp of new knowledge or a new art, is very loth to lose it altogether, especially when it relates to matters important to man in general, for the conduct of his daily life, and the satisfaction of his daily wants, things that come home to men's "business and bosoms." An inspection of the geographical distribution of art and knowledge among mankind, seems to give some grounds for the belief that the history of the lower races, as of the higher, is not the history of a course of degeneration, or even of equal oscillations to and fro, but of a movement which, in spite of frequent stops and relapses, has on the whole been forward; that there has been from age to age a growth in Man's power over Nature, which no degrading influences have been able permanently to check.

CHAPTER VIII

HISTORICAL TRADITIONS
AND MYTHS OF OBSERVATION

The traditions current among mankind are partly historical and partly mythical. To the ethnologist they are of value in two very different ways, sometimes as preserving the memory of past events, sometimes as showing by their occurrence in different districts of the world that between the inhabitants of these districts there has been in some way a historical connexion. His great difficulty in dealing with them is to separate the fact and the fiction, which are both so valuable in their different ways: and this difficulty is aggravated by the circumstance that these two elements are often mixed up in a most complex manner, myths presenting themselves in the dress of historical narrative, and historical facts growing into the wildest myths.

Between the traditions of real events, which are History, and the pure myths, whose origin and development are being brought more and more clearly into view in our own times by the labours of Adalbert Kuhn and Max Müller, and their school, there lie a mass of stories which may be called "Myths of Observation." They are inferences from observed facts, which take the form of positive assertions, and they differ principally from the inductions of modern science in being much more generally crude and erroneous, and in taking to themselves names of persons, and more or less of purely subjective detail, which enables them to assume the appearance of real history. When a savage builds upon the discovery of great bones buried in the earth a story of a combat of the giants and monsters whose remains they are, he constructs a Myth of Observation which may shape itself into the form of a historical tradition, and be all the more puzzling for the portion of scientific truth which it really contains. The object of the present chapter is to collect a quantity of evidence, bearing on the problem how to separate Historical Traditions and Myths of Observation from pure Myths, and from one another.

Though it may not be possible to lay down any general canon of criticism by which the historical and mythical elements of tradition may be separated, it is to some extent possible to judge by internal evidence whether or not a particular legend or episode has a claim to be considered as history. It happens sometimes that a legend contains statements which are hardly likely to have come into the minds of the original narrators of the story, except by actual experience. The Chinese legend which tells us the name of the ancient sage who taught his people to make fire by the friction of wood cannot be taken as it stands for real history, seeing that so many nations ascribe this and other arts to mythic heroes, yet it embodies a recollection of a time when this was the ordinary way of producing fire. So, when the same people tell us that they once used knotted cords like the Peruvian quipus, as records of events, and that the art of writing superseded this ruder expedient, we are in no way called upon to receive the names and dates of the inventors to whom they ascribe these arts; but, at the same time, it is hard to imagine what could have put such an idea into their heads, unless there had been a foundation of fact for the story, in the actual use of quipus in the country before writing became general.

In the traditions which the Polynesians have preserved of their migrations in past times, it is likely that some historic truth may be preserved, and with their help, aided by a closer study of the languages and myths of the district, it may be some day possible for ethnologists to sketch out, at least roughly, the history of the race for ages before the European discovery. Much of the historical value of the South Sea traditions is due to their being commonly preserved in verses kept alive by frequent repetition, and in which even small events are placed on record with an accuracy and permanence that yields only to written history. Thus a question that arose when Ellis was in Tahiti, about a certain buoy that was stolen from the 'Bounty' nearly thirty years before, was settled at once by a couple of lines from a native song,

> O mea eiá e Tareu eiá
> Eiá te poito a Bligh.

> Such a one a thief, and Tareu a thief,
> Stole the buoy of Bligh.[1]

---

[1] Ellis, Polyn. Res., vol. i. p. 287.

Among the mass of Central American traditions which have become known through the labours of the Abbé Brasseur, there occur certain passages in the story of an early migration of the Quiché race, which have much the appearance of vague and broken stories derived in some way from high northern latitudes. The Quiché manuscript describes the ancestors of the race as travelling away from the rising of the sun, and goes on thus:— "But it is not clear how they crossed the sea, they passed as though there had been no sea, for they passed over scattered rocks, and these rocks were rolled on the sands. This is why they called the place 'ranged stones and torn up sands,' the name which they gave it on their passage within the sea, the water being divided when they passed." Then the people collected on a mountain called Chi Pixab, and there they fasted in darkness and night. Afterwards it is related that they removed, and waited for the dawn which was approaching, and the manuscript says:—"Now, behold, our ancients and our fathers were made lords and had their dawn; behold, we will relate also the rising of the dawn and the apparition of the sun, the moon, and the stars." Great was their joy when they saw the morning star, which came out first with its resplendent face before the sun. At last the sun itself began to come forth; the animals, small and great, were in joy; they rose from the watercourses and ravines, and stood on the mountain tops with their heads towards where the sun was coming. An innumerable crowd of people were there, and the dawn cast light on all these nations at once. "At last the face of the ground was dried by the sun: like a man the sun showed himself, and his presence warmed and dried the surface of the ground. Before the sun appeared, muddy and wet was the surface of the ground, and it was before the sun appeared, and then only the sun rose like a man. But his heat had no strength, and he did but show himself when he rose, he only remained like (an image in) a mirror, and it is not indeed the same sun that appears now, they say in the stories."[2]

Obscure as much of this is, there are things in it which agree very curiously with the phenomena of the Arctic regions. The cold and darkness, the sea not like a sea but like rocks rolled on the sand, the long waiting for the sun, and its appearance at last

[2] Brasseur, 'Popol Vuh,' pp. 231–43; 'Mexique,' vol. i. pp. 169–76.

with little strength, and but just rising above the horizon, form a picture which corresponds with the nature of the high north, as much as it differs from that of the tropical regions where the tradition is found. We read of the people of Thule of old, after their 35-day night, climbing hills to look out for the returning sun, as in more modern times of Arctic voyagers going out to watch for the sun towards the close of the long dismal winter.[3] The judgment that it was not indeed the sun of Central America that appeared so strangely, may be placed by the side of a remark made by a savage in another country. Sir George Grey, travelling in Australia, was once telling stories of distant countries to a party of natives round the camp fire; "I now spoke to them of still more northern latitudes; and went so far as to describe those countries in which the sun never sets at a certain period of the year. Their astonishment now knew no bounds: 'Ah! that must be another sun, not the same as the one we see here,' said an old man; and in spite of all my arguments to the contrary, the others adopted this opinion."[4]

The legend of the introduction of rice in Borneo relates how a Dayak climbed up a tree which grew downward from the sky, and so got up to the Pleiades, and there he found a personage who took him to his house and gave him boiled rice to eat. He had never seen rice before, and the story says that when he saw the grains, he thought they were maggots.[5] Now there is a tradition of recent date, among the Keethratlah Indians of British Columbia, which tells in the most graphic way the story of the first appearance of the white men among them; how an Indian canoe was out catching halibut, when the noise of a huge sea-monster was heard, plunging along through the thick mist; the Indians drew up their lines and paddled to shore, when the monster proved to be a boat full of strange-looking men. "The strangers landed, and beckoned the Indians to come to them and bring them some fish. One of them had over his shoulder what was supposed to be a stick; presently he pointed it to a bird that was flying past—a violent poo went forth—down came the bird to the ground. The Indians

---

[3] Procopius, ii. 206; Purchas, vol. iii. p. 499.

[4] Grey, Journals, vol. i. p. 293.

[5] St. John, vol. i. p. 202, and see under Chap. IX.

died! As they revived, they questioned each other as to their state, whether any were dead, and what each had felt. The whites then made signs for a fire to be lighted; the Indians proceeded at once, according to their usual tedious practice, of rubbing two sticks together. The strangers laughed, and one of them, snatching up a handful of dry grass, struck a spark into a little powder placed under it. Instantly another poo!—and a blaze. The Indians died! After this the new-comers wanted some fish boiled: the Indians, therefore, put the fish and water into one of their square wooden buckets, and set some stones on the fire; intending, when they were hot, to cast them into the vessel, and thus boil the food. The whites were not satisfied with this way: one of them fetched a tin kettle out of the boat, put the fish and some water into it, and then, strange to say, set it on the fire. The Indians looked on with astonishment. However, the kettle did not consume; the water did not run into the fire. Then, again, the Indians died! When the fish was eaten, the strangers put a kettle of rice on the fire; the Indians looked at each other, and whispered *Akshahn, ak-shahn!* or 'Maggots, maggots!' "[6]

Again, the Australians have had the same idea of what rice was, for in the Moorunde dialect it is called "yeelilee," or "mag-gots,"[7] a name which, of course, dates from the recent time when foreigners brought it to the country. When, therefore, we are told in the Borneo tale that the first Dayak who saw grains of rice took them for maggots, we are, I think, justified in believing this no-tion to be in Borneo, as elsewhere, a real reminiscence of the introduction of rice into the country, though this piece of actual history comes to us woven into the texture of an ancient myth. There is reason to suppose that rice was introduced into the Ma-lay islands from Asia; in Marsden's time it had not been adopted even in Engano and Batu, which are islands close to Sumatra.[8]

When a tradition is once firmly planted among the legendary lore of a tribe, there seems scarcely any limit to the time through which it may be kept up by continual repetition from one genera-tion to the next; unless such an event as the coming of a stronger

---

6 Mayne, 'British Columbia,' p. 279.

7 Eyre, vol. ii. p. 393.

8 Marsden, pp. 467, 474. See Ellis, 'Madagascar,' vol. i. p. 39.

and more highly cultivated race entirely upsets the old state of society, and destroys the old landmarks. The traditions of the Polynesians, for instance, seem often to be of great age, for they occur among the natives of distant islands whose languages have had time to diverge widely from a common origin; but even the most long-lived stories are fast disappearing, under European influence, from the memory of the people. The historical value of a tradition does not of necessity vary inversely with its age, and indeed this rule-of-three test goes for very little, for some very old stories are, beyond a doubt, of greater historical value than other very new ones current in the same tribe.

There is even a certain amount of evidence which tends to prove that the memory of the huge animals of the quaternary period has been preserved up to modern times in popular tradition. It is but quite lately that the fact of man having lived on the earth at the same time with the mammoth has become a generally received opinion, though its probability has been seen by a few far-sighted thinkers for many years past, and it had been suggested long before the late discoveries in the Drift-beds, that several traditions, found in different parts of the world, were derived from actual memory of the remote time when various great animals, generally thought to have died out before the appearance of man upon the earth, were still alive. The subject is hardly in a state to express a decided opinion upon, but the evidence is worthy of the most careful attention.

Father Charlevoix, whose 'History of New France' was published in 1744, records a North American legend of a great elk. "There is current also among these barbarians a pleasant enough tradition of a great Elk, beside whom others seem like ants. He has, they say, legs so high that eight feet of snow do not embarrass him: his skin is proof against all sorts of weapons, and he has a sort of arm which comes out of his shoulder, and which he uses as we do ours."[9] It is hard to imagine that anything but the actual sight of a live elephant can have given rise to this tradition. The suggestion that it might have been founded on the sight of a mammoth frozen with his flesh and skin, as they are found in Siberia, is not tenable, for the trunks and tails of these animals

[9] Charlevoix, vol. v. p. 187.

perish first, and are not preserved like the more solid parts, so that the Asiatic myths which have grown out of the finding of these frozen beasts, know nothing of such appendages. Moreover, no savage who had never heard of the use of an elephant's trunk would imagine from a sight of the dead animal, even if its trunk were perfect, that its use was to be compared with that of a man's arm.

The notion that the Indian story of the Great Elk was a real reminiscence of a living proboscidian, is strengthened by a remarkable drawing (Fig. 19) from one of the Mexican picture-writings. It represents a masked priest sacrificing a human victim, and

FIG. 19

Humboldt copies it in the 'Vues des Cordillères' with the following remarks:—"I should not have had this hideous scene engraved, were it not that the disguise of the sacrificing priest presents some remarkable and apparently not accidental resemblance with the Hindoo Ganesa [the elephant-headed god of wisdom]. The Mexicans used masks imitating the shape of the heads of the serpent, the crocodile, or the jaguar. One seems to recognize in the sacrificer's mask the trunk of an elephant or some pachyderm resembling it in the shape of the head, but with an upper jaw furnished with incisive teeth. The snout of the tapir no doubt protrudes a little more than that of our pigs, but it is a long way from the tapir's snout to the trunk figured in the 'Codex Borgianus.' Had the peoples of Aztlan derived from Asia some vague notions of the elephant, or, as seems to me much less probable, did their traditions reach back to the time when America was still inhabited by these gigantic animals, whose petrified skeletons are found buried in the marly ground on the very ridge of the Mexican Cordilleras?''[10] It may be worth while to notice in connexion with Humboldt's remarks, that when Mr. Bates showed a picture of an elephant to some South American Indians, they settled it that the creature must be a large kind of tapir.[11]

Attempts have been made by other writers to connect the memory of animals now extinct, with mythological tales current in the regions to which they belong. Dr. Falconer is disposed to connect the huge elephant-fighting and world-bearing tortoises of the Hindoo mythology with a recollection of the time when his monstrous Himalayan tortoise, the *Colossochelys atlas,* the restoration of which forms so striking an object in the British Museum, was still alive.[12] The savage tribes of Brazil have traditions about a being whom they call the Curupíra. Sometimes he is described as a kind of orang-utan, being covered with long, shaggy hair, and living in trees. At others he is said to have cloven feet, and a bright red face. He has a wife and children, and sometimes comes down to the roças to steal the mandioca. Similar to, or the same as this being, is the Caypór, whom the Indians, in their masquerades, represent as a bulky, misshapen monster, with red skin and long shaggy red hair, hanging halfway down his back.[13] With reference to these Brazilian stories, Mr. Carter Blake remarks—"In Brazil the Indians had a tradition of a gigantic anthropoid ape, the cayporé, which represented the African gorilla. No such ape exists in the present day; but in the post-pliocene in Brazil, remains have been preserved of an extinct ape (*Protopithecus antiquus*) four feet high, which might possibly have lived down to the human period, and formed the subject of the tradition."[14] Lastly, Colonel Hamilton Smith has collected a

10 Humboldt, Vues des Cord., pl. xv.; Borgia MS. in Kingsborough, vol. iii.
11 Bates, 'Amazons,' vol. ii. p. 128.
12 Falconer, 'Palæontological Memoirs,' London, 1868, vol. i. p. 375.
13 Bates, 'Amazons,' vol. i. p. 73; vol. ii. p. 204.
14 C. Carter Blake in Tr. Eth. Soc. 1863, p. 169.

quantity of evidence, thought by him to bear on the preservation of the memory of extinct creatures, adding to Father Charlevoix's great Elk, and the Père aux Bœufs from Buffon, a North American "Naked Bear," and an East Indian "Elephant-Horse," etc., and endeavouring to identify them in nature.[15]

To proceed now from the traditions which have, or may set up some sort of claim to have, a historical foundation, to the Myths of Observation, which are so often liable to be confounded with them: it is to be noticed that if the inference from facts, which forms the basis of such a myth, should happen to be a correct one, and if the story should also happen to have fairly dropped out of sight the evidence out of which it grew, its separation from a real tradition of events may be hardly possible. Fortunately for the ethnologist, it is very common for such stories to betray their unhistoric origin in one or both of these ways, either by recording things which seemed indeed probable when the myths arose, but which modern knowledge repudiates, or by having embodied with them the facts which have been appealed to for ages as confirmation of their truth, but which we are now in a position to recognize at once as the very basis on which their mythical structure was raised.

A good example of a Myth of Observation is a story current in Egypt in Strabo's time, but which he, having indeed a considerable knowledge of geology, declines to believe. "But one of the wondrous things," he says, "which we saw about the pyramids, must not be passed over. There lie in front of the pyramids certain heaps of the masons' rubbish, and among these there are found pieces in shape and size like lentils, and in some, as it were, half-peeled grains. They say, the leavings of the workmen's food have been turned into stone, but this is not likely, for at home among us there is a longish ridge of hill in a plain, and this is full of lentil-like stones of tufa, etc."[16]

To men whose country has the open sea to its west it seems that the sun plunges at night into its waters. Now the sun is evidently a mass of matter at a distance, and very hot, and when red-hot bodies come in contact with water there follows a hissing noise;

---

[15] C. Hamilton Smith, Nat. Hist. of Human Sp., pp. 104–6.

[16] Strabo, xvii. 1, 34.

and thus the inference is easy and straightforward, that when the sun dips into the waves such a sound ought to be heard. From the inference that the hissing might be heard, to the assertion that it has actually been heard, is the easy step by which the crude argument of early science passes into the full-grown Myth of Observation. In two distant countries where the world seems to end westward in the boundless ocean, the story is to be found. The Sacred Promontory, that is Cape St. Vincent, Strabo says, is the westernmost point, not of Europe alone, but of the whole habitable earth, and there Posidonius tells how the vulgar say the sun goes down larger on the ocean-coast, and with a noise almost as it were the sea hissing as the sun plunges into its depths and is quenched; but this is false, as well as that the night follows instantly upon its setting. So in the Pacific, in some of the Society Islands, the name for sunset means the falling of the sun into the sea, and the sun itself is thought to be a substance resembling fire. Mr. Ellis asked them how they knew it fell into the sea, and they said they had not seen it, but some people of Borabora or Maupiti, the most western islands, had once heard the hissing occasioned by its plunging into the ocean.[17]

From the incredulous geographer who records the stories of the fossil lentils and the hissing sun, yet another Myth of Observation may be taken, which shows well the easy transition from "it may have been," to "it was," which lies at their root. Mr. Catlin, in one of his journeys, says that he came to a place where he saw rocks "looking as if they had actually dropped from the clouds in such a confused mass, and all lay where they had fallen." So in old times, a round plain between Marseilles and the mouths of the Rhone was called the "stony" plain, from its being covered with stones as big as a man's fist. You would think, says Pomponius Mela, that the stones had rained there, so many are they, and so far and wide do they lie.[18] Now Æschylus, says Strabo, having perceived the difficulty of accounting for these stones, or having heard about it from some one else, has wrested the whole matter into a myth. In some lines of his, preserved to us by

[17] Strabo, iii. 1, 5. Ellis, Polyn. Res., vol. ii. p. 414. See also Bastian, vol. ii. p. 58. Tac. Germ., c. 45.

[18] Catlin, vol. ii. p. 70. Mela, ii. c. 5.

Strabo's quotation of them, Prometheus, explaining to Hercules his way from the Caucasus to the Hesperides, tells him how when his missiles fail him in his fight with the Ligurians, and the soft earth will not even afford him a stone, Jove, pitying his defence-less state, will rain down a shower of round pebbles over the ground, hurling which he will easily rout his foes.[19]

Fossil remains have for ages been objects of curious speculation to mankind. In the most distant regions where huge bones have been found, they have been explained, truly enough, as being the bones of monstrous beasts, and as plausibly, though, as later investigations have shown within the last century, not so correctly, as bones of giants. Given the belief that the earth was formerly inhabited by monsters and giants, the myth-making power of the human mind gave "a local habitation and a name" wherever it was required, and the battles of these monsters with each other, and with man, were worked into the general mass of popular tradition, with gradually increasing fulness and accuracy-of detail. The Asiatic sagas which have grown out of the finding of the frozen mammoths, and the fossil remains of these and other great extinct animals, are excellent cases in point. Many of them have been collected and criticized in an admirable paper published more than twenty years ago by Von Olfers, of Berlin.[20]

The Siberians are constantly finding bones and teeth of mammoths imbedded in the faces of cliffs or river banks at some depth below the surface. Often a mass of earth or gravel falls away from such a cliff, and exposes such remains. How could they have got there? A plausible explanation suggested itself, that the creature was a huge burrowing animal, and lived underground. Not only the skeleton, but the body in tolerable preservation with flesh and skin being found in a frozen state in high Northern latitudes, the notion grew up that it was a monstrous kind of burrowing rat, and it is described in Chinese books under such names as *fen-shu*, or "digging rat," *yen-men*, or "burrowing ox," *shu-mu*, "mother of mice," and so on. A difficulty which suggested itself to the

19 Strabo, iv. 1, 7.

20 J. F. M. v. Olfers, 'Die Ueberreste vorweltlicher Riesenthiere in Beziehung zu Ostasiatischen Sagen und Chinesischen Schriften' (Berlin Acad., 1839); Berlin; 1840.

native Siberian geologists was met in a characteristic manner. It was strange that whenever they came upon a mammoth imbedded in a cliff, it was always dead. It must be a creature unable to bear the air or the light, and when in the course of its subterranean wanderings it breaks through to the outer air it dies immediately. With so much knowledge of the natural history of the creature to start from, other details grow round it in the usual way. Yakuts and Tunguz have seen the earth heave and sink, as a mammoth walked beneath. It frequents marshes, and travels underground, never appearing above the surface of the earth or water during the day, but has been seen at dawn in lakes and rivers, just as it dived below. The account of it given in the Chinese Encyclopædia of Kang-hi is as follows:—

Fen-shu.—The cold is extreme and almost continual on the coast of the Northern Sea, beyond the Tai-tong-Kiang; on this coast is found the animal *Fen-shu,* which resembles a rat in shape, but is as big as an elephant; it dwells in dark caverns, and ever shuns the light. There is got from it an ivory as white as that of the elephant, but easier to work, and not liable to split. Its flesh is very cold, and excellent for refreshing the blood. The ancient book *Shin-y-King* speaks of this animal in the following terms:— "There is in the extreme north, among the snows and ice which cover this region, a *shu* (rat), which weighs up to a thousand pounds, its flesh is very good for those who are heated. The *Tse-shu* calls it *fen-shu,* and speaks of another kind which is of less size; it is only, says this authority, as large as a buffalo, it burrows like the moles, shuns the light, and almost always stays in its underground caves. It is said that it would die if it saw the light of the sun, or even of the moon."[21]

The story of the mammoth being a burrowing animal, which has arisen from the finding its remains exposed in cliffs or banks deep below the surface, becomes the more valuable as evidence of the growth of myths, from the fact that on the other side of the world a like story has developed itself from a like origin. When Darwin visited certain cliffs of the river Parana, between Buenos Ayres and Santa Fé, where many bones of Mastodons are found, he says, "The men who took me in the canoe, said they

---

[21] Mém. conc. les Chinois, vol. iv. p. 481. Klemm, C. G., vol. vi. p. 471.

had long known of these skeletons, and had often wondered how they had got there: the necessity of a theory being felt, they came to the conclusion that, like the bizcacha, the mastodon was formerly a burrowing animal."[22] The bizcacha is a small rabbit-like rodent, common on the Pampas.

Other fossil remains besides those of the mammoth have given rise to myths of observation in Siberia. The curved tusks of the *Rhinoceros tichorhinus* are something like the claws of a monstrous bird, and when both tusks are found united by part of the skull, the whole might very well be taken by a man totally ignorant of anatomy, for the bird's foot with two claws. The Siberians not only believe the horns of the rhinoceros to be the claws of an enormous bird, and call them "birds' claws" accordingly, but a family of myths has developed itself out of this belief, how these winged monsters lived in the country in the time of the ancestors of the present inhabitants, who fought with them for the possession of the land. One story tells how the country was wasted by one of them, till a wise man fixed a pointed iron spear on the top of a pine tree, and the bird alighted there, and skewered itself upon the lance.

Adolf Erman connects with much plausibility the well-known *rukh* of the Arabian Nights, and the *griffin* (γρύψ) of Herodotus, with the tales of monstrous birds current in the gold-producing regions of Siberia; and he even suggests the remark that gold-bearing sand really underlies the beds which contain these fossil "birds' claws" as an explanation of the passage, "it is said that the Arimaspi, one-eyed men, seize (the gold) from underneath the griffins" (λέγεται δὲ ὑπὲκ τῶν γρυπῶν ἀρπάζειν Ἀριμασποὺς ἄνδρας μουνοφθάλμους).[23] At about the same time as Herodotus, Ctesias brings out more fully the familiar figure of the griffin. "There is also gold," he says, "in the Indian country, not found in the streams and washed, as in the river Pactolus; but there are many and great mountains, wherein dwell the griffins, four-footed birds of the greatness of the wolf, but with legs and claws like lions. The feathers on the rest of their bodies are black, but red on the breast. Through them it is that the gold in the mountains, though

22 Darwin, p. 127.

23 Herod., iii. 116. Erman, Reise, vol. i. pp. 711–2.

plentiful, is most difficult to get."[24] That the Siberian myths of monstrous birds have passed into the mediæval notions of the griffins admits of no question whatever. Albertus Magnus describes them as quadrupeds, with birds' beaks and wings; they dwell in Scythia, and possess the gold, and silver, and precious stones. The Arimaspi fight with them. In its nest the griffin lays the agate for its help and medicine. It is hostile to men and horses: it has long claws, which are made into goblets; they are as big as ox-horns, as indeed the creature itself is bigger than eight lions; of its feathers are made strong bows, arrows, and lances.[25] With regard to this description, it is to be observed that the horns, cut in slices, are really used for plating bows;[26] but the bird's quills, as they are still considered to be in the country where they are found, are the leg-bones of other animals.[27] The rhinoceros horns, supposed to be griffins' claws, were mounted in gold and silver in Europe in the middle ages, and preserved as relics in churches. There is or was one in Corpus Christi College, Cambridge, mounted on little gilt claws, which sufficiently show what it was thought to be.

The Chinese idea that the mammoth was a huge rat, and the very name of "Mother of Mice" given to it, fit curiously with a set of North American stories, which may have a like origin in the finding of fossil remains of enormous size. The name of the "Père aux Bœufs," probably the translation of a native Indian name, was given to an extinct animal whose huge bones were found on the banks of the Ohio.[28] The Indians of New France, Father Paul le Jeune relates in 1635, "say besides, that all the animals of each species have an elder brother, who is as the beginning and origin of all the race, and this elder brother is marvellously great and powerful. The elder brother of the beavers,

24 Ctesias, 'De Rebus Indicis,' 12.

25 Klemm, C. G., vol. i. p. 155, and see p. 101.

26 Olfers, p. 12.

27 Erman, vol. i. p. 711. See Lane, 'Thousand and One Nights,' vol. ii. p. 538; vol. iii. p. 85.

28 Buffon, Hist. Nat. (ed. Sonnini), vol. xxviii. p. 264.

they told me, is perhaps as big as our hut.''[29] There are current among the Iroquois, says Morgan, fables of a buffalo of such huge dimensions as to thresh down the forest in his march.[30] And lastly, in one of the North American tales of the Sun-catcher, we find a creature to which the name of "Mother of Mice" may well belong. When the sun was to be set free from the snare, the animals debated who should go up and sever the cord, and the dormouse went, "for at this time the dormouse was the largest animal in the world; when it stood up it looked like a mountain." The whole story, which goes on to tell how it came to pass that the dormice are but small creatures now, is given here in the next chapter.

The native tribes of the lower end of South America explained the reason why they, unlike the Spaniards, had no herds of cattle in their country, by an interesting story, which has the air of a myth of observation founded upon the examination of caves containing fossil bones. They had a multiplicity of inferior deities below the two great powers of Good and Evil, who, there as elsewhere on the American continent, are above all. Each of the lower deities presides over one particular caste or family of Indians, of which he is supposed to have been the creator. "Some make themselves of the caste of the tiger, some of the lion, some of the guanaco, and others of the ostrich, etc. They imagine that these deities have each their separate habitations, in vast caverns under the earth, beneath some lake, hill, etc.; and that when an Indian dies, his soul goes to live with the deity who presides over his particular family, there to enjoy the happiness of being eternally drunk. They believe that their good deities made the world, and that they first created the Indians in their caves, gave them the lance, the bow and arrows, and the stone-bowls to fight and hunt with, and then turned them out to shift for themselves. They imagine that the deities of the Spaniards did the same by them;

---

29 Le Jeune, Relations (1634), vol. i. p. 46. A remarkable resemblance appears in the description of the Slavonic Buyán, the ocean-island of the blest, where are to be found the Snake older than all snakes, the prophetic Raven, elder brother of all ravens, the Bird, largest and oldest of all birds, with iron beak and copper claws, and the Mother of Bees, eldest among bees; Ralston, 'Songs of the Russian People,' p. 375. [Note to 3rd Edition.]

30 Morgan, p. 166.

but that instead of lances, bows, etc., they gave them guns and swords. They suppose that when the beasts, birds, and lesser animals were created, those of the more nimble kind came immediately out of their caves; but that the bulls and cows being the last, the Indians were so frightened at the sight of their horns, that they stopped up the entrance of their caves with great stones. This is the reason they give why they had no black cattle in their country till the Spaniards brought them over, who more wisely had let them out of the caves."[31]

The possibility that the Brazilian belief in the caypor, or wild ape-like being of the woods, may be derived from a recollection of a great extinct ape, has been already mentioned, but there is a circumstance which rather favours the idea of its being a myth, founded on the examination of fossil bones. Like the mammoth and the mastodon, and the creators of the beasts and birds, he is thought to live underground. "They believe he has subterranean campos and hunting grounds in the forest, well stocked with pacas and deer."[32] It is possible, too, that the notion of subterranean animals, who die if they see the daylight, like the mammoths of Siberia, may be traced in various stories. Thus, the Fijians tell a tale of two rocks, male and female Lado, which are two deities who were turned by the sight of daylight into stone;[33] and in the West Indies there were men who dwelt in Cimmerian darkness in their caves, and coming out were turned into stones and trees by the sight of the sun.[34]

Tales of giants and monsters, which stand in direct connexion with the finding of great fossil bones, are scattered broadcast over the mythology of the world. Huge bones, found at Punto Santa Elena, in the north of Guayaquil, have served as a foundation for the story of a colony of giants who dwelt there.[35] The whole area of the Pampas is a great sepulchre of enormous extinct animals; no wonder that one great plain should be called the "field of the giants," and that such names as "the hill of the

---

[31] Thos. Falkner, 'A Description of Patagonia,' etc.; Hereford, 1774, p. 114.

[32] Bates, vol. ii. p. 204. [33] Seemann, 'Viti,' p. 66.

[34] Oviedo, in Purchas, vol. v. p. 959.

[35] Humboldt, Vues des Cord., pl. 26. Cieza de Leon, p. 189. Rivero and Tschudi, Ant. Per. p. 51.

giant," "the stream of the animal," should be guides to the geologist in his search for fossil bones.[36]

In North America it is the same. The fossil bones of Mexico are referred to the giants who dwelt in the land in early times, and were found living in the plains of Tlascala by the Olmecs, who came there before the Toltecs. At the time of the conquest, Bernal Diaz was told of their huge stature and their crimes; and, to show him how big they were, the people brought him a bone of one of them, which he measured himself against, and it was as tall as he, who was a man of reasonable stature. He and his companions were astonished to see those bones, and held it for certain that there had been giants in that land.[37] The Indians of North America tell how their mythic hero, Manabozho, "killed the ancient monsters whose bones we now see under the earth." They use pieces of the bones of thse monsters as charms, and most likely the pieces of bone drawn in their pictures as instruments of magic power are such. They tell of giants who could stride over the largest rivers, and the tallest pine-trees. The Winnebagos say their monstrous medicine animal still exists, and they have pieces of the bones which belong to them, which they use as charms. The Dacotas use such bones for "medicine," and say they belong to the great horned water-beast, the Unk-a-ta-he. Hiawatha helped the Indians to subdue the great monsters that overran the country. The "Tom Thumb" of the Chippewas killed the giants and hacked them into little pieces, saying, "Henceforth let no man be larger than you are now," and so men became of their present size.[38] There are plenty more such stories. One mentioned by Dr. Wilson has the interesting feature that monsters and giants both perished by the thunderbolts of the Great Spirit, and in another all the monsters were thus slain except the Big Bull, who went off to the Great Lakes.[39] It must be borne in mind, however, that in speculating on the origin of tales such

[36] Darwin, in Narr., vol. iii. p. 155.

[37] Bernal Diaz, Conq. de la Nueva España; Madrid, 1795, vol. i. p. 350. Tylor, 'Mexico,' p. 236. Clavigero, vol. i. p. 125. Humboldt, Vues des Cord., pl. 26.

[38] Schoolcraft, part i. pp. 319, 390; part ii. pp. 175, 224; part iii. pp. 232, 315, 319.

[39] Wilson, 'Prehistoric Man,' vol. i. p. 112.

as these, possible recollections of contests of men with huge animals now extinct must be taken into consideration, as well as inferences from the finding of large bones, and sometimes even both causes may have worked together.

In the Old World, myths both old and new connected with huge bones, fossil or recent, are common enough.[40] Marcus Scaurus brought to Rome, from Joppa, the bones of the monster who was to have devoured Andromeda, while the vestiges of the chains which bound her were to be seen there on the rock;[41] and the sepulchre of Antæus, containing his skeleton, 60 cubits long, was found in Mauritania.[42]

Don Quixote was beforehand with Dr. Falconer in reasoning on the huge fossil bones so common in Sicily as remains of ancient inhabitants, as appears from his answer to the barber's question, how big he thought the giant Morgante might have been? ". . . Moreover, in the island of Sicily there have been found long-bones and shoulder-bones so huge, that their size manifests their owners to have been giants, and as big as great towers, for this truth geometry sets beyond doubt." Again, the fossil bones so plentifully strewed over the Sewalik, or lowest ranges of the Himalayas, belonged to the slain Rakis,[43] the gigantic Rakshasas of the Indian mythology. The remains of the Dun Cow that Guy Earl of Warwick slew are or were to be seen in England, in the shape of a whale's rib in the church of St. Mary Redcliffe, and some great fossil bone kept, I believe, in Warwick Castle. "The giant sixteen feet high, whose bones were found in 1577 near Reyden under an uprooted oak, and examined and celebrated in song by Felix Plater, the renowned physician of Basle, has been long ago banished by the later naturalists into a very distant department of zoology; but the giant has from that time forth got a firm standing ground beside the arms of Lucerne, and will keep it, all critics to the contrary notwithstanding."[44]

It would be tedious to enumerate more instances in which traditions of giants and huge beasts have been formed both in

---

[40] In Polynesia, see Mariner, vol. i. p. 313.

[41] Plin., ix. 4; v. 14.   [42] Strabo, xvii. 3, 8.

[43] Torrens, 'Ladâk,' etc., p. 87.

[44] Olfers, p. 3. See also Grimm, D. M. p. 522.

ancient and modern times from the finding of great fossil bones. But the remarks of St. Augustine on a great fossil tooth he saw are worthy of attention, as throwing some light on the connexion of such bones with the belief that man was once both enormously larger and longer-lived than he is now, and that his stature has diminished in the course of ages to its present dimensions; as it is held by the Moslems that Adam was sixty feet high, of the measure of a tall palm-tree, and that the true believers will be restored in Paradise to this original stature of the human race, and that the houris who will attend them will be of proportionate dimensions. It seems as if Linnæus may have held such an opinion, at least his editor gives the following as his reading of a passage in the notes of his northern tour, where unfortunately the original is obscure. "I have a notion that Adam and Eve were giants, and that mankind, from one generation to another, owing to poverty and other causes, have diminished in size. Hence perhaps the diminutive stature of the Laplander."[45]

St. Augustine's observations are contained in his chapter "Concerning the long life of men before the flood, and the greater size of their bodies." He makes these remarks, he says, in case any infidel should raise a doubt about men having lived to so great an age. "So some indeed do not believe that men's bodies were formerly much greater than now." Virgil, he continues, expresses the huge size of the men of former times, how much more then in the younger periods of the world, before the celebrated deluge. "But concerning the magnitude of their bodies, the graves laid bare by age or the force of rivers and various accidents especially convict the incredulous, where they have come to light, or where bones of the dead of incredible magnitude have fallen. I have seen, and not I alone, on the shore by Utica, so huge a molar tooth of a man, that were it cut up into small models of teeth like ours, it would seem enough to make a hundred of them. But this I should think had belonged to some giant; for besides that the bodies of all men were then much larger than ours, the giants again far exceeded the rest."[46]

Among the traditions preserved from remote ages by the human race, there are perhaps none more important to the ethnol-

[45] Linnæus, 'Tour,' vol. i. p. 28.   [46] Aug., 'De Civitate Dei,' xv. 9.

ogist than those which relate, in every great district of the world, and with so much unity combined with so much variety, the occurrence of a great Deluge in long past time. In studying these Diluvial Traditions it is of the highest consequence that he should be able to separate the results of the memory of real events from those of observation of natural phenomena and of purely mythological development. Humboldt in part states the problem in his remarks on the four devastations of the earth, by famine, fire, hurricane, and deluge, as represented in the Mexican picture-writing. "Whatever may be their true origin, it does not appear less certain that they are fictions of astronomical mythology, modified either by a dim remembrance of some great revolution which our planet has undergone, or in accordance with the physical and geological hypotheses to which the appearance of marine petrifactions and fossil bones gives rise, even among peoples at the greatest distance from civilization."[47]

That the observation of shells and corals in places above the level of the sea, and even on high mountains, should have given rise to legends of great floods which deposited them there, is natural enough, and quite consistent with the growth of myths of monsters and giants from the observation of fossil bones. Marine productions being found at heights of many hundred feet above the sea, the question would evidently occur to the men who speculated so ingeniously about the fossil bones, how did these productions of the sea get upon the mountains? As to fossil crustaceans, the Arabian geographer Abu-Zeyd explains their appearance in Ceylon by setting them down as sea-animals like crawfish, which, when they come out of the sea, are converted into stone,[48] but the appearance of sea-shells on mountains could hardly be so accounted for. Two alternatives suggest themselves to explain the occurrence of shells in such situations; either the sea may have been up to the mountain, or the mountain may have been down in the sea. Modern geologists have in most cases to adopt the latter alternative, but till recent times the former was oftener than not held to be the more probable. Water is the type of all that is movable, fluctuating, unstable, while the firm

[47] Humboldt, Vues des Cord., pl. 26.

[48] Tennent, 'Ceylon,' vol. i. p. 14.

earth is immovable, permanent, solid, and it is not to the purpose to argue that modern knowledge has reversed this older view, with so many other doctrines which seemed to rest on the plain evidence of the senses, and which only failed, as many of our own theories have no doubt to fail, from the narrowness of their range of observation.

The fossils embedded in high ground have been appealed to, both in ancient and modern times, both by savages and civilized men, as evidence in support of their traditions of a flood, and moreover the argument, apparently unconnected with any tradition, is to be found, that because there are marine fossils in places away from the sea, therefore the sea must once have been there. In the Society Islands, tradition tells how a flood that rose over the tops of the mountains, was raised by the sea-god Ruahatu. A fisherman caught his hooks in the hair of the god as he lay sleeping among his coral groves, and woke him, but strange to say, though in his anger he drowned the rest of the inhabitants of the land in the deluge, he allowed the fisherman himself to find safe refuge with his wife and child on a small, low, coral island close to Raiatea, and they repeopled the earth. How the little island was preserved they give no account, but they appeal to the *farero,* coral, and shells found at the tops of the highest mountains, as proof of the inundation.[49] In Samoa it is the universal belief that of old the fish swam where the land now is, and tradition adds that when the waters abated, many of the fish of the sea were left on the land, and afterwards were changed into stones. Hence, they say, there are stones in abundance in the bush and among the mountains, which were once sharks, and other inhabitants of the deep.[50] In the North the Moravian missionary Cranz records that, "The first missionaries found among the Greenlanders a tolerably distinct tradition of the Deluge, of which almost all heathen nations still know something, namely, that the world was once tilted over (umgekantert) and all men were drowned, but some became fire-spirits. The only man who remained alive, smote afterwards with his stick upon the ground, and there came out a woman, with whom he peopled the earth again. They tell moreover that far up in the country, where men

---

[49] Ellis, Polyn. Res., vol. ii. p. 58.   [50] Turner, 'Polynesia,' p. 249.

could never have dwelt, there are found all sorts of remains of fishes, and even bones of whales on a high mountain; wherefrom they make it clear that the earth was once flooded."[51] It is interesting to compare this argument with the explanation the Kamchadals give of the bones of whales, which in their country also are found on high mountains. They fear all high mountains, says Steller, especially volcanos, and also hot springs, and believe that some mountains are the abodes of spirits. "When one asks them what the devils do up there, they reply 'they cook whales.' I asked, where they got them? The answer was, they go down to the sea at night and catch so many, that one brings home five to ten of them, one hanging to each finger. When I asked, how do you know this? They said their old people had always said so and believed it themselves. Withal they appealed to the observation, that there were many bones of whales found on all burning mountains. I asked whence come the flames there sometimes, and they answered, when the spirits have heated up their mountains as we do our *yurts,* they fling the rest of the brands out up the chimney, so as to be able to shut up. They said moreover, God in heaven sometimes does so too at the time when it is our summer and his winter, and he warms up his yurt; whereby they explain the veneration of the lightning."[52]

In the geological theories of classical times, the inference from fossil shells found inland, high or low above the sea level, was commonly that the sea had once been there. Herodotus argues from the shells on the mountains in Egypt,[53] and Xanthus from the fossil shells, like cockles and scallops, which he had seen far from the sea, that there had been sea in old times where the land had since been left dry. Eratosthenes notices the existence of quantities of oyster-shells and bits of wreck of sea-going ships near the temple of Ammon, far inland in Lybia, while Strabo expresses the opinion that this temple was once close to the sea, though since thrown inland by the retiring of the waters.[54] Describing the region of Numidia farther west, Pomponius Mela relates that, "Inland and far enough from the coast (if the thing

---

[51] Cranz, p. 262. Again recently, C. F. Hall, 'Life with the Esquimaux'; London, 1864, vol. ii. p. 318.

[52] Steller, p. 47.   [53] Herod., ii. 12.   [54] Strabo, i. 3, 4.

be credible) they tell that in a wondrous way the spines of fish, and fragments of murex and oyster-shells, stones worn in the ordinary manner by the waves and not differing from those of the sea, anchors fixed in the rocks, and other similar signs and vestiges of the sea that once spread to those places, exist and are found on the barren plains."[55] So Ovid says in his remarkable statement of the Pythagorean doctrines—

> Et procul a pelago conchæ jacuere marinæ
> Et vetus inventa est in montibus anchora summis,

and argues thence that sea has been converted into land.[56]

In the Chinese Encyclopædia from which I have already quoted two remarkable passages, an account is to be found bearing on the present subject. *"Eastern Tartary.*—In travelling from the shore of the Eastern Sea toward Che-lu, neither brooks nor ponds are met with in the country, although it is intersected by mountains and valleys. Nevertheless there are found in the sand very far away from the sea, oyster-shells and the shields of crabs. The tradition of the Mongols who inhabit the country is, that it has been said from time immemorial that in remote antiquity the waters of the deluge flooded the district, and when they retired, the places where they had been made their appearance covered with sand. . . . However it may have happened, to follow the great geographer Ti-chi, a part of this country is in great plains, where several hundred leagues are found to have been covered by the waters and since abandoned; this is why these deserts are called the Sandy Sea, which indicates that they were not originally covered with sand and gravel."[57]

Again, the presence of fossil shells on high mountains has long been adduced as evidence of the Noachic flood. Thus Tertullian connects the sea-shells on mountains with the reappearance of the earth from below the waters,[58] and the argument may be followed up through later times, and was current in England till quite recently. In the ninth edition of Horne's 'Introduction to the Scriptures,' published in 1846, the evidence of fossils is con-

[55] Mela, i. c. 6.   [56] Ov. Met., xv. 264.

[57] Mém. conc. les Chinois, vol. iv. p. 474. Klemm, C. G., vol. vi. p. 467.

[58] Tert., 'De Pallio,' ii. H. F. Link, 'Die Urwelt,' etc.; Berlin, 1821, p. 4.

fidently held to prove the universality of the Deluge; but the argument disappears from the next edition, published ten years later.

To the statements of classical writers as to anchors and pieces of wreck being found inland, some more modern accounts must be added. From time to time, whether from upheaval of the earth's surface or other geological changes, ships and things belonging to them have been found far inland, in places for ages out of reach of navigable waters. Buffon speaks of fragments of vessels being found in a mountain lake in Portugal, far from the sea, and mentions a statement of Sabinus, in his commentary on the lines just quoted from Ovid, that in the year 1460 a vessel was found with its anchors, in a mine in the Alps.[59] This is, no doubt, the same story that Antonio Galvano refers to, when he says, "Thus they tell of finding hulls of ships and iron anchors in the mountains of Switzerland very far inland, where it appears that there was never sea nor salt water."[60]

The bearing of such phenomena on the formation of diluvial traditions is clearly shown by their having been repeatedly claimed, like the fossil shells, as evidence of the former presence of the sea, and even of the Biblical deluge. It is not, however, necessary, from this point of view, that the accounts in question should all be true; it is enough that they should be believed and reasoned upon. In the seventeenth century, Fray Pedro Simon relates that some miners, running an adit into a hill near Callao, "met with a ship which had on top of it the great mass of the hill, and did not agree in its make and appearance with our ships," whence people judged that it had been left there by the Flood, and the fact is cited in proof of the habitation of the country in antediluvian times.[61] Writing in 1730, Strahlenberg gives it as his opinion that mammoth bones in Siberia are relics of the Deluge, and goes on to add a like example, that some thirty years earlier the whole lower hull of a ship with a keel was found in Barabinsk Tartary, where nevertheless there is no ocean.[62] Lastly,

59 Buffon, 'Théorie de la Terre,' vol. iii. p. 119.

60 Galvano, p. 26.

61 Simon, 'Noticias Historiales,' etc.; Cuenca, 1627, p. 31.

62 Strahlenberg, 'Das Nord und Ostliche Theil von Europa und Asien;' Stockholm, 1730, p. 396. C. Hamilton Smith, p. 45.

in Scotland it is quite a common thing for ancient canoes hollowed from a single tree to be found buried in places remote from navigable channels, while the skeletons of whales are found in similar situations. Sir John Clerk thus remarks upon a canoe found near Edinburgh in 1726. "The washings of the river Carron discovered a boat, 13 or 14 feet underground; it is 36 feet in length, and 4.5 in breadth, all of one piece of oak. There were several strata above it, such as loam, clay, shells, moss, sand, and gravel; these strata demonstrate it to have been an antediluvian boat."[63]

Both in Scotland and in South America, upheaval of land in more or less modern times is a recognized fact, and the finding of boats, as of various other productions of human art, in places where they could hardly have been placed by man, is readily accounted for between this upheaval and the effects of ordinary accumulation and degradation.

Geological evidence bearing on traditions of a Deluge is scarce. Sir Charles Lyell seems disposed to adopt the view of old writers that some of the South American deluge traditions are connected with the memory of local floods, such as are known to happen there. Dr. Szabó says that the Hungarians still preserve traditions of their plains having been once covered by a freshwater sea, the waters of which afterwards escaped through the narrows of the Iron Gate. The draining of the country in this manner is considered by Dr. Szabó as having really happened, so that this may be a case of tradition handing down the memory of a geological change from a very remote period.[64] It would require a large body of scientific evidence of this character to make possible a thorough investigation of the Diluvial traditions of the world, and any attempt to draw a distinct line between the claims of Hisory and Mythology must in the meantime be premature.

It fortunately happens that the difficulty in analysing the Diluvial traditions into their historical and mythological elements is one which only partially affects their use to ethnology. Were they merely stories current in various parts of the world, saying little more than that there was once a great flood, or giving de-

---

[63] Bibl. Topog. Brit.; London, 1790, vol. iii. part i. p. 241. Wilson, 'Archæology, etc., of Scotland,' p. 32.

[64] Geol. Journal, Feb. 1863.

tails only harmonizing within limited districts, they might be explained as independent Myths of Observation. But the general state of things found over the world is widely different from this. The notion of men having existed before this flood, and having been all destroyed except a few who escaped and repeopled the earth, does not flow so immediately from the observation of natural phenomena that we can easily suppose it to have originated several times independently in such a way, yet this is a feature common to a great number of flood traditions. Still more strongly does this argument apply to the occurrence of some form of raft, ark, or canoe, in which the survivors are usually saved, unless, as in some cases, they take refuge directly on the top of some mountain which the waters never cover. The idea is indeed conceivable, if somewhat farfetched, that from the sight of a boat found high on a mountain there might grow a story of the flood which carried it there, while the people in it escaped to found a new race. But it lies outside all reasonable probability to suppose such circumstances to have produced the same story in several different places, nor is it very likely that the dim remembrances of a number of local floods should accord in this with the amount of consistency that is found among the flood traditions of remote regions of the world. The occurrence of an ark in the traditions of a deluge found in so many distant times and places, favours the opinion of these being derived from a single source.

As to Myths of Observation in general, the line of demarcation which separates them on the one hand from traditions of real events, and on the other from more purely mythic tales, is equally hard to draw. Even the stories which have their origin in a mere realized metaphor, or a personification of the phenomena of nature, will attach themselves to real persons, places, or objects, as strongly as though they actually belonged to them. To the subjective mind of the myth maker, every hill and valley, every stone and tree, that strikes his attention, becomes the place where some mythic occurrence happened to gods, or heroes, or fair women, or monsters, or ethereal beings. When once the tale is made, the rock or tree becomes evidence of its truth to future generations: "the bricks are alive at this day to testify it; therefore, deny it not."

CHAPTER IX

GEOGRAPHICAL DISTRIBUTION OF MYTHS

The student of the early History of Mankind finds in Comparative Mythology the same use and the same difficulty which lie before him in so many other branches of his subject. He can sometimes show, in the mythical tales current among several peoples, coincidences so quaint, so minute, or so complex, that they could hardly have arisen independently in two places, and these coincidences he claims as proofs of historical connexion between the tribes or nations among whom they are found. But his great difficulty is how to be sure that he is not interpreting as historical evidence analogies which may be nothing more than the results of the like working of the human mind under like conditions. His ever-recurring problem is to classify the crowd of resemblances which are continually thrusting themselves upon him, so as to keep those things which are merely similar apart from those which, having at some spot of the earth's surface their common source and centre of diffusion, are really and historically united.

No attempt is made in the present chapter to lay down definite rules for the solution of this important problem, but a few illustrations are given of the more general analogies running through the Folk-lore of the world, which Ethnology, for the present at least, has to set aside; and then a few facts are stated, bearing on the diffusion of Myths by recognised channels of intercourse, with the view of introducing a group of similar episodes, which it is for the reader to reject as caused by independent growth or modern transmission, or to accept as a contribution to the early History of the New World.

Firstly, then, there are found among savage tribes myths like in their character, and therefore no doubt in their origin, to those of the great Aryan race which have in our own times been so successfully traced to the very point where they arose out of the contemplation of Nature. No one has yet done for the myths of the lowest tribes what has been done for those of our more highly developed race by Kuhn and Müller, and their school in Germany and England; but Schirren, by his treatment of the gods and mythic ancestors of the South Sea Islanders as personifications of the phenomena of nature, has made an important step toward extending the modern method of interpretation to the Mythology of the World.[1] Still, a very slight acquaintance with the popular tales of America, Polynesia, even Australia and Van Diemen's Land, will show that they are the same in their nature and often in their incidents, by virtue of the like nature of the minds which conceived them.

As Zeus, the personified Heaven of our own race, drops tears on earth which mortals call rain, so does the heaven-god of Tahiti;

> Thickly falls the small rain on the face of the sea,
> They are not drops of rain, but they are tears of Oro.[2]

In the dark patches on the face of the moon, the Singhalese sees the pious hare that offered itself to Buddha to be cooked and eaten, when he was wandering hungry in the forest. The Northman saw there the two children whom Mâni the Moon caught up, as they were taking the water from the well Byrgir, and who are carrying the bucket on the pole between them to this day. Elsewhere in Europe, Isaac has been seen carrying the bundle of wood up Mount Moriah for his own sacrifice, and Cain bringing from his field a load of thorns as his offering to Jehovah. Our own "Man in the Moon" was set up there for picking sticks on a Sunday, and he, too, carries his thorn-bush, as Caliban had seen, "I have seen thee in her, and I do adore thee; my mistress showed me thee, and thy dog and thy bush." The Selish Indians of North-West America have devised their story of the "Toad in the Moon"; the little wolf was in love with the toad, and pursued her one bright moonlight night, till, for a last chance of escape, she made a desperate spring on to the face of the moon, and there

1 Schirren, 'Die Wandersagen der Neuseeländer und der Mauimythos;' Riga, 1856.

2 Ellis, Polyn. Res., vol. i. p. 531.

she is still. In the Samoan Islands in the Central Pacific, the dweller in the moon is a woman. Her name was Sina, and she was beating out paper-cloth with a mallet. The moon was just rising, and looked like a great bread-fruit, so Sina asked her to come down and let her child have a bit of her. But the moon was very angry at the idea of being eaten, and took up Sina, child, and mallet and all, and there they are to be seen to this day.[3]

The heavenly bodies are gods and heroes, and tales of their deeds in love and arms are found among the lower as among the higher races. Apollo and Artemis, Helios and Selene, are brother and sister, and so in the Polar Regions the Sun is a maiden and the Moon her brother. The Esquimaux tale tells how, when the girl was at a festive gathering, some one declared his love for her by shaking her by the shoulders, after the manner of the country. She could not tell who it was in the dark hut, so she smeared her hand with soot, and when he came back, she blackened his face with her hand. When a light was brought, she saw it was her brother, and fled, and he rushed after her. She came to the end of the earth and sprang out into the sky, and he followed her. There they became the Sun and Moon, and this is why the moon is always chasing the sun through the heavens; and the moon is sometimes dark as he turns his blackened cheek towards the earth.[4]

The natives of Van Diemen's Land, whose dismal history is now closing in total extinction, are among the lowest tribes known to Ethnology. Yet to them, as to higher races, the idea is familiar that the stars are men, or beings of a higher order who have appeared as men on earth. Their myth of the two heroes who are now the twin stars Castor and Pollux, is thus told by Milligan, as related by a native of the Oyster Bay Tribe:

"My father, my grandfather, all of them lived a long time ago all over the country; they had no fire. Two black-fellows came, they slept at the foot of a hill,—a hill in my own country. On the summit of a hill they were seen by my fathers, my countrymen,

3 Grimm, D. M., pp. 679–83. Wilson, 'Indian Tribes,' in Tr. Eth. Soc. vol. iv. p. 304. Turner, 'Polynesia,' p. 247. See Mariner, vol. ii. p. 127.

4 Hayes, 'Arctic Boat Journey,' p. 253. Different versions in Cranz, p. 295, Tr. Eth. Soc. vol. iv. p. 147.

on the top of the hill they were seen standing: they threw fire like a star,—it fell amongst the blackmen, my countrymen. They were frightened,—they fled away, all of them; after a while they returned, they hastened and made a fire,—a fire with wood; no more was fire lost in our land. The two black-fellows are in the clouds; in the clear night you see them like two stars.[5] These are they who brought fire to my fathers.

The two blackmen stayed awhile in the land of my fathers. Two women were bathing; it was near a rocky shore, where mussels were plentiful. The women were sulky, they were sad; their husbands were faithless, they had gone with two girls. The women were lonely; they were swimming in the water, they were diving for cray-fish. A sting-ray concealed in the hollow of a rock,—a large sting-ray! The sting-ray was large, he had a very long spear; from his hole he spied the women, he saw them dive: he pierced them with his spear,—he killed them, he carried them away. Awhile they were gone out of sight. The sting-ray returned, he came close to the shore, he lay in still water, near the sandy beach; with him were the women, they were fast on his spear,— they were dead!

The two blackmen fought the sting-ray; they slew him with their spears; they killed him;—the women were dead! The two blackmen made a fire—a fire of wood. On either side they laid a woman,—the fire was between: the women were dead!

The blackmen sought some ants, some large blue ants; they placed them on the bosoms of the women. Severely, intensely were they bitten. The women revived,—they lived once more.

Soon there came a fog, a fog dark as night. The two blackmen went away, the women disappeared: they passed through the fog, the thick dark fog! Their place is in the clouds. Two stars you see in the clear cold night; the two blackmen are there,—the women are with them: they are stars above."[6]

It is not needful to accumulate great masses of such tales as these, in order to show that the myth-making faculty belongs to mankind in general, and manifests itself in the most distant regions, where its unity of principle develops itself in endless va-

5 Castor and Pollux.

6 Milligan, Papers, etc., of R. Soc. of Tasmania, vol. iii. part ii. 1859, p. 274.

riety of form. There may indeed be a remote historical connexion at the root of some of the analogies in myths from far distant regions, which have just been mentioned; but when resemblances in Mythology are brought forward as proofs of such historical connexion, they must be closer and deeper than these. Mythological evidence, to be used for such a purpose, requires a systematic agreement in the putting together of a number of events or ideas, which agreement must be so close as to make it in a high degree improbable that two such combinations should have occurred separately, or at least the tales or ideas found alike in distant regions must be of so quaint and fantastic a character as to make it, on the very face of the matter, unlikely that they should have been invented twice. But it is both easier and safer to appeal to the effects of known intercourse between different peoples in spreading beliefs and popular tales, as evidence of the way in which historical connexion really does record itself in Mythology, than to lay down *à priori* rules as to what the effects of such connexion ought to be.

When we consider how short the time is since the Indians of North America have been acquainted with guns, the fact that there has been recorded, as one of their native beliefs, the notion that there are men who have charmed lives, and can only be killed with a silver bullet, may prepare us for the way in which savages can take up foreign mythology into their own. Again, it might be naturally expected that Bible stories learnt from missionaries, settlers, and travellers, should pass in a more or less altered shape into the folk-lore of savage races. Moffat gives a good instance which happened to himself. He had never succeeded in finding a deluge-tradition in South Africa, but making inquiries in a Namaqua village, he came upon a somewhat intelligent native who had one to tell, so he began with great satisfaction to take it down in writing. By the time it was finished, however, he began to suspect, for it bore the impress of the Bible, though the Hottentot declared that he had received it from his forefathers, and had never seen or heard of a missionary. Mr. Moffat was puzzled, and suspended his judgment till, a little while afterwards, the mystery was unraveled by the appearance of the very missionary from whom the native story-teller had received his teaching.[7] As another case of the same kind, may be quoted the following servile version of the story of Joseph and his brethren, found in Hawaii as the story of Waikelenuiaiku. His father had ten sons and one daughter; he was beloved by his father, and hated by his brethren, and they threw him into a pit, but his eldest brother felt more compassion for him than the rest. He escaped out of the pit, into the country of King Kamohoalii, and there he was confined in a dungeon with the prisoners. He bade his companions dream, and interpreted the dreams of four of them. One had seen a ripe banana, and his spirit ate it, the next dreamt of a banana, and the next of a hog, in the same way, but the fourth dreamt that he saw *awa*, that he pressed out the juice, and his spirit drank it. The three first dreams the foreigner interpreted for evil, and the dreamers were put to death in course of time, but to the fourth he prophesied deliverance and life, and he was saved, and told the King, who set Waikelenuiaiku at liberty, and made him a principal chief in the kingdom.[8]

There is sometimes a crudeness about these tales adopted from foreign sources, which gives us the means of positively condemning them. But the power which myths have of taking root the moment they are transplanted into a new country, often makes it impossible to tell whether they are of old date and historical value, or mere modern intruders. There is reason to believe that a story carried into a distant place by civilized men may spread and accommodate itself to the circumstances of the country, so that in a very few years' time it may be quite honestly collected as a genuine native tale, even by the very people who originally introduced it, like the farmer's hack that he sold in the morning, and bought back in the afternoon with a fresh mane and tail as a new horse. Of course this is the same kind of diffusion of myths which has been going on from remote ages among mankind, one of the very processes which have preserved to Ethnology aids of such high importance for the reconstruction of early history. It is only unfortunate that its results in modern times, by confounding the evidence of early and late intercourse between different peoples, have done so much to impair its historical value.

[7] Moffat, 'Missionary Labours, etc., in S. Africa'; London, 1842, p. 126.

[8] Hopkins, 'Hawaii'; London, 1862, p. 67.

Among the stories found in circulation among outlying races, there are many, beside those relating to a Deluge, which appear to be really united by ancient and deep-lying bonds of connexion with Biblical episodes, and the extreme difficulty, or impossibility, of separating a great part of these ancient stories from those which have grown up in modern times under Christian influences, is a very serious loss to early history. Still it is better to submit to this, than to base Ethnological arguments on evidence that will not bear the test of criticism. It is not only to Scriptural stories that this objection lies. Episodes from the classics and other European sources may be carried into distant lands by colonists and missionaries, and it may be laid down as a general rule, that stories which may have been transplanted in this way in modern times, must be rejected as independent evidence of remote intercourse between distant races among whom they are found. It is when a connexion between two peoples has been already made probable by evidence not liable to be thus impeached, that these stories can be taken into consideration as secondary evidence, which, once proved to be safe, may be of extraordinary interest and value.

Before proceeding to the comparison of a number of American myths with their analogues in the Old World, it is to be premised that the view of a connexion between the inhabitants of America and Asia by no means rests on one of those vague and misty theories, which have too often been allowed to pass current as solid Ethnological arguments. The researches of Alexander von Humboldt brought into view, half a century ago, evidence which goes with great force to prove that the civilization of Mexico and that of Asia have, in part at least, a common origin, and that therefore the population of these regions are united, if not by the tie of common descent and relationship by blood, at least by intercourse, direct or indirect, in past times. Of this evidence, the similarity of the chronological calendars is perhaps the strongest point. Not only are series of names like our signs of the zodiac used to record periods of time, but such series are combined together, or with numbers, in both countries, in a complex, perverse, and practically purposeless manner, which, whatever its origin, can hardly by any stretch of probability be supposed to have come up independently in the minds of two different peoples. The theory of the successive destructions and renovations of the world, at the end of long cycles of years, was pointed out by Humboldt as another bond of connexion between Mexico and the Old World. If these agreements between North America and Asia are to be read as indications of a deep-rooted connexion, this ought to have left many other traces. Of customs, the occurrence of which in America as well as in the Old World would be well explained by such a view, something has already been said. Of the North or South American myths which closely resemble tales current in Asia, Polynesia, and elsewhere in the world, eight are discussed here, the World-Tortoise, the Man swallowed by the Fish, the Sun-Catcher, the Ascent to Heaven by the Tree, the Bridge of the Dead, the Fountain of Youth, the Tail-Fisher, and the Diable Boiteux.

In the Old World, the Tortoise Myth belongs especially to India, and the idea is developed there in a variety of forms. The Tortoise that upholds the earth is called in Sanskrit *Kûrmarâja,* "King of the Tortoises," and the Hindus believe to this day that the world rests upon its back. Sometimes the snake Sesha bears the world on its head, or an elephant carries it upon its back, and both snake and elephant are themselves supported by the great tortoise. The earth, rescued from the deluge which destroys mankind, is set up with the snake that bears it resting on the floating tortoise, and a deluge is again to pour over the face of the earth when the world-tortoise, sinking under its load, goes down into the great waters. When the Daityas and Dânavas churned the Sea of Milk to make the *amrita,* the drink of immortality, they took the mountain Mandara for the churning-stick, and the serpent Vâsuki was the thong that was wound round it, and pulled back and forwards to drive the churn. In the midst of the milky sea, Vishnu himself, in the form of a tortoise, served as a pivot for the mountain as it was whirled around.[9]

9 Boehtlingk & Roth, *s. v.* Kûrma. Wilson, *s. v.* Kûrmarâja. Coleman, p. 12. Vans Kennedy, 'Researches'; London, 1831, pp. 216, 243. Holwell, 'Historical Events,' etc.; London, 1766-7, part ii. p. 109. Falconer, in Proc. Zool. Soc., 1844, p. 86. See Sir W. Jones, in As. Res. vol. ii. p. 119. Baldæus, in Churchill's Voyages, vol. iii. p. 848. Wilson, 'Vishnu Purana'; London, 1840, p. 75. W. v. Humboldt (Kawi-Spr., vol. i. p. 240) says with reference to the Naga Padoha,

The notion of the earth being itself a great tortoise swimming in the midst of the ocean, is thus described by Reinaud:—"According to Varâha-Mihira, the Indians represented to themselves the inhabited part of the world under the form of a tortoise floating upon the water; it is in this sense that they call the World *Kaurma-chakra,* that is to say, 'the wheel of the tortoise.' "[10] And lastly, the ancient Vedic Books of India, which so often supply the means of tracing the most florid developments of mythology back to mere simple child-like views of nature, present, as really existing in very early times, the original idea out of which the whole series of myths of the World-Tortoise seems to have grown. To man in the lower levels of science, the earth is a flat plain over which the sky is placed like a dome, as the arched upper shell of the tortoise stands upon the flat plate below, and this is why the tortoise is the symbol and representative of the world. The analogy of other conceptions of heaven and earth, as formed by the two halves of the shell of Brahma's Egg, or by the two calabashes shut together in the mythology of the Yorubas of Africa,[11] is indeed sufficient to lead us to the opinion that this was the original meaning of the World-Tortoise, but the following passage from Weber will enable us to substitute fact for inference. "The earth is conceived in the Catapatha Brâhmana as the under shell (adharam kapâlam) of the Tortoise Kûrma, which represents the Triple World. The upper shell is the sky, the body lying between the two shells is the atmosphere (nabhas, antari-ksham) which connects them."[12]

There is a curious group of myths, of which an ancient example is preserved in the Zend-Avesta. The hero, Kereçaspa, cooks his

---

the great snake on whose three horns the world rests,—"It seems to me not unlikely, that the idea of a world-bearing elephant lies at the bottom of the whole saga [of the snake, that is] and that the double meaning of Sanskrit nâga, *elephant* and *snake,* has brought confusion into the story."

[10] Reinaud, 'Mémoire sur l'Inde'; Paris, 1849, p. 116.

[11] Pott, 'Anti-Kaulen'; Lemgo, 1863, p. 68.

[12] Weber, 'Indische Studien'; Berlin, 1850, etc.; vol. i. p. 187. See also p. 81. I may mention having set down this conception as the probable basis of the Tortoise-myths before meeting with this direct evidence from ancient India. The coincidence defends such an interpretation of the myths from the charge of being far-fetched and fanciful.

food in a cauldron on the back of the serpent Çruvara, on which the green poison flowed of the thickness of a thumb; the burnt monster dashes away, and returns to the hurrying waters. It is related in the first voyage of Sindbad, that he and his companions came, as they sailed along, to an island like one of the gardens of Paradise, and there they anchored the ship, and went ashore, and lighted fires to cook food. But the island was a great fish, on whose back sand had accumulated, and trees had grown from times of old, and when it felt the fire on its back, it moved and went down to the botom of the sea. This story, which may be also found in Jewish and mediæval European literature, seems to have become combined with the tortoise-myth. In El-Kazwini's account of the animals of the water, there is a version of the story, which describes the creature as a huge tortoise; "The Tortoise," he says, "is a sea and land animal. As to the sea-tortoise, it is very enormous, so that the people of the ship imagine that it is an island. One of the merchants hath related, saying, 'We found in the sea an island elevated above the water, having upon it green plants; and we went forth to it, and dug [holes for fire] to cook; whereupon the island moved, and the sailors said, Come yet to your place; for it is a tortoise, and the heat of the fire hath hurt it; lest it carry you away!—By reason of the enormity of its body,' saith he (i.e. the narrator above mentioned), 'it was as though it were an island; and earth collected upon its back in the length of time, so that it became like land, and produced plants.'" It is remarkable that a similar story, of a monstrous river-tortoise, has been found among the Zulus.[13]

The striking analogy between the Tortoise-myths of North America and India is by no means a matter of new observation; it was indeed remarked upon by Father Lafitau nearly a century and a half ago.[14] Three great features of the Asiatic stories are found among the North American Indians, in the fullest and

---

[13] Avesta (tr. by Spiegel & Bleeck) Yaçna, ix. 34. Lane, 'Thousand and One Nights,' vol. iii. pp. 6, 79, see vol. i. p. 21. Eisenmenger, 'Entdecktes Judenthum,' Königsberg, 1711, part i. p. 399. St. Brandan, ed. T. Wright, London, 1844. Petri Siculi Hist. Manichæorum, recog. Gieseler, Göttingen, 1846, p. 34. Callaway, 'Zulu Nursery Tales,' vol. i. pp. 2, 341.

[14] Lafitau, vol. i. p. 99.

clearest development. The earth is supported on the back of a huge floating Tortoise, the Tortoise sinks under water and causes a deluge, and the Tortoise is conceived as being itself the Earth floating upon the face of the deep.

In the last century, Loskiel, the Moravian missionary, remarked of the North American Indians, that "Some imagine, that the earth swims in the sea, or that an enormous tortoise carries the world on its back."[15] Schoolcraft, an unrivalled authority on Indian mythology within his own district, remarks that the turtle is "an object held in great respect, in all Indian reminiscence. It is believed to be, in all cases, a symbol of the earth, and is addressed as a mother." In the Iroquois mythology, there was a woman of heaven who was called Atahentsic, and one of the six men of heaven became enamoured of her. When it was discovered, she was cast down to earth, and received on the back of a great turtle lying on the waters, and there she was delivered of twins. One was "the Good Mind," the other was "the Bad Mind," and thus the two great powers of the Indian dualism, the Good and Evil Principle, came into the world, and the tortoise expanded and became the earth,[16] or, as it is elsewhere related, the otter and the fishes disturbed the mud at the bottom of the ocean, and drawing it up round the tortoise, formed a small island, which, gradually increasing, became the earth.[17] Father Charlevoix gives two different versions of the story. In one place it is Taronyawagon, the King of Heaven, who gave his wife so mighty a kick that she flew out of the sky and down to earth, and fell upon the back of a tortoise, which, cleaving the waters of the deluge with its feet, at last uncovered the earth, and carried the woman to the foot of a tree, where she was delivered of two sons, and the elder, who was called Tawiskaron, killed his younger brother. In another place the story is like Schoolcraft's.[18] Among the Mandans, Catlin found a legend which brings in the same notion of the World-tortoise, but shows by the difference of the accessory circumstances that it was not in America a mere part of a particular story, but a mythological conception which might be worked into

[15] Loskiel, part i. p. 30.

[16] Schoolcraft, part i. pp. 300, 316.

[17] Coleman, p. 15.

[18] Charlevoix, vol. vi. pp. 146, 65.

an unlimited variety of myths. The tale that the Mandan doctor told Catlin, was that the earth was a large tortoise, that it carried dirt upon its back, and that a tribe of people who are now dead, and whose faces were white, used to dig down very deep in this ground to catch badgers. One day they stuck a knife through the shell of the tortoise, and it sank and sank till the water ran over its back, and they were all drowned but one man.[19] The North American idea that it is the movement of the earth-tortoise which causes earthquakes, adds the last touch to the realism of the whole conception.[20]

The Myth of the World-Tortoise is one of those which have this great value in the comparison of Asiatic and American Mythology, that it leaves not the least opening for the supposition of its having been carried by modern Europeans from the Old to the New World. But it is to be seen, even from the tales which have just been quoted, that it is mixed up in America with incidents and ideas more familiar to the European mind; and the stories told only with reference to the World-Tortoise may serve to give a glimpse into the vast ethnological field which lies in the Red Indian traditions, ready to be worked. The Deluge, Cain and Abel, Ahriman and Ormuzd, Romulus and Remus, all have their analogies among the legends of these wild hunters. In the story which Charlevoix tells just before that which I have quoted, there is Noah's raven and Pandora's casket.

To proceed now to the story of the Man swallowed by the Fish.[21] It is related in the Chippewa tale of the Little Monedo, that there was once a little boy, of tiny stature, and growing no bigger with years, but of monstrous strength. He had done before various wondrous feats, and one day he waded into the lake, and called, "You of the red fins, come and swallow me." Immediately that monstrous fish came and swallowed him, and he, seeing his sister standing in despair on the shore, called out to her, and she tied an old mocassin to a string, and fastened it to a tree near the

---

[19] Catlin, vol. i. p. 181.

[20] J. G. Müller, 'Amerikanische Urreligionen,' pp. 61, 122.

[21] This subject has since been more fully treated by the author in 'Primitive Culture,' chap. ix.

water's edge. The fish said to the boy-man under water, "What is that floating?" The boy-man said to the fish, "Go take hold of it, and swallow it as fast as you can." The fish darted towards the old shoe, and swallowed it; the boy-man laughed to himself, but said nothing till the fish was fairly caught, and then he took hold of the line and hauled himself to shore. When the sister began to cut the fish open she heard her brother's voice from inside the fish, calling to her to let him out, so she made a hole, and he crept through, and told her to cut up the fish and dry it, for it would last them a long while for food.[22]

In the Old World, the Hindoo story of Saktideva tells that there was once a king's daughter who would marry no one but the man who had seen the Golden City, and Saktideva was in love with her; so he went travelling about the world seeking some one who could tell him where this Golden City was. In the course of his journeys he embarked on board a ship bound for the island of Utsthala, where lived the King of the Fishermen, who, Saktideva hoped, would set him on his way. On the voyage there arose a great storm and the ship went to pieces, but a great fish swallowed Saktideva whole. Then driven by the force of fate, the fish went to the island of Utsthala, and there the servants of the King of the Fishermen caught it, and the King wondering at its size had it cut open, and Saktideva came out unhurt, to pass through other adventures, and at last to see the Golden City, and to marry, not the Princess only, but her three sisters beside.[23]

The analogy of these curious tales with the leading episode of the Book of Jonah is of course evident, and it might at first appear as though this very ancient story were possibly the direct origin of one or both of them; as regards dates, the American story has been but recently taken down, and even the Hindoo tale only comes out of a mediæval Sanskrit collection. But both agree in differing from the history of Jonah, in the fish being cut open to let the man out. Something very like this occurs in the myth of the Polynesian Sun-god Maui. He was born on the sea-shore, and his mother flung him into the foam of the surf; then the sea-

[22] Schoolcraft, part iii. pp. 318–20.

[23] Somadeva Bhatta, vol. ii. pp. 118–184.

weed wrapped its long tangles round him, and the soft jelly-fish rolled themselves about him to protect him as he was drifted on shore again, and his great ancestor the Sky, Tama-nui-ki-te-Rangi, saw the flies and the birds collected in clusters and flocks, and ran and stripped the encircling jellyfish off, and behold there lay within a human being; so the old man took the child and carried it home.[24] As the Polynesian Maui is among the clearest and completest personifications of the Sun, there is some force in Schirren's argument that this story means the Sun being set free by the Sky at dawn, from the Earth which covers him at night;[25] for it must be remembered here that one of the most prominent ideas of the Polynesian Mythology is that the Earth is a huge fish, which Maui draws up with his line from the bottom of the sea, and that Maui's death, the sunset, is told in the story of his creeping into the mouth of his great ancestress, Hine-nui-te-po, whom you may see flashing, and, as it were, opening and shutting, where the horizons meets the sky; there Maui crept in, and perished. And not only would such an explanation of the tale of the Red Indian 'Tom Thumb' be a fitting one, in that he, like so many personifications of the Sun in other countries, is a slayer of Giants, but he will appear a few pages further on as the Sun-Catcher in a plain, open Solar myth. In any full discussion of the group of tales, it would be necessary to investigate their correspondence with the European stories of Tom Thumb, who was swallowed by the cow and came out unhurt, and of Little Red Riding-Hood, who was swallowed whole by the wolf, and came out alive when the hunter cut him open.[26]

In the next myth, that of the Sun-Catcher, the Polynesian Sun-god Maui again makes his appearance. He began to think that it was too soon after the rising of the sun that it became night again, and that the sun again sank down below the horizon, every day, every day; so at last he said to his brothers, "Let us now catch the sun in a noose, so that we may compel him to move more slowly, in order that mankind may have long days to labour in to

[24] Grey, Polynesian Mythology,' pp. 18, 31.

[25] Schirren, pp. 143–44, 29. But the legend is very erroneously given.

[26] J. & W. Grimm, 'Märchen,' vol. i. pp. 142, 198, 28.

procure subsistence for themselves.'" Then they began to spin and twist ropes to make a noose to catch the sun in, and thus the art of rope-making was discovered. And Maui took his enchanted weapon, which, like Samson's, was a jaw-bone, the jaw-bone of his ancestress Muri-ranga-whenua, and he and his brothers travelled off through the desert, till they came very far, very far, to the eastward, to the very edge of the place out of which the sun rises. There they set the noose, and at last the sun came up and put his head and fore-paws through it; then the brothers pulled the ropes tight and held them fast, and Maui rushed at him with his magic weapon. Alas! the sun screams aloud, he roars; Maui strikes him fiercely with many blows; they hold him for a long time, at last they let him go, and then, weak from wounds, the sun crept slowly along its course.[27] Another version of the story was taken down in the Samoan Islands. There was once a man who, like the white people, though it was years before pipes, muskets, or priests were heard of, never could be contented with what he had; pudding was not good enough for him, and he worried his family out of all heart with his new ways and ideas. At last he set to build himself a house of great stones, to last for ever; so he rose early and toiled late, but the stones were so heavy and so far off, and the sun went round so quickly, that he could get on but very slowly. One evening he lay awake, and thought and thought, and it struck him that as the sun had but one road to come by, he might stop him and keep him till the work was done. So he rose before the dawn, and pulling out in his canoe as the sun rose, he threw a rope round his neck; but no, the sun marched on and went his course unchecked. He put nets over the place where the sun rose, he used up all his mats to stop him, but in vain; the sun went on, and laughed in hot winds at all his efforts. Meanwhile the house stood still, and the builder fairly despaired. At last the great Itu, who generally lies on his mats, and cares not at all for those he has made, turned round and heard his cry, and, because he was a good warrior, sent him help. He made the *facehere* creeper grow, and again the poor man sprang up from the ground near his house, where he had lain down in despair. He

[27] Grey, 'Polynesian Mythology,' pp. 35–8.

took his canoe and made a noose of the creeper. It was the bad season, when the sun is dull and heavy; so up he came, half asleep and tired, nor looked about him, but put his head into the noose. He pulled and jerked, but Itu had made it too strong. The man built his house—the sun cried and cried, till the island of Savai was nearly drowned; but not till the last stone was laid, was he suffered to resume his career. None can break the *facehere*. It is the Itu's cord.[28]

Other versions of this episode in the great Maui-myth have been taken down in the Pacific Islands,[29] and a like variety is found in the corresponding tales from North America. Among the Ojibwas, the Sun-Catcher is evidently the same personage as the Boy swallowed by the Fish in the last group of stories. At the time when the animals reigned in the earth, they had killed all but a girl and her little brother, and these two were living in fear and seclusion. The boy never grew bigger than a little child, and his sister used to take him out with her when she went to get food for the lodge-fire, for he was too little to leave alone; a big bird might have flown away with him. One day she made him a bow and arrows, and told him to hide where she had been chopping, and when the snow-birds came to pick the worms out of the wood, he was to shoot one. That day he tried in vain to kill one, but the next, toward nightfall, she heard his little footsteps on the snow; he brought in a bird, and told his sister she was to take off the skin and to put half the bird at a time into the pottage, for till then men had not begun to eat animal food, but had lived on vegetables alone. At last the boy had killed ten birds, and his sister made him a little coat of the skins. "Sister," said he one day, "are we all alone in the world? Is there nobody else living?" Then she told him that those they feared, and who had destroyed their relatives, lived in a certain part, and he must by no means go that way; but this only made him eager to go, and he took his bow and arrows and started. When he had walked a long while, he lay down on a knoll, where the sun had melted the snow, and fell fast

28 Walpole, 'Four Years in the Pacific,' vol. ii. p. 375.

29 Turner, 'Polynesia,' pp. 245, 248. Tyerman & Bennet, vol. ii. p. 40; and see vol. i. p. 433. Ellis, Polyn. Res., vol. ii. p. 415.

asleep; but while he was sleeping the sun beat so hot upon him, that his bird-skin coat was all singed and shrunk. When he awoke and found his coat spoilt, he vowed vengeance against the sun, and bade his sister make him a snare. She made him one of deer's sinew, and then one of her own hair, but they would not do. At last she brought him one that was right; he pulled it between his lips, and, as he pulled, it became a red metal cord. With this he set out a little after midnight, and fixed his snare on a spot just where the sun would strike the land, as it rose above the earth's disc, and sure enough he caught the sun, so that it was held fast in the cord and did not rise. The animals who ruled the earth were immediately put into a great commotion. They had no light. They called a council to debate upon the matter, and to appoint some one to go and cut the cord, for this was a very hazardous enterprise, as the rays of the sun would burn whoever came so near. At last the dormouse undertook it, for at this time the dormouse was the largest animal in the world. When it stood up it looked like a mountain. When it got to the place where the sun was snared, its back began to smoke and burn with the intensity of the heat, and the top of its carcass was reduced to enormous heaps of ashes. It succeeded, however, in cutting the cord with its teeth, and freeing the sun; but it was reduced to a very small size, and has remained so ever since.[30]

In this North American tale we have the Sun-Catcher of the South Sea Islands, combined with part of our own Jack and the Beanstalk. As Jack, in spite of his mother's prayers, goes up the ladder that is to take him to the dwelling of the Giant who killed his father, so the boy of the American tale will not heed his sister's persuasion, but goes to seek the enemies who had slain his kindred. In the next two versions also from North America, the incident of the going up a tree to the country in the sky, as Jack goes up his beanstalk, makes its appearance. And in all three, the loosing of the imprisoned sun is told in a story of which the European fable of the Lion and the Mouse might be a mere moralized remnant.

In the story found among the Wyandots, in the seventeenth

---

[30] Schoolcraft, 'Onéota'; New York and London, 1845, p. 75. See *ante*, p. 179.

century, by the missionary Paul le Jeune, it is related that there was a child whose father was killed and eaten by a bear, and his mother by the Great Hare; a woman came and found the child, and adopted him as her little brother, calling him Chakabech. He did not grow bigger than a baby, but he was so strong that the trees served as arrows for his bow. When he had killed the destroyers of his parents, he wished to go up to heaven, and climbed up a tree; then he blew upon it, and it grew up and up till he came up to heaven, and there he found a beautiful country. So he went down to fetch his sister, building huts as he went down to lodge her in; brought her up the tree into heaven, and then broke off the tree low down: so no one can go up to heaven that way. Then Chakabech went out and set his snares for game, but when he got up at night to look at them, he found everything on fire, and went back to his sister to tell her. Then she told him he must have caught the Sun, going along by night he must have got in unawares, and when Chakabech went to see, so it was; but he dared not go near enough to let him out. But by chance he found a little Mouse, and blew upon her till she grew so big that she could set the Sun free, and he went again on his way; but while he was held in the snare, day failed down here on earth.[31]

The first and second American versions of the Sun-Catcher come from near the great lakes, but the third is found among the Dog-Rib Indians, far in the north-west, close upon the Esquimaux who fringe the northern coast. When Chapewee, after the deluge, formed the earth, and landed the animals upon it from his canoe, he "stuck up a piece of wood, which became a fir-tree, and grew with amazing rapidity, until its top reached the skies. A squirrel ran up this tree, and was pursued by Chapewee, who endeavoured to knock it down, but could not overtake it. He continued the chase, however, until he reached the stars, where he found a fine plain, and a beaten road. In this road he set a snare, made of his sister's hair, and then returned to the earth. The sun appeared as usual in the heavens in the morning, but at noon it was caught by the snare which Chapewee had set for the

---

31 Le Jeune (1637) in 'Relations des Jésuites dans la Nouvelle-France'; Quebec, 1858, vol. i. p. 54. Schoolcraft, part iii. p. 320. See also page 203, in the present Chapter.

squirrel, and the sky was instantly darkened. Chapewee's family on this said to him, 'You must have done something wrong when you were aloft, for we no longer enjoy the light of day.' 'I have,' replied he, 'but it was unintentionally.' Chapewee then endeavoured to repair the fault he had committed, and sent a number of animals up the tree to release the sun by cutting the snare, but the intense heat of that luminary reduced them all to ashes. The efforts of the more active animals being thus frustrated, a ground mole, though such a grovelling and awkward beast, succeeded by burrowing under the road in the sky until it reached and cut asunder the snare which bound the sun. It lost its eyes, however, the instant it thrust its head into the light, and its nose and teeth have ever since been brown, as if burnt."[32]

In former editions of this work it was remarked that the origin of the story of the Sun-Catcher is not yet clear, but probably some piece of unequivocal evidence will be found to explain it. There has since been published by the Rev. W. W. Gill a version of the Maui-myth from the Hervey Islands, which looks as though it might be this expected key. Maui plaited six great cocoa-nut fibre ropes to make his royal nooses to catch the sungod, Rā; the first noose he set at the opening where the sun climbs up from Avaiki, the under-world, and the other five one after another further on in the sun's path; as Rā came up in the morning, Maui pulled the first slip-knot, which held him by the feet, the next by the knees, and so on, till the last noose closed round his neck, and Maui made him fast to a point of rock; then Rā, nearly strangled, confessed himself conquered, and promised henceforth to go more slowly through the heavens, that men might have time to get easily through their work. "The sun-god Rā was now allowed to proceed on his way; but Maui wisely declined to take off these ropes, wishing to keep Rā in constant fear. These ropes may still be seen hanging from the sun at dawn, and when he descends into the ocean at night. By the assistance of these ropes he is gently let down into Avaiki, and in the morning is raised up out of the shades. Of course this extravagant myth refers to what English children call 'the sun drawing up water;' or, as these

---

[32] Richardson, Narr. of Franklin's Second Exp.; London, 1828, p. 291.

islanders still say 'Tena te taura a Māui!' 'Behold the ropes of Māui!' "[33]

In connexion with this set of tales, it may be noticed that there are to be found in the Old World ideas of the sun being bound with a cord to hold it in check. In North Germany the townsmen of Bösum sit up in their church tower and hold the sun by a cable all day; taking care of it at night, and letting it up again in the morning. In Reynard the Fox, the day is bound with a rope, and its bonds only let it come slowly on. In a Hungarian tale midnight and dawn are bound, so that they can get no farther towards men.[34] This notion is curiously like the Peruvian story of the Inca who denied the pretension of the Sun to be the doer of all things, for if he were free, he would go and visit other parts of the heavens where he had never been. He is, said the Inca, like a tied beast who goes ever round and round in the same track.[35] The idea is renewed by Wordsworth, that "modern ancient," as Max Müller so truly calls him:—

> Well does thine aspect usher in this Day;
> As aptly suits therewith that modest pace
>   Submitted to the chains
> That bind thee to the path which God ordains
>   That thou shouldst trace,
> Till, with the heavens and earth, thou pass away!

The legend of the Ascent to Heaven by the Tree has just been brought forward in two of its American versions,[36] taken down at periods two centuries apart, and among tribes not only separated by long distance but speaking languages of two distinct families, and yet in both cases embodying also the story of the Sun-Catcher. A further examination of the story of Jack and the Bean-Stalk, and the analogous tales which are spread through the Malay and

[33] Rev. W. W. Gill, 'Myths and Songs from the South Pacific,' London, 1876, p. 62; another version, p. 70, mentions Maui's ropes breaking, till a noose was made of his sister's hair, as in the American story. [Note to 3rd Edition.]

[34] Bastian, vol. ii. p. 58. Grimm, D. M., p. 706. See Steinthal, 'Die Sage von Simson,' in Lazarus & Steinthal's 'Zeitschrift'; Berlin, 1862, vol. ii. p. 141.

[35] Garcilaso de la Vega, part i. viii. 8. See also Acosta, Hist. del Nuevo Orbe, chap. v.

[36] See also Schoolcraft, part iii. p. 547; part i. plate 52, p. 378.

Polynesian districts and North America, will bring into view the vast ramifications of a mythic episode flourishing far and wide in these distant regions, though so scantily represented in the folk-lore of Europe.

Once upon a time there was a poor widow, and she had one son, and his name was Jack. One day she sent him to sell the cow, but when he saw some pretty-coloured beans that the butcher had, he was so delighted that he gave the cow for them and brought his prize home in triumph. When the poor mother saw the beans that Jack had brought home she flung them away, and they grew and grew till next morning they had grown right up into the sky. So Jack climbed up sorely against his mother's will, and saw the fairy, and went to the house of the giant who had killed his father, and stole the hen that laid the golden eggs, and did various other wonderful things, till at last the Giant came running after him and followed him down the bean-stalk, but Jack was just in time to cut the ladder through, and the wicked Giant tumbled down head first into the well, and there he was drowned.

So runs the good old nursery tale of Jack and the Bean-Stalk. That it is found in England and yet is not general in the folk-lore of the rest of our race in Europe is remarkable. Mr. Campbell says it is not known in the Highlands of Scotland, while in Germany Wilhelm Grimm only compares it with two poor, dull little stories, one a version distinctly connected with our English tale, the other perhaps so, but neither worth repeating here.[37]

In another American tradition, found current among the Mandans, the ascent is not from the earth to the sky, but from the regions underground to the surface. It is thus related in the account of Lewis and Clarke's expedition. "Their belief in a future state is connected with this tradition of their origin: the whole nation resided in one large village underground near a subterraneous lake: a grape-vine extended its roots down to their habitation and gave them a view of the light: some of the most adventurous climbed up the vine and were delighted with the sight of the earth, which they found covered with buffalo and rich with

[37] J. & W. Grimm, 'Märchen,' vol. ii. p. 133; vol. iii. pp. 193, 321.

every kind of fruits: returning with the grapes they had gathered, their countrymen were so pleased with the taste of them that the whole nation resolved to leave their dull residence for the charms of the upper region; men, women, and children ascended by means of the vine; but when about half the nation had reached the surface of the earth, a corpulent woman who was clambering up the vine broke it with her weight, and closed upon herself and the rest of the nation the light of the sun. Those who were left on earth made a village below where we saw the nine villages; and when the Mandans die they expect to return to the original seats of their forefathers; the good reaching the ancient village by means of the lake, which the burden of the sins of the wicked will not enable them to cross."[38]

The set of Malayo-Polynesian stories which tell of the climbing from earth to heaven by a tree or vine-like plant is, besides, a good illustration of the unity of the Island Mythology from Borneo to New Zealand. The Dayak tale of the man who went up to heaven and brought down rice has been already cited. It is thus told by Mr. St. John:—"Once upon a time, when mankind had nothing to eat but a species of edible fungus that grows upon rotting trees, and there were no cereals to gladden and strengthen man's heart, a party of Dayaks, among whom was a man named Si Jura, whose descendants live to this day in the Dayak village of Simpok, went forth to sea. They sailed on for some time, until they came to a place at which they heard the distant roar of a large whirlpool, and, to their amazement, saw before them a huge fruit-tree rooted in the sky, and thence hanging down with its branches touching the waves. At the request of his companions, Si Jura climbed among its boughs to collect the fruit which was in abundance, and when he was there he found himself tempted to ascend the trunk and find out how the tree grew in that position. He did so, and at length got so high that his companions in the boat lost sight of him, and after waiting a certain time coolly sailed away loaded with fruit. Looking down from his lofty position, Si Jura saw his friends making off, so he had no other resource but to go on climbing in hopes of reaching some resting-place. He therefore persevered climbing higher and higher, till he reached the roots of the tree, and there he found himself in a new country—that of the Pleiades. There he met a being in form of a man, named Si Kira, who took him to his home and hospitably entertained him. The food offered was a mess of soft white grains—boiled rice. 'Eat,' said Si Kira. 'What, those little maggots?' replied Si Jura. 'They are not maggots, but boiled rice;' and Si Kura forthwith explained the process of planting, weeding, and reaping, and of pounding and boiling rice. . . . So Si Jura made a hearty meal, and after eating, Si Kira gave him seed of three kinds of rice, instructed him how to cut down the forest, burn, plant, weed, and reap, take omens from birds, and celebrate harvest feasts; and then, by a long rope, let him down to earth again near his father's house."[39]

In the Malay island of Celebes, the episode of the heaven-plant occurs in a story no doubt derived from an Arabic source, its theme being that of the tale of Hassan of Bassora in the Arabian Nights.[40] Seven heavenly nymphs came down from the sky to bathe, and they were seen by Kasimbaha, who thought first that they were white doves, but in the bath he saw that they were women. Then he stole one of the thin robes that gave the nymphs their power of flying, and so he caught Utahagi, the one whose robe he had stolen, and took her for his wife, and she bore him a son. Now she was called Utahagi from a single white hair she had, which was endowed with magic power, and this hair her husband pulled out. As soon as he had done it, there arose a great storm, and Utahagi went up into heaven. The child cried for its mother, and Kasimbaha was in great grief, and cast about how he should follow Utahagi up into the sky. Then a rat gnawed the thorns off the rattans, and he clambered up by them

[39] St. John, vol. i. p. 202.

[40] Lane, 'Thousand and One Nights'; vol. iii. ch. 25. The early occurrence of this, which may be called the story of the Swan-coat, in the folk-lore of Northern Europe, is interesting. Among a number of instances, in the Völundarqvitha, three women sit on the shore with their swan-coats beside them, ready to turn into swans and fly away. Or three doves fly down to a fountain and become maidens when they touch the earth. Wielant takes their clothes and will not give them back till one consents to be his wife, etc. etc. Grimm, D. M., pp. 398–402.

with his son upon his back till he came to heaven. There a little bird showed him the house of Utahagi, and after various adventures he took up his abode among the gods.[41]

From Celebes to New Zealand the distance is some four thousand miles, but among the Maoris a tale is found which is beyond doubt connected with this. There was once a great chief called Tawhaki, and a girl of the heavenly race, whose name was Tango-tango, heard of his valour and his beauty and came down to earth to be his wife, and she bore a daughter to him. But when Tawhaki took the little girl to a spring and had washed it, he held it out at arm's length and said, "Faugh, how badly the little thing smells." When Tango-tango heard this, she was bitterly offended and began to sob and weep, and at last she took the child and flew up to heaven with it. Tawhaki tried to stop her and besought her to stay, but in vain, and as she paused for a minute with one foot resting on the carved figure at the end of the ridge-pole of the house, above the door, he called to her to leave him some remembrance of her. Then she told him he was not to lay hold of the loose root of the creeper, which dropping from aloft sways to and fro in the air, but rather to lay fast hold on that which hanging down from on high has again struck its fibres into the earth. So she floated up into the air and vanished, and Tawhaki remained mourning: at the end of a month he could bear it no longer, so he took his younger brother with him, and two slaves, and started to look for his wife and child. At last the brothers came to the spot where the ends of the tendrils which hung down from heaven reached the earth, and there they found an old ancestress of theirs whose name was Matakerepo. She was appointed to take care of the tendrils, and she sat at the place where they touched the earth, and held the ends of one of them in her hands. So next day the younger brother, Karihi, started to climb up, and the old woman warned him not to look down when he was midway between heaven and earth, lest he should turn giddy and fall, and also to take care not to catch hold of a loose tendril. But just at that very moment he made a spring at the

41 Schirren, p. 126. Compare Bornean story, Bp. of Labuan in Tr. Eth. Soc. 1863, p. 27.

tendrils, and by mistake caught hold of a loose one, and away he swung to the very edge of the horizon, but a blast of wind blew forth from thence and drove him back to the other side of the skies, and then another gust swept him heavenwards, and again he was blown down. Just as he reached the ground this time Tawhaki shouted to him to let go, and lo, he stood upon the earth once more, and the two brothers wept over his narrow escape from destruction. Then Tawhaki began to climb, and he went up and up, repeating a powerful incantation as he climbed, till at last he reached the heavens, and there he found his wife and their daughter, and they took her to the water, and baptised her in proper New Zealand fashion. Lightning flashed from Tawhaki's armpits, and he still dwells up there in heaven, and when he walks, his footsteps make the thunder and lightning that are heard and seen on earth.[42]

There are other mythological ways besides the Heaven-tree, by which, in different parts of the world, it is possible to go up and down between the surface of the ground and the sky or the regions below; the rank spear-grass, a rope or thong, a spider's web, a ladder of iron or gold, a column of smoke, or the rainbow. It must be remembered in discussing such tales, that the idea of climbing, for instance, from earth to heaven by a tree, fantastic as it may seem to a civilized man of modern times, is in a different grade of culture quite a simple and natural idea, and too much stress must not be laid on bare coincidences to this effect in proving a common origin for the stories which contain them, unless closer evidence is forthcoming. Such tales belong to a rude and primitive state of the knowledge of the earth's surface, and what lies above and below it. The earth is a flat plain surrounded by

42 Grey, 'Polynesian Mythology,' p. 66, etc. Several incidents are here omitted. In another version Tawhaki goes up not by the creeper but upon a spider's web. (Thomson, N. Z., vol. i. p. 111. Yate, p. 144.) Other stories connected with this series are to be found in the Samoan group. The taro, like the rice in Borneo, is brought down from heaven; there was a heaven-tree, where people went up and down, and when it fell it stretched some sixty miles; two young men went up to the moon, one by a tree, the other on the smoke of a fire as it towered into the sky (Turner, p. 246). In the Caroline Islands, another of these καπνοβάται goes up to heaven on a column of smoke to visit his celestial father (J. R. Forster, Obs. p. 606). In the Tonga Islands, Maui makes the *toa* grow up to heaven, so that the god Etumatubua can come down by it (Schirren, p. 76).

the sea, and the sky forms a roof on which the sun, moon, and stars travel. The Polynesians, who thought, like so many other peoples, ancient and modern, that the sky descended at the horizon and enclosed the earth, still call foreigners *papalangi,* or "heaven-bursters," as having broken in from another world outside. The sky is to most savages what it is called in a South American language, *mumeseke,* that is, the "earth on high"; and we can quite understand the thought of the Mbocobis of Paraguay, that at death their souls would go up to heaven by the tree Llagdigua, which joins earth and sky.[43] There are holes or windows through the sky-roof or firmament, where the rain comes through, and if you climb high enough you can get through and visit the dwellers above, who look, and talk, and live very much in the same way as the people upon earth. As above the flat earth, so below it, there are regions inhabited by men or man-like creatures, who sometimes come up to the surface, and sometimes are visited by the inhabitants of the upper earth. We live as it were upon the ground floor of a great house, with upper storeys rising one over another above us, and cellars down below.

The Bridge of the Dead is one of the well-marked myths of the Old World. The Zarathustrian religion recognizes the bridge Chinvat, made by Ahura-Mazda, whither souls of the dead on their way to give account of their deeds in life must come, the good to pass over, the wicked to fall into the abyss; to this day the

43 Humboldt & Bonpland, vol. ii. p. 276. D'Orbigny, 'L'Homme Américain'; vol. ii. p. 102. A closely related version of the heaven-tree among the Guarayos, Martius, 'Ethnog. Amer.,' vol. i. p. 218. The following are to be added to the group of myths. The Waraus of the Essequibo district lived in heaven till Okonorote went after a shot arrow which had fallen through a hole in the sky; seeing the earth he made a rope ladder by which his people descended, till a fat one stuck in the hole and made return impossible, Bastian, 'Rechtsverhältnisse,' p. 291. The Ahts of Vancouver's Island know of an ascent by a rope to a region above the earth, Sproat, 'Scenes of Savage Life,' London, 1868, p. 176. In the White Nile district, the Kych and Bari say God made all men good, and they lived with him in heaven, but as some of them turned bad he let them down by a rope to the earth; the good could climb up again by this rope to the sky, where there was dancing and beer and all was joyous, but the rope broke (or a bird bit it through) so there is no going up to heaven now; it is closed to men. A. Kaufmann, 'Gebiet des Weissen Flusses,' Brixen, 1861, p. 125. [Note to 3rd Edition.]

Parsi declares in solemn confession of his faith, that he is wholly without doubt in the stepping over the bridge Chinvat.[44] Perhaps it was from this Persian source that the myth found its way into Rabbinical literature,[45] and into the accepted belief of Islam. Over the midst of the Moslem Hell stretches the bridge Es-Sirat, finer than a hair, and sharper than the edge of a sword. There all souls of the dead must pass along, but while the good reach the other side in safety, the wicked fall off into the abyss.[46]

In Scandinavian mythology, the bridge on the Hell-way, where the pale unsubstantial dead ride over the river Gjöll, is part and parcel of the myth of Baldur in the Prose Edda.[47] But it seems rather from the Oriental group just described, that the ideas of the bridge in Christian Europe had their source. The "Brig of Dread, na brader than a thread," sung of in the grand old Lyke-Wake Dirge of our North Country,[48] was a recognized part of the architecture of Purgatory and Hell, to be seen and even passed over by the ecstatic explorers whose visions of the future state were a staple commodity of pious literature in the middle ages. It is thus described when Owayne Miles, one of King Stephen's Knights, descends into St. Patrick's Purgatory:—

> Over the water a brygge there was,
> Forsothe kenere than ony glasse:
> Hit was narowe and hit was hyge,
> Onethe that other end he syge.
> The mydylle was hyge, the ende was lowe,
> Hit ferde as hit hadde ben a bent bowe.
> The develle sayde, "Knyghte, here may thu se
> Into helle the rygte entré;
> Over thys brygge thu meste wende,
> Wynde and rayne we shulle the sende:
> We shulle the sende wynde full goode,
> That shall the caste ynto the floode."

44 Avesta, tr. by Spiegel & Bleeck, vol. i. p. 141, vol. ii. p. 14, vol. iii. p. 163; Alger, 'Doctrine of a Future Life'; New York, 1866, p. 136.

45 Eisenmenger, 'Entd. Judenthum'; part ii. p. 258.

46 Lane, Mod. Eg., vol. i. p. 95.

47 Prose Edda: Gylfaginning, 49. Grimm, D. M., p. 794.

48 Brand, Pop. Ant., vol. ii. p. 275.

But Owayne with prayer passed safely over and reached the Earthly Paradise on the other side.[49] The adaptation of the myth in Paradise Lost is too familiar to be quoted.

Looking to the far East, we find in the Hinduized and Islamized mythology of Java the bridge which leads across the abyss to the single opening in the stone wall round Suralaya, the dwelling of the gods; off this bridge the evildoers fall into the depths below.[50] Other myths from this region have more special and seemingly more local character. The conception of a bridge being needed for the passage of souls is well shown among the Karens of Birmah, who at this day tie strings across the rivers for the ghosts of the dead to pass over to their graves; among these people the Heaven-bridge is a sword, those who cross it become men, those who dare not, women.[51] And among the Idaan of Borneo, the passage for men into paradise is across a long tree, which to those who have not killed a man is scarcely practicable.[52]

In America, the bridge over the abyss is distinct in native mythology. The Greenland angekok, when he has passed through the land of souls, has to cross an awful gulf over a stretched rope, his guardian spirit holding him by the hand, till he reaches the abode of the great female Evil Spirit below the sea.[53] Among the North American Indians the Ojibwa soul has to cross the river of death on the great snake which serves as a bridge,[54] while the Minnetarees, in their way to the mansions of their ancestors after death, have to cross a narrow footing over a rapid river, where the good warriors and hunters pass, but the worthless ones fall in.[55] Catlin's account of the Choctaw belief is as follows:—"Our people all believe that the spirit lives in a future state; that it has a great distance to travel after death towards the west—that it has to cross a dreadful deep and rapid stream, which is hemmed in on both sides by high and rugged hills—over this stream, from

49 T. Wright, 'St. Patrick's Purgatory'; London, 1844, p. 74, and elsewhere.

50 Schirren, pp. 122, 125. For China, see Doolittle, 'Social Life of the Chinese'; vol. i. p. 173.

51 Mrs. Mason, p. 73; Mason in Journ. As. Soc. Bengal, 1865, part ii. p. 197.

52 Journ. Ind. Archip. vol. iii. p. 557.   54 Keating, vol. ii. p. 154.

53 Cranz, Grönland, p. 264.   55 Long's Exp., vol. i. p. 280.

hill to hill, there lies a long and slippery pine-log, with the bark peeled off, over which the dead have to pass to the delightful-hunting grounds. On the other side of the stream there are six persons of the good hunting-grounds with rocks in their hands, which they throw at them all when they are on the middle of the log. The good walk on safely to the good hunting-grounds. . . . The wicked see the stones coming, and try to dodge, by which they fall down from the log, and go thousands of feet to the water, which is dashing over the rocks."[56] In the interior of South America the idea appears again among the Manacicas. Among these people, the Maponos or priests performed a kind of baptism of the dead, and were then supposed to mount into the air, and carry the soul to the Land of the Departed. After a weary journey of many days over hills and vales, through forests, and across rivers and swamps and lakes, they came to a place where many roads met, near a deep and wide river, where the god Tatusiso stood night and day upon a wooden bridge to inspect all such travellers. If he did not consider the sprinkling after death a sufficient purgation of the sins of the departed, he would stop the priest, that the soul he carried might be further cleansed, and if resistance were made, would sometimes seize the unhappy soul and throw him into the river, and when this happened some calamity would follow among the Manacicas at home.[57]

The Bridge of the Dead may possibly have its origin in the rainbow. Among the Northmen the rainbow is to be seen in the bridge Bifröst of the three colours, over which the Æsir make their daily journey, and the red in it is fire, for were it easy to pass over, the Frost-giants and the Mountain-giants would get across it into heaven. In a remark, evidently belonging to the North American story of the Sun-Catcher, the rainbow replaces the tree up which the mouse climbs and gnaws loose a captive in the sky.[58] The rainbow is a ladder by which New Zealand chiefs climb to heaven, and by it the souls of the Philippine islanders

---

[56] Catlin, vol. ii. p. 127. See J. G. Müller, Amer. Urrelig. pp. 87, 286.

[57] Southey, 'Brazil,' vol. iii. p. 186.

[58] Schoolcraft in Pott, 'Ungleichheit der Menschlichen Rassen'; Lemgo, 1856, p. 267.

who died violent deaths were carried to the happy state.[59] The Milky Way, which among the North American Indians is the road of souls to the other world, has also a claim to be considered.[60] As in the Old World, so in the New, the Bridge of the Dead is but an incident, sometimes, but not always or even mostly, introduced into a wider belief that after death the soul of man comes to a great gulf or stream, which it has to pass to reach the country that lies beyond the grave. The Mythology of Polynesia, though it wants the Bridge, develops the idea of the gulf which the souls have to pass, in canoes or by swimming, into a long series of myths.[61] It is not needful to enter here into details of so well-known a feature of the Mythology of the Old World, where the Vedic Yama, King of the Dead, crossed the rapid waters and showed the way to our Aryan fathers; where the modern Hindu hopes by grasping the cow's tail at death to be safely ferried over the dreadful river Vaitaranî; where Charon and his boat, the procession of the dead by water to their long home in modern Brittany as in ancient Egypt, the setting afloat of the Scandinavian heroes in burning ships or burying them in boats on shore, are all instances of its prevalence. In barbaric districts, myths of the river of death may be instanced alike among the Finns and the Guinea negroes, among the Khonds of Orissa and the Dayaks of Borneo.[62] In North America we hear sometimes of the bridge, but sometimes the water must be passed in canoes. The souls come to a great lake where there is a beautiful island, towards which they have to paddle in a canoe of white shining stone. On the way there arises a storm, and the wicked souls are wrecked, and the heaps of their bones are to be seen under water, but the good reach the happy island.[63] So Charlevoix speaks of the souls that are shipwrecked in crossing the river which they have to pass on their long journey towards the west,[64] and with this belief the

59 Polack, N. Z., vol. i. p. 273. Meiners, vol. i. p. 302.

60 Le Jeune (1634), p. 63.

61 Williams, 'Fiji,' vol. i. pp. 244, 205. Schirren, pp. 93, 110, etc.

62 Castrén, p. 129, etc. Bosman, Guinea, in Pinkerton, vol. xvi. p. 401. Macpherson, p. 92. Journ. Ind. Archip., vol. i. p. 31.

63 Schoolcraft, part i. p. 321. Mackenzie, p. cxix.

64 Charlevoix, vol. vi. p. 76

canoe-burial of the North-West and of Patagonia hangs together. How the souls of the Ojibwas cross the deep and rapid water to reach the land of bliss,[65] and the souls of the Mandans travel on the lake by which the good reach their ancient village, while the wicked cannot get across for the burden of their sins,[66] I do not know; but, like the Heaven-Bridge, the Heaven-Gulf which has to be passed on the way to the Land of Spirits, has a claim to careful discussion in the general argument for the proof of historical connexion from Analogy of Myths.[67]

The Fountain of Youth is known to the Mythology of India. The Açvinas let the husband of Sukanyâ go into the lake, whence the bather comes forth as old or as young as he may choose; and elsewhere the "ageless river," *vijarâ nadî,* makes the old young again by only seeing it, or perhaps by bathing in its waters.[68] Perhaps it is this fountain that Sir John Maundevile tells of early in the fourteenth century somewhere about India. "Also toward the heed of that Forest is the Cytee of *Polombe.* And above the Cytee is a grete Mountayne, that also is clept *Polombe;* and of that Mount the Cytee hathe his name. And at the Foot of that Mount, is a fayr Welle and a gret, that hathe odour and savour of alle Spices; and at every hour of the day, he chaungethe his odour and his savour dyversely. And whoso drynkethe 3 tymes fasting of that Watre of that Welle, he is hool of alle maner sykenesse, that he hathe. And thei that dwellen there and drynken often of that Welle, thei nevere han Sekenesse, and thei semen alle ways ȝonge. I have dronken ther of 3 or 4 sithes; and ȝit, methinkethe, I fare the better. Sum men clepen it the Welle of ȝouthe: for thei that often drynken there of, semen alle weys ȝongly, and lyven with outen Sykenesse. And men seyn, that that Welle cometh out of *Paradys:* and therefore it is so vertuous."[69]

When Cambyses sent the Fish-Eaters to spy out the condition of the long-lived Ethiopians, and the messengers wondered to

---

[65] Schoolcraft, part ii. p. 135. [66] Lewis & Clarke, p. 139.

[67] For further remarks on these subjects, see Tylor, 'Primitive Culture,' chaps. xii.–xiv. [Note to 3rd Edition.]

[68] Kuhn, pp. 128, 12.

[69] The Voiage and Travaile of Sir John Maundevile, Kt.'; London, 1725, p. 204.

hear that they lived a hundred and twenty years or more, the Ethiopians took them to a fountain, where, when they had bathed, their bodies shone as if they had been oiled, and smelt like the scent of violets.[70] In Europe, too, stories of miraculously healing fountains have long been current.[71] The Moslem geographer Ibn-el-Wardi places the Fountain of Life in the dark southwestern regions of the earth. El-Khidr drank of it, and will live till the day of judgment; and Ilyas or Elias, whom popular belief mixes not only with El-Khidr, but also with St. George, the Dragon-slayer, has drunk of it likewise.[72] Farther east, the idea is to be found in the Malay islands. Batara Guru drinks from a poisonous spring, but saves himself and the rest of the gods by finding a well of life; and again, Nurtjaja compels the pandit Kabib, the guardian of the caverns below the earth, where flows the spring of immortality, to let him drink of its waters, and even to take some for his descendants.[73] In the Hawaiian legend, Kamapiikai, "the child who runs over the sea," goes with forty companions to Tahiti (Kahiki, that is to say, to the land *far away*), and brings back wondrous tales of Haupokane, "the belly of Kane," and of the *wai ora, waiola,* "water of life," *wai ora roa,* "water of enduring life," which removes all sickness, deformity, and decrepitude from those who plunge beneath its waters.[74] It is perhaps to this story of the Sandwich Islands that Turner refers, when he says that some South Sea islanders have traditions of a river in the spirit-world called "Water of Life," which makes the old young again, and they return to earth to live another life.[75]

One easy explanation of the Fountain of Youth suggests itself at the first glance. Every islander who can see the sun go down old, faint, and weary into the western sea, to rise young and fresh from the waters, has the Fountain of Youth before him; and

[70] Herod. iii. c. 23.

[71] Grimm, D. M., p. 554. Perty, p. 149.

[72] Lane, 'Thousand and One Nights,' vol. i. p. 20. See Bastian, vol. ii. pp. 158, 371.

[73] Schirren, p. 124.

[74] Schirren, p. 80. Ellis, Polyn. Res. vol. ii. p. 47. Ellis, 'Hawaii'; London, 1827, p. 399.

[75] Turner, p. 353.

this explanation of several, at least, of the stories is strengthened by their details, as when the fountain is described as flowing in the regions below, or in the belly of Kane, where the boy who climbs over the sea goes to it; or when, like the dying and reviving sun, Batara Guru is poisoned, but finds the reviving water, and is cured;[76] or when the Moslem associates the drinking from the fountain with Elijah of the chariot of fire and horses of fire, or with St. George, the favourite mediæval bearer of the great Sun-myth. Without further discussing the origin of these myths, it may suffice to point out their occurrence in the New World. The Aleutian islanders had their legend that in the early times men were immortal, and when they grew old had but to spring from a high mountain into a lake whence they came forth in renewed youth. In the West Indies, early in the sixteenth century, Gomara relates that Juan Ponce de Leon, having his government taken from him, and thus finding himself rich and without charge, fitted out two caravels, and went to seek for the island of Boyuca, where the Indians said there was the fountain that turned old men back into youths (a perennial spring, says Peter Martyr, so noble that the drinking of its waters made old men young again). For six months he went lost and famishing among many islands, but of such a fountain he found no trace. Then he came to Bimini, and discovered Florida on Pascua Florida (Easter Sunday), wherefrom he gave the country its name.[77]

To proceed now to the story of the Tail-Fisher. Dr. Dasent, who, in his admirable Introduction to the Norse Tales, has taken the lead in the extension of the argument from Comparative Mythology beyond the limited range within which it is aided by History and Language, has brought the popular tales of Africa and Europe into close connexion by adducing, among others, the unmistakable common origin of the Norse Tale of the Bear who, at the instigation of the Fox, fishes with his tail through a hole in the ice till it is frozen in, and then pulls at it till it comes off, and

---

[76] For etym. etc. of Batara Guru, see W. v. Humboldt, Kawi-Spr., vol. i. p. 100; Schirren, p. 116; also Crawfurd, Introd., p. cxviii. and *s. vv.* batara, guru.

[77] Gomara, Hist. Gen. de las Indias; Medina del Campo, 1553, part i, vol. xxiii. Petri Martyri De Orbe Novo (1516), ed. Hakluyt; Paris, 1587, dec. ii. c. 10. Galvano, p. 123.

the story from Bornu of the Hyæna who puts his tail into the hole, that the Weasel may fasten the meat to it, but the Weasel fastens a stick to it instead, and the Hyæna pulls till his tail breaks; both stories accounting in a similar way, but with a proper difference of local colouring, for the fact that bears and hyænas are stumpy-tailed.[78]

A similar story is told in Reynard the Fox, less appositely, of the Wolf instead of the Bear,[79] and in the Celtic story recently published by Mr. Campbell, it is again the Wolf who loses his tail. In this latter story, by that kaleidoscopic arrangement of incidents which is so striking a feature of Mythology, the losing of the tail is combined with the episode of taking the reflection of the moon for a cheese, which occurs in another connexion in Reynard,[80] and is apparently the origin of our popular saying about the moon being made of green cheese.

> He made an instrument to know
> If the moon shine at full or no;
> That would, as soon as e'er she shone, straight
> Whether 'twere day or night demonstrate;
> Tell what her d'ameter to an inch is,
> And prove that she's not made of green cheese.[81]

Here, of course, "green cheese" means, like τυρὸς χλωρός, fresh, white cheese. In the Highland tale the Fox shows the Wolf the moon on the ice, and tells him it is a cheese, and he must cover it with his tail to hide it, till the Fox goes to see that the farmer is asleep. When the tail is frozen tight the Fox alarms the farmer, and the Wolf leaves his tail behind him.[82]

"The tailless condition both of the bear and the hyæna," Dr. Dasent remarks, "could scarcely fail to attract attention in a race of hunters, and we might expect that popular tradition would attempt to account for both." The reasonableness of this conjec-

[78] Dasent, 'Popular Tales from the Norse'; (2nd ed.) Edinburgh, 1859, pp. 1, 197.

[79] Grimm, 'Reinhart Fuchs,' pp. civ. cxxii. 51.

[80] Grimm, 'Reinhart Fuchs,' p. cxxvii.

[81] 'Hudibras,' part ii. canto iii.

[82] Campbell, 'Popular Tales of the West Highlands'; Edinburgh, 1860, vol. i. p. 272.

ture is well shown in the case of two older shorttailed beasts, in a mythical episode from Central America, which bears no appearance of being historically connected with the rest, but looks as though it had been devised independently to account for the facts. When the two princes Hunahpu and Xbalanqué set themselves one day to till the ground, the axe cut down the trees and the mattock cleared away the underwood, while the masters amused themselves with shooting. But next day, when they came back, they found the trees and creepers and brambles back in their places. So they cleared the ground again, and hid themselves to watch, and at midnight all the beasts came, small and great, saying in their language, "Trees, arise; creepers, arise!" and they came close to the two princes. First came the Lion and the Tiger, and the princes tried to catch them, but could not. Then came the Stag and the Rabbit, and them they caught by their tails, but the tails came off, and so the Stag and the Rabbit have still but "scarce a stump" left them to this day. But the Fox and the Jackal and the Boar and the Porcupine and the other beasts passed by, and they could not catch one till the Rat came leaping along; he was the last and they got in his way and caught him in a cloth. They pinched his head and tried to choke him, and burnt his tail over the fire, and since then the rat has had a hairless tail, and his eyes are as if they had been squeezed out of his head. But he begged to be heard, and told them it was not their business to till the ground, for the rings and gloves and the india-rubber ball, the instruments of the princely game, were hidden in their grandmother's house, and so forth.[83]

The curious mythic art of Tail-fishing only forms a part of the stories how the Bear, the Wolf, and the Hyæna came to lose their tails in Europe and Africa. But this particular idea, taken by itself, has a wide geographical range both in the Old and New Worlds. A story current in India, apparently among the Tamil population of the South, is told by the Rev. J. Roberts, who says, speaking of the jackal, "this animal is very much like the fox of England in his habits and appearance. I have been told, that they often catch the crab by putting their tail into its hole, which the

[83] Brasseur, 'Popul-Vuh,' pp. 118–25.

creature immediately seizes, in hope of food: the jackal then drags it out and devours it."[84]

In North America, the bearer of the story is the racoon. "Lawson relates, that those which formerly lived on the salt waters in Carolina, fed on oysters, which they nimbly snatched when the shell opened; but that sometimes the paw was caught, and held till the return of the tide, in which the animal, though it swims well, was sometimes drowned. His art in catching crabs is still more extraordinary. Standing on the borders of the waters where this shell-fish abounds, he keeps the end of his tail floating on the surface, which the crab seizes, and he then leaps forward with his prey, and destroys it in a very artful manner."[85] In South America, the art is given to two other very cunning creatures, the monkey and the jaguar. I have been informed by one of the English explorers in British Guiana, that it is a current story there, that the monkey catches fish by letting them take hold of the end of his tail. Southey, quoting from a manuscript description of the district flooded by the River Paraguay, called the Lago Xarayes, says "when the floods are out the fish leave the river to feed upon certain fruits: as soon as they hear or feel the fruit strike the water, they leap to catch it as it rises to the surface, and in their eagerness spring into the air. From this habit the Ounce has learnt a curious strategem; he gets upon a projecting bough, and from time to time strikes the water with his tail, thus imitating the sound which the fruit makes as it drops, and as the fish springs towards it, he catches them with his paw."[86] More recently, the story has been told again by Mr. Wallace: "The jaguar, say the Indians, is the most cunning animal in the forest: he can imitate the voice of almost every bird and animal so exactly, as to draw them towards him: he fishes in the rivers, lashing the water with his tail to imitate falling fruit, and when the fish approach, hooks them up with his claws."[87] It may be objected against the use of the tail-fishing story as mythological evidence, that there may possibly be some foundation for it in actual fact;

[84] Roberts, 'Oriental Illustrations,' p. 172.

[85] D. B. Warden, Account of U.S.; Edinburgh, 1819, vol. i. p. 199.

[86] Southey, vol. i. p. 142.   [87] Wallace, p. 455.

and it is indeed hardly more astonishing, for instance, than the jaguar's turning a number of river-turtles on their backs to be eaten at his leisure, a story which Humboldt accepts as true. But the way in which the tail-fishing is attributed in different countries to one animal after another, the bear, the wolf, the hyæna, the jackal, the racoon, the monkey, and the jaguar, authorizes the opinion that, in most cases at least, it is one of those floating ideas which are taken up as part of the story-teller's stock in trade, and used where it suits him, but with no particular subordination to fact.

Lastly, another Old World story which has a remarkable analogue in South America is that of the Diable Boiteux. This, however, in the state in which it is known to modern Europe, is a conception a good deal modified under Christian influences. In the old mythology of our race, it is the Fire-god who is lame. The unsteady flickering of the flames may perhaps be figured in the crooked legs and hobbling gait of Hephæstus, and Zeus casts him down from heaven to earth like his crooked lightnings; while the stories which correspond with the Vulcan-myth on German ground tell of the laming of Wieland, our Wayland Smith, the representative of Hephæstus. The transfer of the lameness of the Fire-god to the Devil seems to belong to the mixture of the Scriptural Satan with the ideas of heathen gods, elves, giants, and demons, which go to form that strange compound, the Devil of popular mediæval belief.[88]

There is something very quaint in the notion of a lame god or devil, but it is quite a familiar one in South Africa. The deity of the Namaquas and other tribes is Tsui'kuap, whose principal attributes seem to be the causing of pain and death. This being received a wound in his knee in a great fight, and "Wounded-knee" appears to be the meaning of his name.[89] Moffat's account, which is indeed not very clear, fits with a late remark made by Livingstone among another people of South Africa, the Bakwains. He observes that near the village of Sechele there is a cave

---

[88] Welcker, 'Griechische Götterlehre'; Göttingen, 1857, etc., vol. i. pp. 661–5. Grimm, D. M., pp. 221, 351, 937–8, 944, 963. See Schirren, p. 164.

[89] Moffat, pp. 257–9.

called Lepelole, which no one dared to enter, for it was the common belief that it was the habitation of the Deity, and that no one who went in ever came out again. "It is curious," he says, "that in all their pretended dreams or visions of their god he has always a crooked leg, like the Egyptian Thau."[90] Even in Australia something similar is to be found. The Biam is held to be like a black, but deformed in his lower extremities; the natives say they got many of the songs sung at their dances from him, but he also causes diseases, especially one which marks the face like small-pox.[91]

The Diable Boiteux of South America is thus described by Pöppig, in his account of the life of the forest Indians of Mainas. "A ghostly being, the Uchuclla-chaqui or Lame-foot, alone troubles the source of his best pleasure and his livelihood. Where the forest is darkest, where only the light-avoiding amphibia and the nocturnal birds dwell, lives this dangerous creature, and endeavours, by putting on some friendly shape, to lure the Indian to his destruction. As the sociable hunters do, it gives the well understood signs, and, never reached itself, entices the deluded victim deeper and deeper into the solitude, disappearing with a shout of mocking laughter when the path home is lost, and the terrors of the wilderness are increasing with the growing shadows of night. Sometimes it separates companions who have gone hunting together, by appearing first in one place, then in another in an altered form; but it never can deceive the wary hunter who in distrust examines the footsteps of his enemy. Hardly has he caught sight of the quite unequal size of the impressions of the feet, when he hastens back, and for long after no one dares to make an expedition into the wilderness, for the visits of the fiend are only for a time."[92] In South America, as in Africa, this is not a mere local tale, but a widely spread belief.

In conclusion, the analogies between the Mythology of America

[90] Livingstone, p. 124. He means, I presume, Pthah, or rather Pthah-Sokari Osiris.

[91] Eyre, vol. ii. p. 362.

[92] Pöppig, 'Reise in Chile,' etc.; Leipzig, 1835, vol. ii. p. 358. Klemm, C. G., vol. i. p. 276.

and of the rest of the world which have been here enumerated, when taken together with the many more which come into view in studying a wider range of native American traditions, and after full allowance has been made for independent coincidences, seem to me to warrant some expectation that the American Mythology may have to be treated as embodying materials common to other districts of the world, mixed no doubt with purely native matter. Such a view would bring the early history of America into definite connexion with that of other regions, over a larger geographical range than that included in Humboldt's argument, and would bear with some force, though of course but indirectly, on the problem of the diffusion of mankind.

CHAPTER X

CONCLUDING REMARKS

It has been intimated that the present series of Essays affords no sufficient foundation for a definite theory of the Rise and Progress of Human Civilization in early times. Nor, indeed, will any such foundation be ready for building upon, until a great deal of preparatory work has been done. Still, the evidence which has here been brought together seems to tell distinctly for or against some widely circulated Ethnological theories, and also to justify a certain amount of independent generalization, and the results of the foregoing chapters in this way may now be briefly summed up, with a few additional remarks.

In the first place, the facts collected seem to favour the view that the wide differences in the civilization and mental state of the various races of mankind are rather differences of development than of origin, rather of degree than of kind. Thus the Gesture-Language is the same in principle, and similar in its details, all over the world. The likeness in the formation both of pure myths and of those crude theories which have been described as "myths of observation," among races so dissimilar in the colour of their skins and the shape of their skulls, tells in the same direction. And wherever the occurrence of any art or knowledge in two places can be confidently ascribed to independent invention, as, for instance, when we find the dwellers in the ancient lake-habitations of Switzerland, and the Modern New Zealanders, adopting a like construction in their curious fabrics of tied bundles of fibre, the similar step thus made in different times and places tends to prove the similarity of the minds that made it. Moreover, to take a somewhat weaker line of argument, the uniformity with which like stages in the development of art and science are found among the most unlike races, may be adduced as evidence on the same side, in spite of the constant difficulty in deciding whether any particular development is due to independent invention, or to transmission from some other people to those among whom it is found. For if the similar thing has been produced in two places by independent invention, then, as has just been said, it is direct evidence of similarity of mind. And on the other hand, if it was carried from the one place to the other, or from a third to both, by mere transmission from people to people, then the smallness of the change it has suffered in transplanting is still evidence of the like nature of the soil wherever it is found.

Considered both from this and other points of view, this uniform development of the lower civilization is a matter of great interest. The state of things which is found is not indeed that one race does or knows exactly what another race does or knows, but that similar stages of development recur in different times and places. There is reason to suppose that our ancestors in remote times made fire with a machine much like that of the modern Esquimaux, and at a far later date they used the bow and arrow, as so many savage tribes do still. The foregoing chapters treating of the history of some early arts, of the practice of sorcery, of curious customs and superstitions, are indeed full of instances of the recurrence of like phenomena in the remotest regions of the world. We might reasonably expect that men of like minds, when placed under widely different circumstances of country, climate, vegetable and animal life, and so forth, should develop very various phenomena of civilization, and we even know by evidence that they actually do so; but nevertheless it strikingly illustrates the extent of mental uniformity among mankind to notice that it is really difficult to find, among a list of twenty items of art or knowledge, custom or superstition, taken at random from a description of any uncivilized race, a single one to which something closely analogous may not be found elsewhere among some other race, unlike the first in physical characters, and living thousands of miles off. It is taking a somewhat extreme case to put the Australians to such a test, for they are perhaps the most peculiar of the lower varieties of Man, yet among the arts, beliefs, and customs, found among their tribes, there are comparatively few that cannot be matched elsewhere. They raise scars on their bodies like African tribes; they circumcise like the Jews and Arabs; they bar marriage in the female line like the Iroquois; they drop out of their language the names of plants and animals which have been used as the personal names of dead men, and make new words to serve instead, like the Abipones of South America; they bewitch their enemies with locks of hair, and pretend to cure the sick by sucking out stones through their skin, as is done in so many other regions. It is true that among their weapons they have one of very marked, perhaps even specific peculiarity, the boomerang, but the rest of their armoury, the spear, the spear-thrower, the club, the throwing-cudgel, are but varieties of instruments common elsewhere, and the same is true of their fire-drill, their stone hatchet, their nets and baskets, their bark canoes and rafts. And while among the Australians there are only a very few exceptions to modify the general rule that whatever is found in one place in the world may be matched more or less closely elsewhere, piecemeal or as a whole, the proportion of such exceptions is smaller, and consequently the uniformity of development more strikingly marked, among most of the other races of the world who have not risen above the lower levels of culture.

In the next place, the collections of facts relating to various useful arts seem to justify the opinion that, in such practical matters at least, the history of mankind has been on the whole a history of progress. Over almost the whole world are found traces of the former use of stone implements, now superseded by metal; rude and laborious means of making fire have been supplanted by easier and better processes; over large regions of the earth the art of boiling in earthen or metal pots over the fire has succeeded the ruder art of stone-boiling; in three distant countries the art of writing sounds is found developing itself out of mere picture-writing, and this phonetic writing has superseded in several districts the use of quipus, or knotted cords, as a means of record and communication. In the chapter particularly devoted to evidence of progress, a number of facts are stated which seem to be records of a forward development in other arts, in times and places beyond the range of history. On the other hand, though arts which flourish in times of great refinement or luxury, and complex processes which require a combination of skill or labour hard to get together, and liable to be easily disarranged, may often degenerate, yet the more homely and useful the art, and the less difficult the conditions for its exercise, the less likely it is to disappear from the world, unless when superseded by some better device. Races may and do leave off building temples and monuments of sculptured stone, and fall off in the execution of masterpieces of metal-work and porcelain, but there is no evidence of any tribe giving up the use of the spindle to twist their thread by hand, or having been in the habit of working the fire-drill with a thong, and going back to the clumsier practice of working it without, and it is even hard to fancy such a thing happening. Since the Hottentots have learnt, within the last two centuries or so, to smelt the iron ore of their country, it is hard to imagine that anything short of extirpating them or driving them into a country destitute of iron, could make them go back to the Stone Age in which their ancestors lived. Some facts are quoted which bear on the possible degeneration of savage tribes when driven out into the desert, or otherwise reduced to destitution, or losing their old arts in the presence of a higher civilization, but there seems ground for thinking that such degeneration has been rather of a local than of a general character, and has rather affected the fortunes of particular tribes than the development of the world at large. I do not think I have ever met with a single fact which seems to me to justify the theory, of which Dr. von Martius is perhaps the leading advocate, that the ordinary condition of the savage is the result of degeneration from a far higher state.[1] The chapter on "Images and Names," which explains the arts of Magic as the effects of an early mental condition petrified into a series of mystic observances carried up into the midst of a higher culture, is indeed in the strongest opposition to the view strongly advocated by degenerationists, that these superstitious practices are mutilated remnants of a high system of belief which

[1] Dr. V. Martius, 'Vergangenheit und Zukunft der Amerikanischen Menschheit'; 1839. It appears, however, that the late Dr. Martius is no longer to be reckoned among the supporters of the degeneration-theory, as in later years he saw cause to reverse his early views. Since the date of the first edition of the present work, he has published his opinion as to the Amazons tribes, that there is no ground for considering their barbarous condition a secondary one, nor that it was preceded by a higher state of morals, or a past civilization. See Martius, 'Beiträge zur Ethnographie Amerika's,' Leipzig, 1867, vol. i. p. 375; also Peschel, 'Völkerkunde,' Leipzig, 1874, p. 137. [Note to 3rd Edition.]

prevailed in former times. So far as may be judged from the scanty and defective evidence which has as yet been brought forward, I venture to think the most reasonable opinion to be that the course of development of the lower civilization has been on the whole in a forward direction, though interfered with occasionally and locally by the results of degrading and destroying influences.

Granting the existence of this onward movement in the lower levels of art and science, the question then arises, how any particular piece of skill or knowledge has come into any particular place where it is found. Three ways are open, independent invention, inheritance from ancestors in a distant region, transmission from one race to another; but between these three ways the choice is commonly a difficult one. Sometimes, indeed, the first is evidently to be preferred. Thus, though the floating gardens of Mexico and Cashmere are very similar devices, it seems more likely that the Mexican *chinampa* was invented on the spot than that the idea of it was imported from a distant region. Though the wattled cloth of the Swiss lake-dwellings is so similar in principle to that of New Zealand, it is much easier to suppose it the result of separate invention than of historical connexion. Though both the Egyptians and Chinese came upon the expedient of making the picture of an object stand for the sound which was the name of that object, there is no reason to doubt their having done so independently.

But the more difficult it is to account for observed facts in this way, and the more necessary it becomes to have recourse to theories of inheritance or transmission to explain them, the greater is their value in the eyes of the Ethnologist. Wherever he can judge that the existence of similar phenomena in the culture of distant peoples cannot be fairly accounted for, except by supposing that there has been a connexion by blood or by intercourse between them, then he has before him evidence bearing upon the history of civilization and on the history of mankind, evidence which shows that such movements as have introduced guns, axes, books, into America—in historic times, have also taken place in unhistoric times among tribes whose ancestors have left them no chronicles of past ages. Thus the appearing of the

Malay smelting-furnace in Madagascar, and of the outrigger canoe in East Australia and the Andaman Islands, may be appealed to as evidence of historical connexion. It is possible that the Ethnographer may some day feel himself justified in giving to this kind of argument a far wider range. He may not perhaps venture on extreme arguments, such, for instance, as to claim for the bow and arrow a common origin wherever it is found, that is, over the whole world with perhaps no exception but part of Polynesia, and part or the whole of Australia. Yet, noticing that the distribution of the potter's art in North America is not sporadic, as if a tribe here and a tribe there had wanted it and invented it, but that it rises northwards in a compact field from Mexico among the tribes East of the Rocky Mountains, he may more forcibly argue that it spread from a single source, and is at once a result and a proof of the transmission of civilization. Indeed, it seems as though the recurrence of similar groups in the inventories of instruments and works of the lower races, so remarkable both in the presence of like things and the comparative absence of unlike ones, might come to supply, in a more advanced state of Ethnography, the materials for an indefinite series of arguments bearing on the early history of man.

It is not to be denied, however, that there is usually a large element of uncertainty in inferences of this kind taken alone, and it is only in special cases that summary generalizations from such evidence can as yet be admitted. Indeed, its proper place is rather as accompanying the argument from language, mythology, and customs, than as standing by itself. Thus the appearance, just referred to, of the Malay blast-furnace in Madagascar has to be viewed in connexion with the affinity in language between Madagascar and the islands of the Eastern Archipelago. Putting the two things together, we may assume that the connexion with Madagascar dates from a time since the introduction of iron-smelting in a part of the great Malayo-Polynesian district, and belongs to that particular group of islands near the Eastern coast of Asia where this immense step in material civilization was made. Again, the philological researches of Buschmann, which have brought into view traces of the Aztec language up into the heart of North America, fifteen hundred miles and more north of the City of Mexico, join with several other lines of evidence in bringing far distant parts of the population of the continent into historical connexion, and in showing, at least, that such communication between its different peoples as may have spread the art of pottery from a single locality is not matter of mere speculation. It is in this way that it will probably be found most expedient to use fragmentary arguments from the distribution of the arts and sciences of savage tribes, in Ethnological districts where a way has been already opened by more certain methods.

In its bearing on the History of Mankind, the tendency of modern research in the region of Comparative Mythology is not to be mistaken. The number of myths recorded as found in different countries, where it is hardly conceivable that they should have grown independently, goes on steadily increasing from year to year, each one furnishing a new clue by which common descent or intercourse is to be traced. Such evidence, as fast as it is brought before the public, is received with the most lively interest; and not only is its value fully admitted, but there may even be observed a tendency to use it with too much confidence in proof of common descent, without enough consideration of what we know of the way in which Mythology really travels from race to race. The cause of the occurrence of a myth, or of a whole family of myths, may be, and no doubt often is, mere intercourse, which has as little to do with common descent as the connexion which has planted the stories of the Arabian Nights among the Malays of Borneo, and the legends of Buddha among the Chinese. On the other hand, the argument from similar Customs has received, as a whole, comparatively little attention, but it is not without importance. Two or three, at least, of the customs remarked upon in the present volume, in the group including the cure by sucking, the couvade, and others, such as the wide-spread superstitions connected with sneezing, on which Mr. Haliburton gave a lecture, in 1863, at Halifax, Nova Scotia,[2] may be adduced as facts for the occurrence of which in so many distant times and places it is hard to account on any other hypothesis than that of deep-lying connexions by blood or intercourse, among races which

2 R. G. Haliburton, 'New Materials for the History of Man'; Halifax, N.S. 1863.

history, and even philology, only know as isolated sections of the population of the world. Whether such customs had one or several original sources, their present diffusion seems in great measure due to propagation from district to district.

On the whole, it does not seem to be an unreasonable, or even an over-sanguine view, that the mass of analogies in Art and Knowledge, Mythology and Custom, confused and indistinct as they at present are, may already be taken to indicate that the civilizations of many races, whose history even the evidence of Language has not succeeded in bringing into connexion, have really grown up under one another's influences, or derived common material from a common source. But that such lines of argument should ever be found to converge in the last instance towards a single point, so as to enable the student to infer from reasoning on a basis of observed facts that the civilization of the whole world has its origin in one parent stock, is a state of things of which not even the most dim and distant view is to be obtained.

On another subject, on which it would not be prudent to offer a definite opinion, a few words may nevertheless be said. Every attempt to trace back the early history of civilization tends, however remotely, towards an ultimate limit—the primary condition of the human race, as regards their knowledge of the laws of nature and their power of modifying the outer world for their own ends. Such lines of investigation as go back from the Bronze or Iron Ages to the time of the use of implements of stone, from the higher to the lower methods of fire-making, from the boat to the raft, from the use of the spindle to the art of hand-twisting, and so on, seem to enable the student to see back through the history of human culture to a state of art and science somewhat resembling that of the savage tribes of modern times. It is useful to work back to this point, at least as a temporary resting-place in the argument, seeing that a state of things really known to exist is generally more convenient to reason upon than a purely theoretical one. But if we may judge that the present condition of savage tribes is the complex result of not only a long but an eventful history, in which development of culture may have been more or less interfered with by degradation caused by war, disease, oppression, and other mishaps, it does not seem likely that any tribe known to modern observers should be anything like a fair representative of primary conditions. Still, positive evidence of anything lower than the known state of savages is scarce in the extreme. That the men whose tools and weapons are found in the Drift Beds, in the Bone Caves, and in the Shell-Heaps of Denmark, were not in the habit of grinding the edges of any of their stone implements, may be instanced as evidence of a singularly low condition of one of the useful arts. The general character of this lowest division of the Stone Age, as exemplified among tribes of remote præ-historic times, seems to place their state of civilization below that recorded among tribes known to travellers or historians.

To turn to a very different department of culture, some of the facts belonging to the history of custom and superstition may for the last time be referred to, as perhaps having their common root in a mental condition underlying anything to be met with now. We have seen prevalent among savages and barbarians a state of mind which helps us to account for the whole business of Magic, including the arts of omen-taking by astrology and other kinds of divination, and of bewitching by means of images and names of persons, with its counter-system of prevention and cure by sympathy, the last including the quaintly instructive custom of the couvade. But it looks as though even savages have but the remains of this magical state of mind inherited from ancestors of yet lower culture, and that they have begun to outgrow it, as the civilized world has more fully done. The early fusion of objective and subjective relations in the mind, of the effects of which in superstitious practices handed down from age to age so much has been said in this book, may perhaps not be fully or exactly represented in the mental state of any living tribe of men.

There have been indeed few more important movements in the course of the history of mankind, than this change of opinion as to the nature and relations of what is in the mind and what is out of it. To say nothing of its vast effects upon Ethics and Religion, the whole course of Science, and of Art, of which Science is a principal element, has been deeply influenced by this mental change. Man's views of the difference between imagination and reality, of the nature of cause and effect, of the connexion between himself and the external world, and of the parts of the external world among themselves, have been entirely altered by it. To the times before this movement had gone too far, belong the developments of Mythology, so puzzling to later ages which had risen to a higher mental state, and had then thrown down the ladder they had climbed by. The modern deciphering of ancient myths has been perhaps more valuable than any direct examination of savage races, in giving us the means of realizing that early state of mind in which there is scarcely any distinct barrier between fact and fancy—to which whatever is similar is the same. If the clouds are driven across the sky like cows from their pasture, they are not merely compared to cows, but are thought and talked of as though they really were cows; if the sun travels along its course like a glittering chariot, forthwith the wheels and the driver and the horses are there; while by treating a name as though it necessarily represented a person, it becomes possible to evolve out of the contemplation of nature those wonderful stories in which even the earth, the sea, and the sky, combine with their natural attributes a kind of half-human personality. The opinion that dreams and phantasms have an objective existence out of the mind that perceives them, and that when two ideas are associated in a man's mind the objects to which those ideas belong must have a corresponding physical connexion, are views over which the long course of observation and study of nature has brought a vast change. These things belong to that early condition of the human mind, from which, to say nothing of the special views of metaphysicians and leaders in science, the ordinary ideas of Man and Nature held by educated men differ so widely. However far these ideas may in their turn be left behind, the growth which can be traced within the range of our own observation and inference, is one of no scant measure. It may bear comparison with one of the great changes in the mental life of the individual man, perhaps rather with the expansion and fixing of the mind which accompanies the passage from infancy into youth, than with the later steps from youth into manhood, or from manhood into old age.

APPENDIX

FIRE, COOKING, AND VESSELS

There are a number of stories, old and new, of tribes of mankind living in ignorance of the art of fire-making. Such a state of things is indeed usually presupposed by the widespread legends of first fire-makers or fire-bringers, and Plutarch, in his essay on the question "Whether water or fire is the more useful?" gives a typical view of the matter. Fire was invented, as they say, by Prometheus, and our life shows that this was not a poetic fiction. For there are some races of men who live without fire, houseless, hearthless, and dwelling in the open air.[1] The modern point of view is, however, very different from Plutarch's, and when the mention of a fireless race appears in company with a Prometheus, mythology, not history, claims it. The mere assertion that in a certain place a race is, or was, to be found living without fire is more difficult to deal with. In examining a collection of such statements, it is well to pay particular attention to the modern ones, on which collateral evidence may be brought to bear.

What is known of the native civilization of the Canary Islands, the making of pottery, the cooking in underground ovens, the use of the fire-drill, leaves no doubt that the Guanches knew how to produce and use fire at the time of the European expeditions in the 14th and 15th centuries. Yet Antonio Galvano, writing his treatise about the middle of the sixteenth century, declares that "in times past they ate raw meat, for want of fire." Farther on in the same book he has another story of a fireless people. In 1529, Alvaro de Saavedra, returning from the Moluccas towards the Pacific coast of Mexico, sailed eastward along the north coast of New Guinea, and having gone four or five degrees south of the Line, crossed again to the north, and discovered an island of tattooed people, which he called Isla de los Pintados, or the isle

Chapter IX in the original.

[1] Plut., 'Aqua an Ignis utilior?'

of painted men. Beyond this island, in 10° or 12° N., they found many small smooth ones together, full of palms and grass, and these they called Los Jardines, "The Gardens." The natives had no domestic animals, they were dressed in a white cloth of grass, ate coco-nuts for bread, and raw fish, which they took in the praus which they made out of drift pine-wood with their tools of shell. They stood in terror of fire, for they had never seen it (espantaram se do fogo, porque nunca o viram).[2] I am not aware that these islands have been identified, but they would seem to be somewhere about the Radack or Chatham group. The account of the natives, to judge by its general consistency with what is known of the common eating of raw vegetables and fish in other coral islands in the Pacific, seems to have come mostly or altogether from an eye-witness, and the statement that they had no fire is not to be summarily set down as a mere fiction, like that about the Canary Islands. It has fortunately happened, however, that a very similar story has come up in our own time about another coral island, under circumstances which allow of its accuracy being tested. When the United States' Exploring Expedition, under Commodore Wilkes, visited Fakaafo or Bowditch Island in 1841, they made the following remarks:—"There was no sign of places for cooking, nor any appearance of fire, and it is believed that all their provisions are eaten raw. What strengthened this opinion, was the alarm the natives felt when they saw the sparks emanating from the flint and steel, and the emission of smoke from the mouths of those who were smoking cigars."[3]

Curiously enough, within the very work which contains these remarks, particulars are given which show that fire was in reality a familiar thing in the island. Mr. Hale, the ethnographer to the expedition, not only mentions the appearance of smoke on the neighbouring Duke of York's Island as being evidence of natives being there, but he gives the name for fire in the language of Fakaafo, *afi*,[4] a most widely-spread Malayo-Polynesian word, cor-

2 Galvano, 'Discoveries of the World'; Hakluyt Soc., London, 1862, pp. 66, 174–9, 238.

3 Wilkes, 'Narr. of U.S. Exploring Exp., 1838–42'; London, 1845, vol. v. p. 18.

4 Hale, 'Ethnography, etc., of U.S. Exp.'; Philadelphia ed. vol. vi. 1846, pp. 149, 363.

responding to the Malay form *api*. Some years later, the Rev. George Turner again mentions this word *afi*, and gives besides a native story about fire, which is an interesting example of the way in which a mere myth may nevertheless be a piece of historical evidence. The account which the inhabitants of Fakaafo give of the introduction of fire among themselves is thus related. "The origin of fire they trace to Mafuike, but, unlike the Mafuike of the mythology of some other islands, this was an old blind *lady*. Talangi went down to her in her lower regions, and asked her to give him some of her fire. She obstinately refused until he threatened to kill her, and then she yielded. With the fire he made her say what fish were to be cooked with it, and what were still to be eaten raw, and then began the time of cooking food." Utter myth as this story is, it yet joins with the evidence of language in bringing the history of the islanders who tell it into connexion with the history of the distant New Zealanders. It belongs to the great Polynesian myth of Maui, who, the New Zealand story says, went away to the dwelling of his great ancestress Mahuika, and got fire from her.[5] And it proves that, even in the past time when these two versions of the story branched off, one to be found in Fakaafo, and the other in New Zealand, not only was fire known, but its discovery had become already a thing of the forgotten past, or a myth would not have been applied to explain it.

In his account of the natives of Fakaafo, Mr. Turner speaks of their recollection of the time when they used fire in felling trees, and he mentions, moreover, some curious native ordinances respecting fire. "No fire is allowed to be kindled at night in the houses of the people all the year round. It is sacred to the god, and so, after sundown, they sit and chat in the dark. There are only two exceptions to the rule: first, fire to cook fish caught in the night, but then it must not be taken to their houses, only to the cooking-house; and second, a light is allowed at night in a house where there happens to be a confinement."[6] It is likely that Wilkes may have misinterpreted the surprise of the natives at seeing cigars smoked, and fire produced from the flint and steel,

[5] Sir G. Grey, 'Polynesian Mythology'; London, 1855, pp. 45–9.

[6] Turner, 'Polynesia,' pp. 527–8, and Vocab.

as well as the eating of raw fish and the absence of signs of cooking in the dwellings. If the similar story of the islanders of Los Jardines really came from an eye-witness, it may have arisen in much the same way. In Kotzebue's time, the people of the Radack group (which may be perhaps the very Jardines in question) were just as much astonished at the smith's forge, though fire was a well-known thing to them.[7]

The circumstances of Magalhaens' discovery of the Ladrones or Marian Islands, and the Philippines, in 1521, are known to us from the narrative of his companion Antonio Pigafetta,[8] who describes the manners and customs of the natives, but without a hint that fire was anything strange to them. This preposterous addition must be sought in later authors. In 1652, Horn, not content with quoting Galvano's stories of the Canaries and Los Jardines, adds the natives of the Philippines as a race destitute of fire.[9] But the story of the Ladrone Islanders is even more remarkable than this.

The arts of these people are described by Pigafetta with some detail. He mentions the slight clothing of bark worn by the women, the mats and baskets, the wooden houses, the canoes with outriggers, and he notices that the natives had no weapons but lances pointed with fish bones, and had no notion of what arrows were. They stole everything they could lay hands on, and at last Magalhaens went on shore with forty men, burnt forty or fifty of their houses, and killed seven of the people. A hundred and eighty years afterwards the Jesuit Father Le Gobien brought out a new feature in the story. "What is most astonishing, and what people will find it hard to believe, is that they had never seen fire. This so necessary element was entirely unknown to them. They neither knew its use nor its qualities; and they were never more surprised than when they saw it for the first time on the descent that Magellan made on one of their islands, where he burnt some fifty of their houses, to punish these islanders for the trouble they had

---

[7] Otto v. Kotzebue, 'Entdeckungs-Reise'; Weimar, 1821, vol. ii. p. 67.

[8] Pigafetta, 'Viaggio fatto attorno il Mondo,' 1556. Eng. Trans. in Pinkerton, vol. xi.

[9] Hornius, 'De Originibus Americanis'; The Hague, 1652, pp. 204. 51. See Goguet, vol. i. p. 69.

given him. They at first regarded the fire as a kind of animal which attached itself to the wood on which it fed. The first who came too near it having burnt themselves frightened the rest, and only dared look at it from afar; for fear, they said, of being bitten by it, and lest this terrible animal should wound them by its violent breath," etc. etc. He goes on to tell how they soon got accustomed to it and learnt to use it.[10]

It is a curious illustration of the change in historical criticism that has come since 1700, that the Jesuit historian should have expected so singular a story, not mentioned by the eye-witness who described the discovery, to be received without the production of the slightest evidence, a hundred and eighty years after date, and that the public should have justified his confidence in their credulity by believing and quoting his account. Whether he took it directly from any other book or not I cannot tell; but it is to be observed, that if we add Galvano's story about Los Jardines to Pigafetta's mention of Magalhaens burning the houses of the Ladrone Islanders, we may account for the sources of all Father Le Gobien's story, except the idea of the fire being an animal, which may be supplied out of Herodotus. "By the Egyptians also it hath been held that fire is a living beast, and that it devours everything it can seize, and when filled with food it perishes with what it has devoured."[11]

There are stories of fireless men in America, to which I can only refer. Father Lafitau speaks indefinitely of there being such.[12] Father Lombard, of the Company of Jesus, writing in 1730 from Kourou, in French Guyana, gives an account of the tribe of Amikouanes on the river Oyapok, who are also called "long-eared Indians," their ears being stretched to their shoulders. This nation, he says, which has been hitherto unknown, is extremely savage; they have no knowledge of fire.[13]

It is a very curious thing that one of the oldest stories of a race of fireless men is also the newest. In Ethiopia, says the geographer

10 Le Gobien, 'Histoire des Isles Marianes'; Paris, 1700, p. 44.

11 Herod., iii. 16.

12 Lafitau, 'Mœurs des Sauvages Amériquains'; Paris, 1724, vol. i. p. 40.

13 'Lettres Édifiantes et Curieuses'; Paris, 1731, vol. xx. p. 223. Goguet, l. c.

Pomponius Mela, "there are people to whom fire was so totally unknown before the coming of Eudoxus, and so wondrously were they pleased with it when they saw it, that they had the greatest delight in embracing the flames and hiding burning things in their bosom till they were hurt."[14] Pliny places these fireless men in his catalogue of monstrous Ethiopian tribes, between the dumb men and the pygmies. To some, he says, the use of fire was unknown before the time of Ptolemy Lathyrus, king of Egypt.[15] His mention of the name of Ptolemy Lathyrus shows that he, too, is quoting the voyages of Eudoxus of Cyzicus. Whether there was such a person as Eudoxus, and whether he really made the voyages attributed to him or not, is not very clear; but his story, like that of Sindbad, embodies notions current at the time it was written. And with such tenacity does the popular mind hold on to old stories, that now, after a lapse of some two thousand years, the fireless men and the pygmies are brought by the modern Ethiopians into even closer contact than in the pages of Pliny. Dr. Krapf was told that the Dokos, men four feet high, living south of Kaffa and Susa, subsisted on roots and serpents, and were not acquainted with fire.[16] As far as the pygmies are concerned, there appears to be a foundation for the story, in a race of small men really living there. Krapf was shown a slave four feet high, who, they told him, was a Doko. But between four feet and three spans, the height assigned by Pliny to pygmy races elsewhere,[17] there is a difference. Nor is this the only instance of the wonderful permanence of old stories in this part of the world, quite irrespectively of their being true. Within no great distance, an old negro gave Mr. Petherick an account of the monstrous men he had met with on his travels, the men with four eyes, the men with eyes under their arm-pits, the men with long tails, and the men whose ears were so big that they covered their bodies;[18] so nearly has the modern African kept to the wonder-tales that were current in the time of Pliny.[19]

An unquestionable account of a fireless tribe would be of the

---

[14] Mela, iii. c. 9.   [15] Plin., vi. 35, and see ii. 67.

[16] Krapf, Travels, etc., in East Africa; London, 1860, p. 51, etc. See Perty, 'Grundzüge der Ethnographie'; Leipzig, 1859, p. 248.

[17] Plin., vii. 2.   [18] Petherick, p. 367.   [19] Plin., vi. 35, vii. 2.

highest interest to the ethnographer, proving, as it would do, a great step forward made by the races who can produce fire, for this is an art which, once learnt, could hardly be lost. But when we see that stories of such tribes have been set up again and again without any sound basis, while further information, when brought to bear on a series of such stories, tells against them so far as it goes, we are hardly warranted in trusting others of the same kind just because we have no means of testing them. A cause is required for the appearance of such stories in the world, but it does not follow that this cause must be the real existence of fireless tribes; a mere belief in their existence will answer the purpose, and this belief is known to have been current for ages, especially coming out in the Prometheus-legends of various regions of the world. Experience shows how such an idea, when once fairly afloat, will assert itself from time to time in stories furnished with place, date, and circumstance. It must be remembered, too, that the fireless men form only one of a number of races mentioned by writers, old and new, as being distinguished by the want of something which man usually possesses, who have no language, no names, no idea of spiritual beings, no dreams, no mouths, no heads, or no noses, but whose real existence more accurate knowledge has by no means tended to confirm.

In connexion with the stories of fireless tribes, some accounts of a kind of transitional state may be mentioned here. Mr. Backhouse was told by a native of Van Diemen's Land, that his ancestors had no means of making fire before their acquaintance with Europeans. They got it first from the sky, and preserved it by carrying firebrands about with them, and if these went out, they looked for the smoke of the fire of some other party, or for smouldering remains of a lately-abandoned fire of their own.[20] This curious account fits with the Tasmanian myth recorded by Mr. Milligan, which tells how fire was thrown down like a star by two black-fellows, who are now in the sky, the twin stars Castor and Pollux.[21] Moreover, Mr. Milligan himself, on the question

[20] Backhouse, 'Australia,' p. 99.

[21] See Chapter IX. Mr. Calder in Journ. Anthrop. Inst. vol. iii. p. 19, accounts for the Tasmanians' non-use of the friction-apparatus by stating that the trees of the country are mostly too hard and uninflammable for the purpose. [Note to 3rd Edition.]

being put to him, has answered it in a way very much corresponding to Mr. Backhouse's account, to the effect that the Tasmanians
never produced fire by artificial means at all, but always carried
it with them from one camping place to another. Again, a statement of the same kind is reported to have been made by Mr. Mac
Dougall Stuart at the 1864 Meeting of the British Association, that
fire was obtained by the natives of the southern part of Australia
by the friction of two pieces of wood over a bunch of dry grass;
but that in the north this mode is unknown, firebrands being
constantly carried about and renewed, and if, by any accident,
they become extinguished, a journey of great length has to be
undertaken in order to obtain fire from other natives.[22] So Mr.
Angas declares that some tribes of West Australia have no means
of kindling fire, but if it goes out they get it from some encamp-
ment near; they say that their fire formerly came down from the
north.[23] With these statements two things must be borne in mind.
The simple apparatus for making fire by friction was in common
use among Australian tribes, and in Tasmania. And it has been
several times remarked that Australians, although acquainted
with the art of making new fire with this instrument, yet finding
the process troublesome, especially in wet weather, carry burning
brands about with them everywhere, so as to be able to light a
fire at a moment's notice.[24]

The accounts, then, of the finding of fireless tribes are of a
highly doubtful character; possibly true to some extent, but not
probably so. Of the existence of others who are possessed of fire,
but cannot produce it for themselves, there is more considerable
evidence. But, on the other hand, both the possession of fire, and
the art of making it, belong certainly to the vast majority of
mankind, and have done so as far back as we can trace. The
methods, however, which have been found in use for making fire
are very various. A survey of the condition of the art in different
parts of the world, as known to us by direct evidence, is enough

[22] 'Athenæum,' Oct. 15, 1864, p. 503.

[23] Angas, 'Savage Life'; vol. i. p. 112.

[24] Oldfield in Tr. Eth. Soc., vol. iii. p. 283. Dumont d'Urville, 'Voyage de
l'Astrolabe'; vol. i. p. 95. See Sir John Lubbock's remarks on accounts of tribes
without fire, or without the art of fire-making, in 'Prehistoric Times,' pp. 433,
439, 547.

to make it probable that nearly all the different processes found in use are the successors of ruder ones; and, besides this, there is a mass of indirect evidence which fills up some of the shortcomings of history, as it does in the investigation of the Stone Age. Among some of the highest races of mankind, the lower methods of fire-making are still to be seen cropping out through the higher processes by which, for so many ages, they have been overlaid. The friction of two pieces of wood may perhaps be the original means of fire-making used by man; but, between the rudest and the most artificial way in which this may be done, there is a considerable range of progress.

FIG. 20

One of the simplest machines for producing fire is that which may be called the "stick-and-groove." A blunt-pointed stick is run along a groove of its own making in a piece of wood lying on the ground, somewhat as shown in the imaginary drawing, Fig. 20. Mr. Darwin says that the very light wood of the *Hibiscus tiliaceus* was alone used for the purpose in Tahiti. A native would produce fire with it in a few seconds; he himself found it very hard work, but at length succeeded. This stick-and-groove process has been repeatedly described in the South Sea Islands, namely, in Tahiti, New Zealand, the Sandwich, Tonga, Samoa, and Radack groups;[25] but I have never found it distinctly mentioned

[25] Darwin, in Narr., vol. iii. p. 488. Polack, vol. i. p. 165. Tyerman and Bennet, vol. i. p. 141. Buschmann, 'Iles Marquises,' etc.; Berlin, 1843, pp. 140–1. Mariner, Vocab., *s. vv. tolo-afi, tolonga, cownatoo.* S. S. Farmer, 'Tonga,' etc.: London, 1855, p. 138. Walpole, 'Four Years in the Pacific'; London, 1849, vol. ii. p. 377. Kotzebue, vol. iii. p. 154. See mention of fire made by rubbing, not drilling, two pieces of wood, in Rochefort, 'Iles Antilles,' p. 440.

out of this region of the world. Even should it be known else-where, its isolation in a particular district round which other processes prevail would still be an ethnographical fact of some importance. It is to be noticed also, that it comes much nearer than "fire-drilling" to the yet simpler process of striking fire with two pieces of split bamboo. The silicious coating of this cane makes it possible to strike fire with it; and this is done in Eastern Asia, and also in the great Malay islands of Borneo and Sumatra,[26] at or near the source whence the higher Polynesian race is sup-posed to have spread over the Pacific Islands. But it would appear

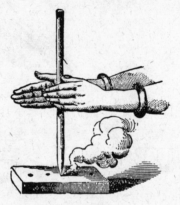

FIG. 21

that the striking fire with bamboo, simple as it seems, is for some reason not so convenient as the use of the more complex friction-apparatus; for Marsden seems to consider the fire-drill as the regular native instrument in Sumatra, though he says he has also seen the same effect produced more simply by rubbing one bit of bamboo, with a sharp edge, across another.

By a change in the way of working, the "stick-and-groove" becomes the "fire-drill." I have been obliged to coin both these terms, no suitable ones being forthcoming. The fire-drill, in its simplest form, is represented in Fig. 21; and Captain Cook's re-marks on it and its use, among the native tribes of Australia, may

26 Bowring, vol. i. p. 206. St. John, vol. i. p. 137. Marsden, p. 60. See Tennent, 'Ceylon,' vol. i. p. 105.

serve also as a general description of it all over the world, setting aside minor details. "They produce fire with great facility, and spread it in a wonderful manner. To produce it they take two pieces of dry soft wood; one is a stick about eight or nine inches long, the other piece is flat: the stick they shape into an obtuse point at one end, and pressing it upon the other, turn it nimbly by holding it between both their hands, as we do a chocolate mill, often shifting their hands up, and then moving them down upon it, so increase the pressure as much as possible. By this method they get fire in less than two minutes, and from the smallest spark they increase it with great speed and dexterity."[27] The same instrument is known in Tasmania.[28] It appears usual both in Australia and elsewhere to lay the lower piece on the ground, holding it firm with feet or knees. A good deal may depend on the kind of wood used, and its dryness, etc., for in some countries it seems to take much more time and labour, two men often working it, one beginning at the top of the stick when his companion's hands have come down nearly to the bottom, and so on till the fire comes.

Contrasting with the isolation of the stick-and-groove in a single district, the geographical range of the simple fire-drill is immense. Its use among the Australians, and Tasmanians, forms one of the characters which distinguish their culture from that of the Polynesians; while it appears again among the Malays in Sumatra[29] and the Carolines.[30] It was found by Cook in Unalashka,[31] and by the Russians in Kamchatka; where, for many years, flint and steel could not drive it out of use among the natives, who went on carrying every man his fire-sticks.[32] It remains in use among the Lepchas of Sikkim, a Tibetan race of Northern India.[33] There is reason to suppose that it prevailed in India before the Aryans invaded the country, bringing with them an improved apparatus, for at this day it is used by the Yenadis, indegenes of South India,[34] and by the wild Veddahs of Ceylon,

27 Cook, First Voy. H., vol. iii. p. 234. Angas, S. Australia, pl. 27.

28 Lubbock, p. 440.

29 Marsden, p. 60.

30 Kotzebue, vol. iii. p. 154.

31 Cook, Third Voy., vol. ii. p. 513.

32 Kracheninnikow, p. 30.

33 Latham, Descr. Eth., vol. i. p. 89.

34 Shortt, in Tr. Eth. Soc., vol. iii. p. 376.

a race so capable of resisting foreign innovation that they have not learnt to smoke tobacco.[35] It prevails, or has done so within modern times, in South and West Africa,[36] and it was in use among the Guanches of the Canary Islands in the seventeenth century.[37] In North America it is described among Esquimaux and Indian tribes.[38] It was in use in Mexico,[39] and Fig. 22, taken from an ancient Mexican picture-writing, shows the drill being twirled; while fire, drawn in the usual conventional manner, comes out from the hole where the point revolves. It was in use in Central America,[40] in the West Indies,[41] and in South America, down as far as the Straits of Magellan.[42]

FIG. 22

The name of "fire-drill" has not, however, been adopted merely with reference to this simplest form. This rude instrument is, as may well be supposed, very wasteful of time and power, and it has been improved by several contrivances which so closely cor-

35 Tennent, 'Ceylon,' vol. ii. p. 451. Bailey in Tr. Eth. Soc., 1863, p. 291.

36 Casalis, p. 129. Klemm, C. W., part i. p. 67. Koelle, 'Kanuri Vocab.'; p. 413.

37 Glas, 'Canary Islands'; London, 1764, p. 8.

38 Klemm, C. G., vol. ii. p. 239. Schoolcraft, part i. p. 214. Loskiel, p. 70, Lafitau, 'Mœurs des Sauvages Amériquains'; Paris, 1724, vol. ii. p. 242.

39 Kingsborough, Selden MS., Vatican MS.

40 Brasseur, 'Popol-Vuh,' pp. 64, 218, 243.

41 Oviedo, 'Hystoria General de las Indias'; Salamanca, 1547, vi. 5.

42 Spix and Martius, vol. ii. p. 387, and plates. Purchas, vol. iii. p. 983; vol. iv. p. 1345. Molina, vol. ii. p. 122. Dobrizhoffer, vol. ii. p. 118. Garcilaso de la Vega, 'Commentarios Reales' (2nd ed.); Madrid, 1723, p. 198.

respond to those applied to boring-tools, that the most convenient plan is to classify them together. Even the clumsy plan of the simple fire-drill has been found in use for boring holes. It has been mentioned at page 163, as in use for drilling hard stone among rude Indians of South America, and, what is much more surprising, the natives of Madagascar bored holes by working their drill between the palms of their hands,[43] though they were so far advanced in the arts as to make and use iron tools, and of course the very drills worked in this primitive way were pointed with iron.

FIG. 23

The principle of the common carpenter's brace, with which he works his centre-bit, is applied to fire-making by a very simple device represented in Fig. 23, which is drawn according to Mr. Darwin's description of the plan used by the Gauchos of the Pampas; "taking an elastic stick about eighteen inches long, he presses one end on his breast, and the other (which is pointed) in a hole in a piece of wood, and then rapidly turns the curved part, like a carpenter's centre-bit."[44] The Gauchos, it should be observed, are not savages, but half-wild herdsmen of mixed European, Indian, and African blood, who would probably only use such a means of kindling fire when the flint and steel were for the moment not at hand, and their fire-drill is not only like the carpenter's brace, but most likely suggested by it.

[43] Ellis, 'Madagascar,' vol. i. p. 317.
[44] Darwin, in Narr., vol. iii. p. 488.

To wind a cord or thong round the drill, so as, by pulling the two ends alternately, to make it revolve very rapidly, is a great improvement on mere hand-twirling. As Kuhn has pointed out, this contrivance was in use for boring in Europe in remote times; Odysseus describes it in telling how he and his companions put out the eye of the Cyclops:

οἱ μὲν μοχλὸν ἑλόντες ἐλάϊνον, ὀξὺν ἐπ᾽ ἄκρῳ
ὀφθαλμῷ ἐνέρεισαν. ἐγὼ δ᾽ ἐφύπερθεν ἀερθεὶς,
δίνεον. ὡς ὅτε τις τρυπῷ δόρυ νήϊον ἀνὴρ
τρυπάνῳ, οἱ δέ τ᾽ ἔνερθεν ὑποσσείουσιν ἱμάντι
ἀψάμενοι ἑκάτερθε, τὸ δὲ τρέχει ἐμμενὲς αἰεί.[45]

They then seizing the sharp-cut stake of the wood of the olive
Thrust it into his eye, the while I standing above them,
Bored it into the hole:—as a shipwright boreth a timber,
Guiding the drill that his men below drive backward and forward,
Pulling the ends of the thong while the point runs round without ceasing.

In modern India, butter-churns are worked with a cord in this way, and the Brahmans still use a cord-drill in producing the sacred fire, as will be more fully stated presently. Half-way round the world, the same thing is found among the Esquimaux. Davis (after whom Davis's Straits are named) describes in 1586 how a Greenlander "beganne to kindle a fire in this maner: he tooke a piece of a board wherein was a hole halfe thorow: into that hole he puts the end of a round stick like unto a bedstaffe, wetting the end thereof in Trane, and in fashion of a turner with a piece of lether, by his violent motion doeth very speedily produce fire."[46] The cut, Fig. 24, is taken from a drawing of the last century, representing two Esquimaux making fire, one holding a cross-piece to keep the spindle steady and force it well down to its bearing, while the other pulls the thong.[47] This form of the apparatus takes two men to work it, but the Esquimaux have devised a modification of it which a man can work alone. Sir E. Belcher thus describes its use for drilling holes by means of a

[45] Kuhn, 'Herabkunft des Feuers,' p. 39. Hom. Od., ix. 382.

[46] Hakluyt, vol. iii. p. 104.

[47] Henry Ellis, 'Voyage to Hudson's Bay'; London, 1748, pp. 132, 234.

point of green jade:—"The thong . . . being passed twice round the drill, the upper end is steadied by a mouthpiece of wood, having a piece of the same stone imbedded, with a countersunk cavity. This held firmly between the teeth directs the tool. Any workman would be astonished at the performance of this tool on ivory; but having once tried it myself, I found the jar or vibration on the jaws, head, and brain, quite enough to prevent my repeating it."[48] There is a set of Esquimaux apparatus for making

Fig. 24

fire in the same manner, in the Edinburgh Industrial Museum, and Fig. 25 is intended to show the way in which it is worked. The thong-drill with the mouthpiece has been found in use in the Aleutian Islands, both for boring holes and for making fire.[49] Lastly, there is a kind of cord-drill used by the New Zealanders in boring holes through hard greenstone, etc., in which the spindle itself is weighted. It is described as a "sharp wooden stick ten inches long, to the centre of which two stones are attached, so as to exert pressure and perform the office of a fly-wheel. The requisite rotatory motion is given to the stick by two strings

48 Sir E. Belcher, in Tr. Eth. Soc., 1861, p. 140.

49 Kotzebue, vol. iii. p. 155.

pulled alternately."[50] There must of course be some means of keeping the spindle upright. The New Zealanders do not seem to have used their drill for fire-making as well as for boring, but to have kept to their stick-and-groove.

To substitute for the mere thong or cord a bow with a loose string, is a still further improvement, for one hand now does the work of two in driving the spindle. The centre, in which its end turns, may be held down with the other hand, or (as is very usual), set against the breast of the operator. The bow-drill thus

FIG. 25

formed, is a most ancient and well-known boring instrument, familiar to the artisan in modern Europe as it was in ancient Egypt. The only place where I have found any notice of its use for fire-making is among the North American Indians. The plate from which Fig. 26 is taken is marked by Schoolcraft as representing the apparatus used by the Sioux, or Dacotahs. They, as well as the Naskapee Indians of Canada, whom Dr. D. Wilson notices as making fire with a bow-drill, may possibly have caught the idea from the European boring instrument.[51]

Lastly, there is a curious little contrivance, known to English toolmakers as the "pump-drill," from its being worked up and

50 Thomson, 'New Zealand,' vol. i. p. 203.

51 Schoolcraft, part iii. pl. 28. D. Wilson, 'Prehistoric Man'; vol. ii. p. 375.

down like a pump. That kept in the London tool-shops is all of metal, expanding into a bulb instead of the disk shown in Fig. 27, which represents the kind used in Switzerland, consisting of a wooden spindle, armed with a steel point, and weighted with a wooden disk. A string is made fast to the ends of the cross-piece, and in the middle to the top of the spindle. As the hand brings the cross-piece down it unwinds the cord, driving the spindle round; as the hand is lifted again, the disk, acting as a fly-wheel,

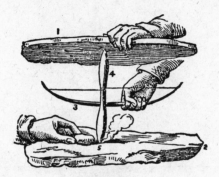

FIG. 26

FIG. 27

runs on and re-winds the cord, and so on. Holtzappfel says that
the pump-drill is as well known among the Oriental nations as
the breast-drill, though it is little used in England except by
china and glass menders.[52] Perhaps it may have found its way
over from Asia to the South Sea Islands; at any rate it is found
there. Fig. 28 shows it as used in Fakaafo or Bowditch Island,
differing from the Swiss form only in being armed with a stone

FIG. 28

instead of a steel point, and in having no hole through the cross-
piece.[53] Mr. Turner describes it in the neighbouring Samoan or
Navigators' Islands, as pointed with a nail or a sail-needle, got
from the foreigners,[54] but the specimen presented by him to the
Hunterian Museum at Glasgow has a stone point. The natives
use it for drilling their fish-hooks made of shell; for which purpose, as for drilling holes in china, it is peculiarly adapted, the
lightness and evenness of its pressure lessening the danger of

[52] Holtzappfel, 'Turning and Mechanical Manipulation'; London, 1856, vol.
ii. p. 557.

[53] Wilkes, U.S. Exp., vol. v. p. 17.   [54] Turner, p. 273.

cracking these brittle materials. One would think that this quality would make the pump-drill particularly unsuitable for fire-making; but nevertheless, by making it very large and heavy, it has been turned to this service in North America, among the Iroquois Indians. Fig. 29 (drawn to a small scale) represents their apparatus, which is thus described by Mr. Lewis H. Morgan:— "This is an Indian invention, and of great antiquity. . . . It consisted of an upright shaft, about four feet in length, and an inch in diameter, with a small wheel set upon the lower part,

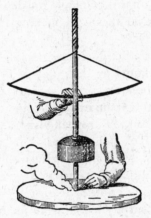

FIG. 29

to give it momentum. In a notch at the top of the shaft was set a string, attached to a bow about three feet in length. The lower point rested upon a block of dry wood, near which are placed small pieces of punk. When ready to use, the string is first coiled around the shaft, by turning it with the hand. The bow is then pulled downwards, thus uncoiling the string, and revolving the shaft towards the left. By the momentum given to the wheel, the string is again coiled up in a reverse manner, and the bow again drawn up. The bow is again pulled downwards, and the revolution of the shaft reversed, uncoiling the string, and recoiling it as before. This alternate revolution of the shaft is continued, until sparks are emitted from the point where it rests upon the piece of dry wood below. Sparks are produced in a few moments by the intensity of the friction, and ignite the punk, which speedily furnishes a fire."[55]

It is now necessary to notice other methods of producing fire which have been found in use in various parts of the world. There is a well-known scientific toy made to show that heat is generated by the compression of air. It consists of a brass tube closed at one end, into which a packed piston is sharply forced down, thus igniting a piece of tinder within the tube. It is curious to find an apparatus on this principle (made in hard wood, ivory, etc.) used as a practical means of making fire in Birmah, and even among the Malays.[56]

The natives of Tierra del Fuego are notably distinguished from their northern neighbours by their way of fire-making. In 1520, Magalhaens on his famous voyage visited the gigantic Patagonians, who thought the Spaniards had come down from heaven, and who, explaining to the European visitors the native theology, told them of their chief god, Setebos. The savages from whom Shakespeare borrowed these traits to furnish the picture of the "servant-monster," Caliban,[57] showed their manner of making fire, which was by the friction of two pieces of wood.[58] But the Fuegians have for centuries used a higher method, striking sparks with a flint from a piece of iron pyrites upon their tinder. This process is described as still in use,[59] and is evidently what Captain Wallis meant by saying (in 1767), that "To kindle a fire they strike a pebble against a piece of mundic."[60] A much earlier account of the same thing appears in the voyage of Sarmiento de

[55] L. H. Morgan, 'League of the Iroquois'; Rochester, U.S., 1851, p. 381.

[56] Bastian, 'Oestl. Asien,' vol. ii. p. 418; Cameron, 'Malayan India,' p. 136.

[57] Cal.—"Hast thou not dropped from heaven?" ('Tempest,' act ii. scene 2.)
    Cal.— . . . .
    "It would control my dam's god, Setebos." (Id., act. i. scene 2.)

[58] Pigafetta, in Pinkerton, vol. xi. Their process was the simplest hand-drilling, as appears (1577–80) from the account in Drake's 'World Encompassed,' Hak. Soc. 1854, p. 48.

[59] W. P. Snow, 'Tierra del Fuego,' etc.; vol. ii. p. 360.

[60] Wallis, in Hawkesworth, vol. i. p. 171.

Gamboa, in 1579–80.[61] Iron pyrites answers extremely well instead of the steel, and was found in regular use in high northern latitudes in America, among the Slave and Dog Rib Indians.[62] It is probably the "iron-stone" which the Esquimaux called *ujarak-saviminilik,* and from which they strike fire with a fragment of flint,[63] and is perhaps referred to in Father Le Jeune's statement that the Algonquin Indians strike fire with two minerals *(pierres de mine).*[64] The use of iron pyrites for striking fire was known to the Greeks and Romans, and it shared with flint the name of *fire*-stone, πυρίτης, *pyrites,* which it and some other metallic sulphurets have since taken entire possession of.

The Alashkans are reported to obtain fire by striking together two pieces of quartz rubbed with sulphur over some dry grass or moss, strewed with feathers where the sulphur falls; and similar descriptions of the process are given in the adjacent islands.[65] Father Zucchelli, who was a missionary in West Africa about the beginning of last century, gives the following account of the way in which, he says, the negroes made fire on their journeys:— "When they found a fire-stone (Feuerstein) on the road, they lay down by it on their knees, took a little piece of wood in their hands, and threw sand between the stone and the wood, rubbing them so long against one another till the wood began to burn, and herewith they all lighted their pipes, and so went speedily forth again smoking on their journey."[66] It is possible that not flint (as is usual), but pyrites, may here be meant by *feuerstein.*

61 Sarmiento de Gamboa, 'Viage al Estrecho de Magallanes'; Madrid, 1768, p. 229. "Y unos pedazos de pedernal, pasados, y pintados de margaxita de oro y plata: y preguntándoles que para qué era aquello? dixeron por señas, que para sacar fuego; y luego uno de ellos tomó unas plumas de las que trahía, y sirviéndole de yesca, sacó fuego con el pedernal. Paréceme que es (casca?) de metal de plata ú oro de veta, porque es al natural como el *curiquixo de porco* en el Pirú."

62 Mackenzie, 'Voyages'; London, 1801, p. 38. Klemm, C. G., vol. ii. p. 26.

63 Hayes, 'Arctic Boat Journey'; London, 1860, p. 217.

64 Le Jeune, 'Relation,' etc. (1634); Paris, 1635, p. 91. Lafitau, vol. ii. p. 242.

65 Billings, 'Exp. to N. Russia'; p. 159. Cook, 3rd Voy., vol. ii. p. 513. Kotzebue, vol. iii. p. 155.

66 Zucchelli, 'Merkwürdige Missions- und Reise-Beschreibung nach Congo'; Frankfort, 1715, p. 344.

The flint and steel may have come into use at any time after the beginning of the Iron age, but history fails to tell us the date of its introduction in Greece and Rome, China, and most other districts of the Old World. In modern times it has made its way with iron into many new places, though it has not always been able to supersede the fire-sticks at once; sometimes, it seems, from a difficulty in getting flints. For instance it was necessary in Sumatra to import the flints from abroad, and thus they did not come immediately into general use among the natives; and there may perhaps be a similar reason for the fire-drill having held its ground to this day among some of the iron-using races of Southern Africa.

The Greeks were familiar with the use of the burning-lens in the time of Aristophanes, who mentions it in the 'Clouds,' in a dialogue between Socrates and Strepsiades:—

Socrates. Very good: now I'll set you another smart question. If some one entered an action against you to recover five talents, tell me, how would you cancel it?

. . . .

Strepsiades. I have found a very clever way to cancel the suit, as you will agree yourself.
Socrates. What kind of way?
Strepsiades. Have you ever seen that stone in the druggists' shops, that pretty, transparent one, that they light fire with?
Socrates. The crystal, you mean?
Strepsiades. I do.
Socrates. Well, what then?
Strepsiades. Suppose I take this, and when the clerk enters the suit, I stand thus, a long way off, towards the sun, and melt out the letters.
Socrates. Very clever, by the Graces![67]

At a much later period Pliny mentions that glass balls with water put into them, when set opposite to the sun, get so hot as to set clothes on fire; and that he finds surgeons consider the best means of cautery to be a crystal ball placed opposite to the sun's rays.[68] The Chinese commonly use the burning-lens to light fire with, as well as the flint and steel, and we hear of the Siamese using it to produce new sacred fire.[69]

[67] Aristoph., Nubes, 757, etc.   [68] Pliny, xxxvi. 67, xxxvii. 10.
[69] Davis, vol. iii. p. 51. Bastian, 'Oestl. Asien,' vol. iii. p. 516.

The fact that fire may be produced by reflecting the sun's rays with mirrors was known as early as Pliny's time (A.D. 23–79), as he remarks, "seeing that concave mirrors placed opposite to the sun's rays ignite things more easily than any other fire."[70] There is some reason to suppose that the knowledge of this phenomenon worked backwards into history, attaching itself to two famous names of old times, Archimedes and Numa Pompilius. The story of Archimedes setting the fleet on fire at Syracuse with burning mirrors, probably unknown as it was to historians for centuries after his time, need not be further remarked on here; but the story of Numa reappears on the other side of the world, under circumstances which make its discussion a matter of importance to ethnography.

It is related by Plutarch in his life of Numa, written in the first century, that among the ordinances made for the Vestal Virgins when they were established in Rome, there was the following. If the sacred fire which it was their duty to keep continually burning should happen to go out, it was not to be lighted again from another fire, but new fire was to be made by lighting from the sun a pure and undefiled flame. "And they kindle it especially with vessels which are shaped hollow from the side of an isosceles triangle with a (vertical) right angle, and converge from the circumference to a single centre. When such an instrument is set opposite to the sun, so that the impinging rays from all sides crowd and fold together round the centre, it divides the rarefied air, and quickly kindles the lightest and driest matters applied to it, the beams acquiring by the repulsion a body and fiery stroke."[71] Stories of Numa's ordinances will hardly be claimed as sober history, though it is possible that such a process as this may have been used, at least in late times, to rekindle the fire of Vesta. But there is in Festus another account of the way in which this was done, having in its favour every analogy from the practices of kindling the sacred fire among our Indo-European race, both in Asia and in Europe. "If the fire of Vesta were extinguished, the virgins were scourged by the priests, whose practice it was to drill into a board of auspicious wood till the fire came,

---

[70] Pliny, ii. 111.   [71] Plutarch, 'Vita Numæ,' ix. 7.

which was received and carried to the temple by the virgin, in a brazen colander."[72]

The parallel passage to that in the life of Numa is to be found in the account of the feast of Raymi, or the Sun, celebrated in ancient Peru, according to Garcilaso de la Vega, whose 'Commentaries' were first published in 1609–16, the Spanish discovery having taken place in 1527. He says this festival was celebrated at the summer solstice. "The fire for this sacrifice had to be new, given, as they said, by the hand of the sun. For which purpose they took a great bracelet, which they call *Chipana* (like the others which the Incas commonly wore on the left wrist), which bracelet the high priest kept; it was larger than the common ones, and had as its medallion a concave cup like a half orange, highly polished; they set it against the sun, and at a certain point where the rays issuing from the cup came together, they put a little finely-carded cotton, as they did not know how to make tinder, which shortly took fire, as it naturally does. With this fire, thus given by the hand of the Sun, the sacrifice was burnt, and all the meat of the day was roasted. And they carried some of the fire to the Temple of the Sun, and to the House of the Virgins, where they kept it up all the year, and it was a bad omen if they let it out in any way. If, on the eve of the festival, which was when the necessary preparations for the following day were made, there was no sun to light the new fire, they made it with two thin smooth sticks as big as one's little finger, and half a yard long, boring one against the other (*barrenando uno con otro*); these little sticks are cinnamon coloured, and they call both the sticks themselves and the fire-making *V-yaca*, one and the same term serving for noun and verb. The Indians use them instead of flint and steel, and carry them on their journeys to get fire when they have to pass the night in uninhabited places," etc.[73]

---

[72] Festus. "Ignis Vestæ si quando interstinctus esset, virgines verberibus afficiebantur a pontificibus, quibus mos erat tabulam felicis materiæ tamdiu terebrare, quousque exceptum ignem cribro æneo virgo in ædem ferret." See Val. Max., I. i. 6.

[73] Garcilaso de la Vega, p. 198.

If circumstantiality of detail were enough to make a story credible, we might be obliged to receive this one, and even to argue on the wonderful agreement of the manner of kindling the sacred fire in Rome and in Peru. But the coincidences between Garcilaso's Virgins of the Sun and Plutarch's Vestal Virgins go farther than this. We are not only expected to believe that there were Virgins of the Sun, that they kept up a sacred fire whose extinction was an evil omen, and that this fire was lighted by the sun's rays concentrated in a concave mirror. We are also told that in Cuzco, as in Rome, the virgin found unfaithful was to be punished by the special punishment of being buried alive.[74] This is really too much. Whatever may be the real basis of fact in the accounts of the Virgins of the Sun and the feast of Raymi, the inference seems, to me at least, most probable, that part or all of the accessory detail is not history, but the realization of an idea of which Garcilaso himself strikes the key-note when he says of this same feast of Raymi, that it was celebrated by the Incas "in the city of Cozco, *which was another Rome*" (*que fue otra Roma*).[75] Those who happen to have experience of the old chroniclers of Spanish America know how the whole race was possessed by a passion for bringing out the Old World stories in a new guise, with a local habitation and a name in America. Garcilaso's story of the burning-mirror, supposing it to be an adaptation from Plutarch, would not even be the best illustration of this modern phase of Mythology; that distinction must be reserved for the reproduction by another chronicler of another of Plutarch's stories, that of the shout that was raised when the Roman Herald proclaimed the liberty of the Greeks,—such a shout that it brought the crows tumbling down into the race-course from the sky above.[76] The Incas, says Sarmiento, "were so feared, that if they went out through the kingdom, and allowed a curtain of their litters to be lifted that their vassals might

[74] Garcilaso de la Vega, p. 109. Compare Diego Fernandez, 'Hist. del Peru,' Seville, 1571; "y nadie podia tratar, ni conversar con estas Mamaconas. Y si alguno lo intentaua, luego le interrauan biuo."

[75] Garcilaso de la Vega, p. 195.

[76] Plut. T. Quinct. Flaminius, x.

see them, they raised so great an acclamation that they made the birds fall from where they were flying above, so that the people could catch them in their hands."[77]

Against the abstract possibility of Garcilaso's story of the lighting of the sacred fire with concave mirrors, there is no more to be said than against Plutarch's. With a good parabolic mirror only two inches in diameter, I have lighted brown paper under an English sun of no extraordinary power, and other surfaces which will make a good caustic will answer, though of course they have less burning power than a paraboloid of revolution of equal size. There is even a material basis out of which the Peruvian story may have grown. In the ancient tombs of Peru, mirrors both of pyrites and obsidian have been found. Some, three or four inches in diameter, were probably mere broken nodules of pyrites, polished on the flat side, but one is mentioned measuring about a foot and a half (probably in circumference), which had a beautifully-polished concave surface, so as to magnify objects considerably,[78] and such a mirror may have been used for making fire. Indeed, the objection to the story of the Virgins of the Sun is not that any of the details I have mentioned must of necessity be untrue, but that the apparent races of absorption from Plutarch invalidate whatever rests on Garcilaso de la Vega's unsupported testimony.

To conclude the notice of the art of fire-making in general, its last phase, the invention of lucifer matches in our own day, is fast spreading over the world, and bringing most other fire-making instruments down to the condition of curious relics of a past time.

But though some of the higher methods date far back in the history of the Old World, the employment of the wooden friction-apparatus in Europe, even for the practical purposes of ordinary life, has come up through the classical and mediæval times into the last century, and for all we know it may still exist. Pliny speaks of its finding a use among the outposts of armies and among shepherds, a stone to strike fire with not being always to

[77] Sarmiento, MS. cited in Prescott, Peru, vol. i. p. 25.

[78] Juan & Ulloa, 'Relacion Historica'; Madrid, 1748, p. 619.

be had;[79] and in a remarkable account dating from 1768, which will be quoted presently, its use by Russian peasants for making fire in the woods is spoken of as an existing custom, just as, at a much more recent date, it is mentioned that the Portuguese Brazilians still have recourse to the fire-drill, when no other means of getting a light are forthcoming.[80] For the most part, however, the early use of the instrument in the Old World is only to be traced in ancient myths, in certain ceremonial practices which have been brought down unchanged into a new state of culture, and in descriptions by Greek and Roman writers of the art. It had lost, even then, its practical importance in everyday life, though lingering on, as it still does in our own day, in rites for which it was necessary to use pure *wild fire,* not the tame fire that lay like a domestic animal upon the hearth.

The traditions of inventors of the art of fire-making by the friction of wood have in so far an historical value, that they bring clearly into view a period when this was the usual practice. There is a Chinese myth that points to such a state of things, and which moreover presents, in the story of the "fire-bird," an analogy with a set of myths belonging to our own race, which may well be due to a deep-lying ethnological connexion. "A great sage went to walk beyond the bounds of the moon and the sun; he saw a tree, and on this tree a bird, which pecked at it and made fire come forth. The sage was struck with this, took a branch of the tree and produced fire from it, and thence this great personage was called Suy-jin."[81] The friction-apparatus itself, apparently of the kind spoken of here as the fire-drill, is mentioned in Morrison's Chinese Dictionary. "*Suy,* an instrument to obtain fire. A speculum for obtaining fire from the sun is called *suy* or *kin-suy*. *Muh-suy,* an utensil to procure fire from wood by rotatory fric-

[79] Pliny, xvi. 77.

[80] Pr. Max. v. Wied., 'Reise nach Brasilien' (1815–7), vol. ii. p. 19. Hyltén-Cavallius, 'Wärend och Wirdarne,' Stockholm, 1863–4, vol. i. p. 189, states that within a generation there were old foresters in districts of Sweden who could still practise the ancient art of making fire by violently twirling a dry oak stick with their hands against a dry piece of wood. See also the account of the *gnid-eld* or "rubbing-fire," which was carried over the land as "need-fire." [Note to 3d Edition.]

[81] Goguet, vol. iii. p. 281. See Kuhn, p. 28, etc.

tion. *Suy-jin-she*, the first person who procured fire for the use of man." The very existence of a Chinese name for the fire-drill shows that it is, or has been, in use in the country.

The absence of evidence relating to fire-making in the Bible is remarkable. If, indeed, the following passage from the cosmogony of Sanchoniathon be founded on a Phœnician legend, it preserves an old Semitic record of the use of the fire-stick. "They say that from the wind Kolpia, and his wife Baan, which is interpreted Night, there were born mortal men, called Æon and Protogonos; and Æon found how to get food from trees. And those born from them were called Genos and Genea, and they inhabited Phœnicia. . . . Moreover, they say that, again, from Genos, son of Æon and Protogonos, they were born mortal children, whose names were Phos, Pur, and Phlox (Light, Fire, and Flame). These, they say, found out how to make fire from the friction of pieces of wood, and taught its use."[82] Fire-making by friction is not unknown to the Arabs, their instrument being the simple fire-drill.

Though direct history does not tell us that the Finns and Lapps used the fire-drill before they had the flint and steel, there is a passage safely preserving the memory of its use in a Finnish poem, whose native metre is familiar to our ears from its imitation in 'Hiawatha';

> Panu parka, Tuonen poika,
> kirnusi tulisen kirnun,
> säkeisin säihytteli,
> pukemissa puhtaissa,
> walkehissa waatteissa.

> Panu, the poor son of Tuoni,
> Churning fiercely at the fire-church,
> Scattering fiery sparks around him,
> Clothèd in a pure white garment,
> In a white and shining garment.[83]

It is, however, by our own race that the most remarkable body of evidence of the ancient use of the fire-drill has been preserved. The very instrument still used in India for kindling the sacrificial fire seems never to have changed since the time

---

[82] Euseb., Præp. Evang. i.x.   [83] Kuhn, p. 110.

when our ancestors left their eastern home to invade Europe. It is thus described:—"The process by which fire is obtained from wood is called churning, as it resembles that by which butter in India is separated from milk. . . . It consists in drilling one piece of arani-wood into another by pulling a string tied to it with a jerk with the one hand, while the other is slackened, and so alternately till the wood takes fire. The fire is received on cotton or flax held in the hand of an assist-ant Brahman."[84] By this description it would seem that the Indian instrument is the same in principle as the Esquimaux thong-drill, shown in Fig. 23. It is driven by a three-stranded cord of cowhair and hemp; and there is probably a piece of wood pressed down upon the upper end of the spindle, to keep it down to its bearing.[85] In the name of Prometheus, the fire-maker, the close connection with the Sanskrit name of this spindle, *pramantha,* has never been broken. Possibly both he and the Chinese Suy-jin may be nothing more than personifica-tions of the fire-drill.

Professor Kuhn, in his mythological treatise on 'Fire and Ambrosia,' has collected a quantity of evidence from Greek and Latin authors, which makes it appear that the fire-making in-strument, whose use was kept up in Europe, was not the stick-and-groove, but the fire-drill. The operation is distinctly described as boring or drilling; and it seems, moreover, that the fire-drill was worked in ancient Europe, as in India and among the Esquimaux, with a cord or thong, for the spindle is compared to, or spoken of as, a τρύπανον, which instrument, as appears in the passage quoted from the Odyssey at page 256, was a drill driven by a thong.[86]

The traces of the old fire-making in modern Europe lie, for the most part, in close connexion with the ancient and wide-

[84] Stevenson, Sama Veda, p. 7.

[85] If so, the upper and lower blocks may be the *upper and lower arani,* and the spindle the *pramantha,* or *ćâtra.* See Kuhn, pp. 13, 15, 78; also Boehtlingk and Roth, s. v. *arani, ćâtra.* The anointing with butter (Kuhn, p. 78), corre-sponds to the use of train oil by the Esquimaux.

[86] Kuhn, 'Herabkunft des Feuers,' etc., pp. 36–40, citing Theophrastus, Hesy-chius, Simplicius, Festus, etc.

spread rite of the New Fire, which belongs to the Aryans among other branches of the human race, and especially with one variety of this rite, which has held its own even in Germany and England into quite late times, in spite of all the efforts of the Church to put it down. This is what the Germans call *nothfeuer,* and we, *needfire;* though whether the term is to be understood literally, or whether it has dropped a guttural, and stands for fire made by *kneading* or rubbing, is not clear.

What the nature and object of the needfire is, may be seen in Reiske's account of the practice in Germany in the seventeenth century:—"When a murrain has broken out among the great and small cattle, and the herds have suffered much harm, the farmers determine to make a needfire. On an appointed day there must be no single flame of fire in any house or on any hearth. From each house straw, and water, and brushwood must be fetched, and a stout oak-post driven fast into the ground, and a hole bored through it; in this a wooden windlass is stuck, well smeared with cart-pitch and tar, and turned round so long that, with the fierce heat and force, it gives forth fire. This is caught in proper materials, increased with straw, heath, and brushwood, till it breaks out into a full needfire; and this must be somewhat spread out lengthways between walls or fences, and the cattle and horses hunted with sticks and whips two or three times through it," etc.[87] Various ways of arranging the apparatus are mentioned by Reiske and other authorities quoted by Grimm, such as fixing the spindle between two posts, etc. How the spindle is turned is sometimes doubtful; but in several places the Indian practice of driving it with a rope wound round it, and pulled backwards and forwards, comes clearly into view; while sometimes a cart wheel is spun round upon an axle; or a spindle is worked round with levers, or two planks are rubbed violently together, till the fire comes.[88]

The needfire seems to have been kept up in late years in Germany. In Great Britain the most modern account I have

[87] Grimm, D. M., p. 570. Cord fire-drill used as toy in Switzerland, *ibid.* p. 573.

[88] Grimm, D. M., pp. 570–9. See *ante,* p. 253, note.

met with dates from 1826.[89] The 'Mirror' of June 24th of that year takes from the 'Perth Courier' a description of the rite, as performed not far from Perth, by a farmer who had lost several cattle by some disease:—"A few stones were piled together in the barn-yard, and wood-coals having been laid thereon, the fuel was ignited by *will-fire,* that is, fire obtained by friction: the neighbours having been called in to witness the solemnity, the cattle were made to pass through the flames, in the order of their dignity and age, commencing with the horses and ending with the swine."

Some varieties of the rite of the New Fire, connected with the Sun-worship so deeply rooted in the popular mind from before the time of the Vedas, were countenanced, or at least tolerated, by the Church. Such are the bonfires at Easter, Midsummer Eve, and some other times; and, in one case, there is ground for supposing that the old rite was taken up into the Roman Church, in the practice of putting out the church candles on Easter Eve, and lighting them again with consecrated new-made fire,—

> On Easter Eve the fire all is quencht in every place,
> And fresh againe from out the flint is fetcht with solemne grace:
> The priest doth halow this against great daungers many one,
> A brande whereof doth every man with greedie mind take home,
> That, when the feareful storme appears, or tempest black arise,
> By lighting this he safe may be from stroke of hurtful skies.[90]

Here the traces of the Indian mythology come out with beautiful clearness. The lightning is the fire that flies from the heavenly fire-churn, as the gods whirl it in the clouds. The New Fire is its representative on earth; and, like the thunder-bolt, preserves from the lightning flash the house in which it is, for the lightning strikes no place twice.

It has been stated by Montanus that in very early times the perpetual lamps in churches were lighted by fire made by friction of dry wood.[91] But in the ceremony of later times the flint

[89] Kuhn, p. 45. Wuttke, 'Deutscher Volksaberglaube'; Hamburg, 1860, p. 92. Brand, vol. iii. p. 286.

[90] Brand, 'Popular Antiquities'; London, 1853, vol. i. p. 157.

[91] Kelly, 'Curiosities of European Tradition,' p. 47.

and steel has superseded the ancient friction-fire; and, indeed, the Western clergy, as a rule, discountenanced it as heathenish. In the Capitularies of Carloman, in the eighth century, there is a prohibition of "illos sacrilegos ignes quos *niedfyr* vocant."[92] The result of this opposition by the Church was, in great measure, to break the connexion between the old festivals of the Sun, which the Church allowed, and the lighting of the needfire, which is so closely connected with the Sun-worship in our ancient Aryan mythology. Still, even in Germany, there are documents that bring the two together. A glossary to the Capitularies says, "the rustic folks in many places in Germany, and indeed on the feast of St. John the Baptist, pull a stake from a hedge and bind a rope round it, which they pull hither and thither till it takes fire," etc.; and a Low German book of 1593 speaks of the *"nodfüre,* that they sawed out of wood" to light the St. John's bonfire, and through which the people leapt and ran, and drove their cattle.[93]

It appears, however, that the Eastern and Western churches differed widely in their treatment of the old rite. The Western clergy discountenanced, and, as far as they could, put down the needfire: but in Russia it was not only allowed, but was (and very likely may be still) practised under ecclesiastical sanction, the priest being the chief actor in the ceremony. This interesting fact seems not to have been known to Grimm and Kuhn, and the following passage, which proves it, is still further remarkable as asserting that the ancient fire-making by friction was still used in Russia for practical as well as ceremonial purposes in the last century. It is contained in an account of the adventures of four Russian sailors, who were driven by a storm upon the desert island of East-Spitzbergen.[94] "They knew, however, that if one rubs violently together two pieces of dry wood, one hard and the other soft, the latter will catch fire. Besides this being the way in which the Russian peasants obtain fire when they are in the woods, there is also a religious ceremony, performed in

92 Cap. Carlomanni in Grimm, D. M., p. 570.

93 Grimm, D. M., pp. 570, 579. See also Migne, Lex s. v. "Nedifri."

94 P. L. le Roy, 'Erzählung der Begebenheiten,' etc.; Riga, 1760. (An E. Tr. in Pinkerton, vol. i.)

every village where there is a church, which could not have been
unknown to them. Perhaps it will be not disagreeable for me here
to give an account of this ceremony, though it does not belong
to the story. The 18th of August, Old Style, is called by the
Russians *Frol i Lavior*, these being the names of two martyrs,
called Florus and Laurus in the Roman Kalendar; they fall,
according to this latter, on the 29th of the said month, when
the Festival of the Beheading of John is celebrated. On this
day the Russian peasants bring their horses to the village church,
at the side of which they have dug the evening before a pit with
two outlets. Each horse has his bridle, which is made of lime-
tree bark. They let the horses, one after the other, go into this
pit, at the opposite outlet of which the priest stands with an
asperging-brush in his hand, with which he sprinkles them with
holy water. As soon as the horses are come out, their bridles
are taken off, and they are made to go between two fires, which
are kindled with what the Russians call *Givoy agon*, that is,
'living fire,' of which I will give the explanation, after remarking
that the peasants throw the bridles of the horses into one of
these fires to burn them up. Here is the manner of kindling
this *Givoy agon*, or living fire. Some men take hold of the
ends of a maple staff, very dry, and about a fathom long. This
staff they hold fast over a piece of birch-wood, which must also
be very dry, and whilst they vigorously rub the staff upon the
last wood, which is much softer than the first, it inflames in a
short time, and serves to kindle the pair of fires, of which I have
just made mention."

To sum up now, in a few words, the history of the art of
making fire, it appears that the common notion that the friction
of two pieces of wood was the original method used, has strong
and wide-lying evidence in its favour, and very little that can be
alleged against it. It has been seen that in many districts where
higher methods have long prevailed, its former existence as a
household art is proved by traces that have come down to us in
several different ways. Where the use of pyrites for striking
fire is found existing in company with it in North America, it is
at least likely that the fire-stick is the older instrument. Perhaps the most notable fact bearing on this quesion is the use of

pyrites by the miserable inhabitants of Tierra del Fuego. I do not know that the fire-sticks have ever been seen among them, but it seems more reasonable to suppose that they were used till they were supplanted by the discovery of the fire-making property of pyrites, than to make so insignificant a people an exception to a world-wide rule. This art of striking fire instead of laboriously producing it with the drill is not, indeed, the only thing in which the culture of this race stands above that of their northern neighbours, for, as has been mentioned, these last were found using no navigable craft but rafts, while the Fuegians had bark canoes, and those by no means of the lowest quality. It is worthy of note that the Peruvians, though they had pyrites, and broke the nodules to polish the faces into mirrors, do not seem to have used it to strike fire with. If they did not, their civilization stood in this matter below that of the much-despised Fuegians. The ancient Mexicans also made mirrors of polished pyrites, and perhaps they may have used it to strike fire;[95] but the wooden friction-apparatus was certainly common among them. Even the fire-drills of Peru and Mexico were of the simplest kind, twirled between the hands without any contrivance to lessen the labour, so that even the rude Esquimaux and Indian tribes have reached, in this respect, a higher stage of art than these comparatively civilized peoples.

To turn now from the art of making fire to one of its principal uses to mankind. The art of Cooking is as universal as Fire itself among the human race; but there are found, even among savages, several different processes that come under the general term, and a view of the distribution of these processes over the world may throw some light on the early development of Human Culture.

Roasting or broiling by direct exposure to the fire seems the one method universally known to mankind, but the use of some kind of oven is also very general. The Andaman Islanders keep fire continually smouldering in hollow trees, so that they have only to clear away the ashes at any time to cook their little pigs

[95] It seems by a passage in Boturini (p. 18), that he had some reason to think they used flint to strike fire with, and if so, as they had no iron, they probably used pyrites.

and fish.[96] In Africa the natives take possession of a great ant-hill, destroy the ants, and clear out the inside, leaving only the clay walls standing, which they make red hot with a fire, so as to bake joints of rhinoceros within.[97] But these are unusual expedients, and a much commoner form of savage oven is a mere pit in the ground. In the most elaborate kind of this cooking in underground ovens, hot stones are put in with the food, as in the familiar South-Sea Island practice, which is too well known to need description. The Malagasy plan seems to be the same;[98] but the Polynesians and their connexions have by no means a monopoly of the art, which is practised with little or no difference in other parts of the world. In the Morea, the traveller's dinner is often prepared by making a fire in a hole in the ground, in which a kid or lamb is afterwards placed, and covered in by a stone made hot for the purpose. The Canary Islanders buried meat in a hole in the ground, and lighted a fire over it;[99] and a similar practice is still sometimes found in the island of Sardinia,[100] while among the Beduins, and in places in North and South America, the process comes even closer to that used in the South Seas.[101] It is this wide diffusion of the art which makes it somewhat doubtful whether Klemm is right in considering its occurrence in Australia as one of the results of intercourse with more civilized islands. The natives cook in underground ovens on very distant parts of the coast; sometimes hot stones are used, and sometimes not.[102]

When meat or vegetables are kept for many hours on a grating above a slow fire, the combination of roasting and smoking brings the food into a state in which it will keep for a

96 Mouat, p. 308.

97 Klemm, C. G., vol. iii. p. 222. Moffat, Missionary Labours, etc., in S. Africa; London, 1842, p. 521.

98 Ellis, Madagascar, vol. i. p. 72.

99 Barker-Webb and Berthelot, vol. i. part i. p. 134.

100 Maury, 'La Terre & l'Homme'; Paris, 1857, p. 572.

101 Klemm, C. G., vol. ii. p. 26; vol. iv. p. 120. FitzRoy, in Tr. Eth. Soc., 1861, p. 4.

102 Cook, 1st Voy. H., vol. iii. p. 233. Lang, p. 347. Grey, Journals, vol. i. p. 176; vol. ii. p. 274. Klemm, C. G., vol. i. p. 307. Eyre, vol. ii. p. 289.

long while, even in the tropics. Jean de Lery, in the account of his adventures among the Indians of Brazil, about 1557, describes the wooden grating set up on four forked posts, "which in their language they call a *boucan*"; on this they cooked food with a slow fire underneath, and as they did not salt their meat, this process served them as a means of keeping their game and fish.[103] To the word *boucan* belongs the term *boucanier, bucaneer,* given to the French hunters of St. Domingo, from their preparing the flesh of the wild oxen and boars in this way, and applied less appropriately to the rovers of the Spanish Main. The process has been found elsewhere in South America,[104] and perhaps as far North as Florida.[105] The Haitian name for a framework of sticks set upon posts, *barbacoa*, was adopted into Spanish and English; for instance, the Peruvian air-bridges, made over difficult ground by setting up on piles a wattled flooring covered with earth, are called *barbacoas*;[106] and Dampier speaks of having "a Barbacue of split Bambooes to sleep on."[107] The American mode of roasting on such a framework is the origin of our term to *barbecue,* though its meaning has changed to that of roasting an animal whole. The art of bucaning or barbecuing, as practised by the Americans, is found in Africa, in Kamchatka, the Eastern Archipelago, and the Pelew Islands;[108] and it merges into the very common process of smoking meat to make it keep.

The mere inspection of these simple and wide-spread varieties of cooking gives the ethnographer very little evidence of the way in which they have been invented and spread over the world. But from the more complex art of Boiling there is something to be

---

[103] Lery, Hist. d'un Voy., etc., 1600, p. 153. Southey, Brazil, vol. i. p. 216; vol. iii. pp. 337, 361. The word *boucan* seems connected with that now commonly used in Brazil. "*Mocaém,* donde fisemos *moquem,* assar na labareda." Dias Dic. da Lingua Tupy.

[104] Wallace, p. 220. Humboldt and Bonpland, vol. ii. p. 556. Purchas, vol. v. p. 899.

[105] Hakluyt, vol. iii. p. 307.   [106] Tschudi, 'Peru,' vol. ii. p. 202.

[107] Dampier, vol. ii. part i. p. 90.

[108] Burton, 'Central Africa,' vol. ii. p. 282. Kracheninnikow, p. 46. Dampier, vol. iii. part ii. p. 24. Keate, p. 203. See Earl, 'Papuans,' p. 165.

learnt. There are races of mankind, such as the Fuegians and the Bushmen, who do not seem to have known how to boil food when they first came into the view of Europe, while the higher peoples of the world, and a great proportion of the lower ones, have had, so long as we know anything of them, vessels of pottery or metal which they put liquids into, and set over the fire to boil. Between these two conditions, however, there lies a process which has been superseded by the higher method within modern times over a large fraction of the earth's surface, and which there is some reason to believe once extended much further. It is even likely that the art of Boiling, as commonly known to us, may have been developed through this intermediate process, which I propose to call *Stone-Boiling*.

There is a North American tribe who received from their neighbours the Ojibwas, the name of Assinaboins, or "Stone-Boilers," from their mode of boiling their meat, of which Catlin gives a particular account. They dig a hole in the ground, take a piece of the animal's raw hide, and press it down with their hands close to the sides of the hole, which thus becomes a sort of pot or basin. This they fill with water, and they make a number of stones red-hot in a fire close by. The meat is put into the water, and the stones dropped in till the meat is boiled. Catlin describes the process as awkward and tedious, and says that since the Assinaboins had learnt from the Mandans to make pottery, and had been supplied with vessels by the traders, they had entirely done away the custom, "excepting at public festivals; where they seem, like all others of the human family, to take pleasure in cherishing and perpetuating their ancient customs."[109] Elsewhere among the Sioux or Dacotahs, to whom the Assinaboins belong, the tradition has been preserved that their fathers used to cook the game in its own skin, which they set up on four sticks planted in the ground, and put water, meat, and hot stones into it.[110] The Sioux had the art of stone-boiling in common with the mass of the northern tribes. Father Charlevoix, writing above a century ago, speaks of the Indians of the North as using wooden kettles and boiling the water in them by throwing in red-hot

[109] Catlin, vol. i. p. 54.   [110] Schoolcraft, part ii. p. 176.

stones, but even then iron pots were superseding both these vessels and the pottery of other tribes.[111] To specify more particularly, the Micmacs and Souriquois,[112] the Blackfeet and the Crees,[113] are known to have been stone-boilers; the Shoshonees or Snake Indians, like the far more northerly tribes of Slaves, Dog-Ribs, etc.,[114] still make, or lately made, their pots of roots plaited or rather twined so closely that they will hold water, boiling their food in them with hot stones;[115] while west of the Rocky Mountains, the Indians used similar baskets to boil salmon, acorn porridge, and other food in,[116] or wooden vessels such as Captain Cook found at Nootka Sound, and La Pérouse at Port Français.[117] Lastly, Sir Edward Belcher met with the practice of stone-boiling in 1826 among the Esquimaux of Icy Cape.[118]

So instantly is the art of stone-boiling supplanted by the kettles of the white trader, that, unless perhaps in the northwest, it might be hard to find it in existence now. But the state of things in North America, as known to us in earlier times, is somewhat as follows. The Mexicans, and the races between them and the Isthmus of Panama, were potters at the time of the Spanish discovery, and the art extended northward over an immense district, lying mostly between the Rocky Mountains and the Atlantic, and stretching up into Canada. In Eastern North America the first European discoverers found the art of earthenware-making in full operation, and forming a regular part of the women's work, and on this side of the continent, as high at least as New England, the site of an Indian village may be traced, like so many of the ancient settlements in the Old World, by innumerable fragments of pottery. But the Stone-Boilers extended far south on the Pacific side, and also occupied what may be roughly called the northern half of North America.

In that north-eastern corner of Asia which is of such extreme interest to the ethnographer, as preserving the lower human

111 Charlevoix, vol. vi. p. 47.   114 Mackenzie, p. 37, and see p. 207.

112 Schoolcraft, part i. p. 81.   115 Schoolcraft, part i. p. 211.

113 Harmon, p. 323.   116 Schoolcraft, part iii. pp. 107, 146.

117 Cook, Third Voy., vol. ii. p. 321. Klemm, C. G., vol. ii. pp. 26, 69.

118 Belcher, in Tr. Eth. Soc., vol. i. 1861, p. 133.

culture so near the high Asiatic civilization, and yet so little influenced by it, the art of Stone-boiling was found in full force. The Kamchadals, like some American tribes, used hollowed wooden troughs for the purpose, and long resisted the use of the iron cooking pots of the Russians, considering that the food only kept its flavour properly when dressed in the old-fashioned way.[119]

Thus the existence of a great district of Stone-Boilers in Northern Asia and America is made out by direct evidence, but beside this we know of the practice in a southern district of the world.

In Australia, Mr. T. Baines mentions native cooking-places seen on the Victoria River in 1855–6, small holes in the ground, where fish, water-tortoise, and, in one instance, a small alligator, had been made to boil by the immersion of heated stones in the water.[120] Thus the Australians, at least in modern times, must be counted as stone-boilers. Concerning the New Zealanders, Captain Cook made a remark that "having no vessel in which water can be boiled, their cooking consists wholly of baking and roasting."[121] But the inference that people who have no vessel that will stand the fire must therefore be unable to boil food is not a sound one. There is evidence that the Maoris knew the art of stone-boiling, though they used it but little. It is found among them under circumstances which give no ground for supposing that it was introduced after Captain Cook's visit. The curious dried human heads of New Zealand, which excel any mummies that have ever been made in the preservation of the features of the dead, were first brought over to England by Cook's party. From a careful description of the process of preparing them, made since, it appears that one thing was to parboil them (as we used to do traitors' heads for Temple Bar), and this was contrived by throwing them "into boiling water, into which red-hot stones are continually cast, to keep up the heat."[122] A remark made by another writer places the existence of stone-boiling as a

119 Kracheninnikow, p. 30. Erman, Reise, vol. iii. p. 423.

120 Baines, in Anthrop. Rev., July, 1886, p. civ.

121 Cook, First Voy. H., vol. iii. p. 55; also Third Voy., vol. i. p. 158.

122 Yate, 'New Zealand,' p. 132.

native New Zealand art beyond question. "The New Zealanders, although destitute of vessels in which to boil water, had an ingenious way of heating water to the boiling point, for the purpose of making shell-fish open. This was done by putting red-hot stones into wooden vessels full of water."[123] When, therefore, we find them boiling and eating the berries of the *Laurus tawa,* which are harmless when boiled, but poisonous in their raw state, it is not necessary to suppose this to have been found out since Captain Cook's time, as the boiling was probably done before with hot stones.[124]

In several other Polynesian islands, it appears from Cook's journals that stone-boiling was in ordinary use in cookery. The making of a native pudding in Tahiti is thus described. Breadfruit, ripe plantains, taro, and palm or pandanus nuts, were rasped, scraped, or beaten up fine, and baked separately. A quantity of juice, expressed from cocoa-nut kernels, was put into a large tray or wooden vessel. The other articles, hot from the oven, were deposited in this vessel, and a few hot stones were also put in to make the contents simmer. Few puddings in England, he says, equal these. In the island of Anamooka, they brought him a mess of fish, soup, and yams stewed in cocoa-nut liquor, "probably in a wooden vessel, with hot stones." The practice seems to have existed in the Marquesas, and in Huaheine he describes the preparation of a dish of *poi* in a wooden trough with hot stones.[125] What the Polynesian notion of a pudding is, as to size, may be gathered from the account of two missionaries who arrived at the island of Rurutu, and were received by a native who paddled out to meet them through a rough sea, in a wooden *poi*-dish, seven feet long and two and a half wide.[126]

I fear that the Tahitian recipe for making *poi* must spoil the good old story of Captain Wallis's tea-urn. A native who was breakfasting on board the Dolphin saw the tea-pot filled from the urn, and presently turned the cock again and put his hand

[123] Thomson, 'New Zealand,' vol. i. p. 160.

[124] Yate, p. 43.

[125] Cook, Third Voy., vol. ii. p. 49; vol. i. p. 233. Second Voy., vol. i. p. 310. First Voy. H., vol. ii. p. 254.

[126] Tyerman & Bennet, vol. i. p. 493.

underneath, with such effects as may be imagined. Captain Wallis, knowing that the natives had no earthen vessels, and that boiling in a pot over a fire was a novelty to them, and putting all these things together in telling the story, interpreted the howls of the scalded native as he danced about the cabin, and the astonishment of the rest of the visitors, as proving that the Tahitians "having no vessel in which water could be subjected to the action of fire, . . . had no more idea that it could be made hot, than that it could be made solid."[127] No doubt the natives were surprised at hot water coming out of so unlikely a place, but the world seems to have accepted both the story and the inference without stopping to consider that hot water could not be much of a novelty among people to whom boiled pudding was an article of daily food. Captain Wallis's story (as is so commonly the case with accounts of savages) may be matched elsewhere. "And we went now," says Kotzebue, in the account of his visit to the Radack islands, "to Rarick's dwelling, where the kettle had already been set on the fire, and the natives were assembled round it, looking at the boiling water, which seemed to them alive." Yet on another island of the same chain it is remarked that the *mogomuk* is made by drying the root of a plant, and pressing the meal into lumps; when it is to be eaten, some of this is broken off, stirred with water in a cocoa-nut shell, and boiled till it swells up into a thick porridge ("und kocht ihn, bis er zu einem dicken Brei aufquillt,") etc.[128]

Though the natives of the islands mentioned, and no doubt of many others, were still stone-boilers in Cook's time, pottery had already made its appearance in Polynesia, in districts so situated that the art may reasonably be supposed to have travelled from island to island from the Eastern Archipelago, where perhaps the Malays received it from Asia. By Cook and later explorers earthen vessels were found in the Pelew, Fiji, and Tonga groups, and in New Caledonia.[129] By this time it is likely that these and Euro-

127 Wallis, H., vol. i. pp. 246, 264.

128 Kotzebue, vol. ii. pp. 47, 65.

129 Cook, Second Voy., vol. i. p. 214; vol. ii. p. 105. Third Voy., vol. i. p. 375. Klemm, C. G., vol. iv. p. 272. Williams, 'Fiji,' vol. i. p. 69. Turner, p. 424. Mariner, vol. ii. p. 272. Keate, p. 336.

pean vessels may have put an end to stone-boiling in Polynesia, so that its displacement by the introduction of pottery and metal will have taken place by the same combination of the influence of neighbouring tribes and of Europeans which have produced a similar effect in North America.

There is European evidence of the art of stone-boiling. The Finns have kept up into modern times a relic of the practice. Linnæus, on his famous Lapland Tour, in 1732, recorded the fact that in East Bothland "The Finnish liquor called Lura is prepared like other beer, except not being boiled, instead of which red-hot stones are thrown into it."[130] Moreover, the quantities of stones, evidently calcined, which are found buried in our own country, sometimes in the sites of ancient dwellings, give great probability to the inference which has been drawn from them, that they were used in cooking. It is true that their use may have been for baking in underground ovens, a practice found among races who are Stone-boilers, and others who are not. But it is actually on record that the wild Irish, of about 1600, used to warm their milk for drinking with a stone first cast into the fire.[131]

In Asia[132] I have met with no positive evidence of cookery by stone-boiling beyond Kamchatka, but some extremely rude boiling-vessels have been observed among Siberian tribes, the use of which is either to be explained by the absence or scarcity of earthenware or metal pots, or by the keeping up of old habits belonging to a time of such absence or scarcity. The Dutch envoy, Ysbrants Ides, remarks of the Ostyaks, "I have also seen a copper kettle among them, and some other kettles of bark sewed together, in which they can boil food over the hot coals, but not in the flame of the fire."[133] Now just such bark-kettles as these have been

---

130 Linnæus, Tour, vol. ii. p. 231. Such beer, called Steinbir, is made in Carinthia, by throwing hot stones into the vat. See W. O. Stanley, 'Memoirs on Ancient Dwellings in Holyhead,' p. 19. [Note to 3rd Edition.]

131 J. Evans, in Archæologia, vol. xli.

132 Dr. Hooker found baths of hollowed trees at Bhomsong, heated with hot stones, 'Himalayan Journals,' vol. i. p. 305. Compare a similar process in N. W. America, Tr. Eth. Soc., vol. iv. p. 290.

133 E. Ysbrants Ides, 'Reize naar China'; Amsterdam, 1710, p. 27.

seen in use among a North American tribe on the Unijah, or Peace River, near the Rocky Mountains. They were stone-boilers, using for this purpose the regular *watape* pots, or rather baskets, of woven roots of spruce fir, but they had also kettles, "made of spruce-bark, which they hang over the fire, but at such a distance as to receive the heat without being within reach of the blaze; a very tedious operation."[134] In Siberia, among the Ostyaks, the practice has been observed of using the paunch of the slaughtered beast as a vessel to cook the blood in over the fire,[135] and the same thing has been noticed among the Reindeer Koriaks.[136] Thus the story told by Herodotus of the Scythians, who, when they had not a suitable cauldron, used to boil the flesh of the sacrificed beast in its own paunch,[137] seems to give a glimpse of a state of things in the centre of Asia, resembling that which has continued into modern times in the remote North-East. It is thus not unlikely that the use of stone-boiling, to meet the want of suitable vessels for direct boiling over the fire, may once have had a range in Asia far beyond the Kamchatkan promontory.[138]

It may be that the more convenient boiling in vessels set over the fire was generally preceded in the world by the clumsier stone-boiling, of which the history, so far as I have been able to make it out from evidence within my reach, has thus been sketched. Of vessels used for the higher kind of boiling, as commonly known to us, something may now be said.

It is not absolutely necessary that vessels of earthenware, metal, etc., should be used for this purpose. Potstone, lapis ollaris, has been used by the Esquimaux, and by various Old World peoples, to make vessels which will stand the fire.[139] The Asiatic paunch-kettles have just been mentioned, and kettles of skins have been

[134] Mackenzie, p. 207.

[135] Erman (E. Tr.), vol. ii. pp. 456, 467.

[136] Kracheninnikow, p. 142.

[137] Herod., iv. 61.

[138] The frequent use of wicker baskets for holding liquids, in Africa, may have a bearing on the history of stone-boiling. See mention of hot stones for melting or boiling fat, in Bleek, 'Reynard in Africa,' pp. 8–10.

[139] Cranz, p. 73; Linnæus, vol. i. p. 356; Klemm, C. G., vol. ii. p. 266. Mem. Anthrop. Soc. vol. i. 1863–4, pp. 297–8.

described among the Esquimaux,[140] and even among the wild Irish[141] and the inhabitants of the Hebrides, of whose way of life George Buchanan gives the following curious account:—"In food, clothing, and all domestic matters, they use the ancient parsimony. Their meat is supplied by hunting and fishing. The flesh they boil with water in the paunch or hide of the slaughtered beast; out hunting they sometimes eat it raw, when the blood has been pressed out. For drink they have the broth of the meat. Whey that has been kept for years, they also drink greedily at their feasts. This kind of liquor they call bland."[142] Beside these animal materials, parts of several plants will answer the purpose, as the bark used for kettles in Asia and America, the spathes of palms, in which food is often boiled in South America,[143] the split bamboos in which the Dayaks, the Sumatrans, and the Stiêns of Cambodia, boil their rice, and cocoa-nut shells, as just mentioned in the Radack group; Captain Cook saw a cocoa-nut shell used in Tahiti, to dry up the blood of a native dog in, over the fire.[144] These facts should be borne in mind in considering the following theory of the Origin of the Art of Pottery.

It was, I believe, Goguet who first propounded, in the last century, the notion that the way in which pottery came to be made, was that people daubed such combustible vessels as these with clay, to protect them from the fire, till they found that the clay alone would answer the purpose, and thus the art of pottery came into the world. The idea was not a mere effort of his imagination, for he had met with a description of the plastering of wooden vessels with clay in the southern Hemisphere. It is related that a certain Captain Gonneville sailed from Honfleur in 1503, doubled the Cape of Good Hope, and came to the Southern Indies (apparently the east coast of South America). There he found a gentle and joyous people, living by hunting and fishing,

140 Martin Frobisher, in 'Hakluyt,' vol. iii. pp. 66, 95.

141 Evans, l. c.

142 'Rerum Scoticarum Historia, auctore Georgio Buchanano Scoto'; (ad ex.) Edinburgh, 1528, p. 7.

143 Spix and Martius, vol. ii. p. 688. Wallace, p. 508.

144 St. John, vol. i. p. 137. Marsden, p. 60. Mouhot, vol. ii. p. 245. Cook, Third Voy., vol. ii. p. 35. See Coleman, p. 318; Mariner, vol. ii. p. 272.

and a little agriculture, and he speaks of cloaks of mats and skins, feather work, bows and arrows, beds of mats, villages of thirty to eighty huts of stakes and wattles, etc., "and their household utensils of wood, even their boiling-pots, but plastered with a kind of clay, a good finger thick, which prevents the fire from burning them."[145] The theory of the origin of pottery which Goguet founded upon this remarkable account, is corroborated by a quantity of evidence which has made its appearance since his time.

The comparison of two accounts of vessels found, one among the Esquimaux, the other among their neighbours the Unalashkans (whose language contains proofs of intimate contact with them[146]), may serve to give an idea of the way in which clay may come to supersede less convenient materials, and a gradual approach be made towards the potter's art. When James Hall was in Greenland, in 1605, he found the natives boiling food over their lamps, in vessels with stone bottoms, and sides of whale's fins.[147] In Unalashka, Captain Cook found that some of the natives had got brass kettles from the Russians, but those who had not, made their own "of a flat stone, with sides of clay, not unlike a standing pye."[148] He thought it likely that they had learnt to boil from the Russians, but the Russians could hardly have taught them to make such vessels as these, and the appearance of a kettle with a stone bottom (no doubt potstone), and sides of another material, at the two opposite sides of America, gives ground for supposing it to have been in common use in high latitudes.

From the examination of an earthen vessel from the Fiji Islands, Dr. D. S. Price considers that it was very likely made by moulding clay on the outside of the shell or rind of some fruit. The vessel in question is made watertight after the South American manner by a varnish of resin. The evident and fre-

---

[145] Goguet, vol. i. p. 77. 'Mémoires touchant l'Établissement d'une Mission Chrestienne dans le troisième monde, autrement appellé la Terre Australe,' etc.; Paris, 1663, pp. 10–16.

[146] Buschmann, Azt. Spr., p. 702.

[147] Purchas, vol. iii. p. 817.

[148] Cook, Third Voy., vol. ii. p. 510.

quent adoption of gourd-shapes in the earthenware of distant parts of the world does not prove much, but as far as it goes it tells in favour of the opinion that such gourd-like vessels may be the successors of real gourds, made into pottery by a plastering of clay. Some details given in 1841 by Squier and Davis, in their account of the monuments in the Mississippi Valley, are much more to the purpose. "In some of the Southern States, it is said, the kilns, in which the ancient pottery was baked, are now occasionally to be met with. Some are represented still to contain the ware, partially burned, and retaining the rinds of the gourds, etc., over which they were modelled, and which had not been entirely removed by the fire. . . . Among the Indians along the Gulf, a greater degree of skill was displayed than with those on the upper waters of the Mississippi and on the lakes. Their vessels were generally larger and more symmetrical, and of a superior finish. They moulded them over gourds and other models and baked them in ovens. In the construction of those of large size, it was customary to model them in baskets of willow or splints, which, at the proper period, were burned off, leaving the vessel perfect in form, and retaining the somewhat ornamental markings of their moulds. Some of those found on the Ohio seem to have been modelled in bags or nettings of coarse thread or twisted bark. These practices are still retained by some of the remote western tribes. Of this description of pottery many specimens are found with the recent deposits in the mounds."[149] Prince Maximilian of Wied makes the following remark on some earthen vessels found in Indian mounds near Harmony, on the Wabash river:—"They were made of a sort of grey clay, marked outside with rings, and seem to have been moulded in a cloth or basket, being marked with impressions or figures of this kind."[150]

It has been thought, too, that the early pottery of Europe retains in its ornamentation traces of having once passed through a stage in which the clay was surrounded by basketwork or netting, either as a backing to support the finished vessel, or as a

[149] Squier & Davis, pp. 195, 187. See the account in J. D. Hunter, 'Memoirs of Captivity among the Indians,' London, 1823, p. 289; also Rau, 'Indian Pottery,' in Smithsonian Report, 1866.

[150] Pr. Max. Voyage, vol. i. p. 192. Klemm, C. G., vol. ii. p. 66.

mould to form it in. Dr. Klemm advanced this view twenty years ago. "The imitation (of natural vessels) in clay presupposes numerous trials. In the Friendly Islands, we find vessels which are still in an early stage; they are made of clay, slightly burnt, and enclosed in plaited work; so also the oldest German vessels seem to have been, for we observe on those which remain an ornamentation in which plaiting is imitated by incised lines. What was no longer wanted as a necessity was kept up as an ornament."[151]

Dr. Daniel Wilson made a similar remark, some years later, on early British urns which, he says, "may have been strengthened by being surrounded with a platting of cords or rushes. . . . It is certain that very many of the indented patterns on British pottery have been produced by the impress of twisted cords on the wet clay,—the intentional imitation, it may be, of undesigned indentations originally made by the platted net-work on ruder urns," etc.[152] Mr. G. J. French mentions experiments made by him in support of his views on the derivation of the interlaced or guilloche ornaments on early Scottish crosses, etc., from imitation of earlier structures of wicker-work. He coated baskets with clay, and found the wicker patterns came out on all the earthen vessels thus made, and he seems to think that some ancient urns still preserved were actually moulded in this way, judging from the lip being marked as if the wicker-work had been turned in over the clay coating inside.[153]

Taken all together, the evidence of so many imperfect and seemingly transitional forms of pottery makes it probable that it was through such stages that the art grew up into the more perfect form in which we usually find it, and in which it has come to be clearly understood that clay, alone or with some mixture of sand or such matters to prevent cracking, is capable of being used without any extraneous support.

Such is the evidence by means of which I have attempted to trace the progress of mankind in three important arts, whose

[151] Klemm, C. G., vol. i. p. 188.

[152] Wilson, Archæology, etc., of Scotland, p. 289.

[153] G. J. French, An Attempt, etc.; Manchester (printed), 1858.

early history lies for the most part out of the range of direct record. Its examination brings into view a gradual improvement in methods of producing fire; the supplanting of a rude means of boiling food by a higher one; and a progress from the vessels of gourds, bark, or shell of the lower races to the pottery and metal of the higher. On the whole, progress in these useful arts appears to be the rule, and whether its steps be slow or rapid, a step once made does not seem often to be retraced.

INDEX

Abipones, 117, 124
Adobe, 84
Aeolian flutes, 152–3
Africa, beast-fables of, 7, 225
Alphabets and syllabaria, 86–89; finger, 12
America, civilization connected with Old World, 199 ff.
Andaman Islanders, 137
Archimedes, his burning mirrors, 265
Architecture, evidence of progress in, 141–42
Articulation of deaf-mutes, 59–62
Australians, 118, 122, 150–52, 232, 281

Baking in hollow trees, ant-hills, pits, 276 ff.
Bamboo, fire produced from, 252
Barbecue, 278
Beast-fables, 6–7, 225 ff.
Bee-hunting, Australian and American method of, 152
Bellows for iron-smelting, 142
Bewitching: by images, 102–5, 107; by earth-cutting, 103; by names, 107–11; by locks of hair, parings of nails, leavings of food, 111–14; by symbolic charms, 114–16; by the evil eye, 116; by "wishing," 116
Bible, tales derived from, 197–99
Blast pump for iron smelting, 142–43, 237
Boats, 137; remains on mountains, 189–92
Boiling, 278–90; with hot stones, 278–88; vessels, 284–88
Bolas, 152
Bones burnt for fuel, 158
Boomerang, 150, 162, 234
Bridge of Dead, 218–23
Burial in canoes, 222

Burning lens, 264
Burning mirror, 265–68
Bushmen, 64, 160

Calculation by stones, 138
Calendars: North American Indian, 76; Mexicans, 77–78, 199–200
Caliban, 262
Cherokees, their syllabarium, 88
Chinampas, 146–47
Chinese, their phonetic writing, 85–86
Chocolate, 153
Churn worked with cord, 256
Cistercians, their gesture language, 32–34
Civilization: progress of, 2, 101, 126, 128, 232; decline of, 156–66, 235
Climbing by hoops, 145
Cloth of fibre bundles, 163–64
Cock and bull stories, 6–7
Colors of feathers changed in live birds, 152
Cooking, 276–86; en papillote, 148; roasting and broiling, 276; baking, 276–78; underground ovens, 277; bucaning or barbecuing, 277–78; boiling, 278–86; stone-boiling, 279–85
Cord, hand-twisted, 163–64

Dasent, Dr., his argument from beast-fables, 225–26
Dead, names not mentioned, 120–25
Deaf-and-dumb: mental condition and education, 11 ff., 57–62; of themselves utter words, 60–62; lip imitation of words, 61
Decline of culture, 156–63, 235; A. von Humboldt on, 162; Dr. Von Martius' theory of, 235
Degeneration theory, 235

Deluge, 75, 186–92, 197
Devil, attributes of fire-god given to, 229
Digger Indians, 161
Divination, 130
Dolls and toys, 90–92
Dreams and phantasms, argument from, 4–6
Drills, for boring holes and for fire-making, 163, 254–62
Dumb, becomes term for foreign, barbarian, stupid, young, 26

Eclipse, 139
Effigies, 106
Eggs, artificial hatching of, 156
Egypt: hieroglyphics in, 83–86; Coptic alphabet in, 86; decline in arts, 156–57
Evil eye, 46, 116

Finns, as stone-boilers, 284
Fire, myths of origins of, 242 ff., 269–75
Fire: new, 265–75; Vestal, 265–66; in Peru, 266; in India, 270–71; on Easter eve, 273; in Russia, 275; *see also* Needfire
Fire: races reported to be destitute of, Gaunches, 242; Islanders of Los Jardines, 243; of Fakaafo, 243–44; of the Ladrones and Philippines, 246–47; tribe in French Guiana, 247; Ethiopian tribes, 248
Fire-drill: simple, 252–55, 266–76; as carpenter's brace, 255; thong-drill, 256; bow-drill, 258; pump-drill, 258–62
Fire-making: Tasmanians and Australians, 249–50; methods in different countries, 250 ff.; stick and groove, 251–52; with bamboo, 252; with fire-drill, 252–61; with iron pyrites, 262–63, 275; with stones, 263; with flint and steel, 264; with burning lens, 264; with burning mirror, 265; with lucifer matches, 268; with wooden friction apparatus, 268 ff.; early evidence in different countries, 268–76
Fire-syringe, 262
Flint and steel, 264

Floating gardens, 146–48
Footprints, 114 ff., 158
Fork, eating, 148 ff.
Fossil bones, shells, myths of observation with, 176–92
Fountain of Youth, 223–25
Fuegians, 262, 276, 279

Gauchos, 255
Gesture-language, 9–68; of deaf-and-dumb, 13–26; nature of, 10 ff.; arbitrary signs, 16 ff.; epithets, 18; absence of grammatical categories, 19, 55; grammar and syntax, 19–25; of savage tribes, 26–32; of Cistercian monks, 32–34; the pantomime, 35–37; as an accompaniment to speech, 44 ff.; common to mankind, 47; evidence of mental similarity, 47; compared with speech, 51–59; prepositions, 54; as original utterance of man, 57; for numerals, 66
Gesture-signs, 31, 35–46; translated in language, 30–40; nodding and shaking head, 30, 45; kissing hand, 31; sign of benediction, 31; beckoning, 37; snapping fingers, 37–38; grasping and shaking hands, 38–39; crouching, bowing, kneeling, 39–40; gestures of prayer, 41 ff.; rubbing noses, kissing, blowing, 44; signs of contempt, 45; against the evil eye, 46
Giants, 177–85
Glass, legend of invention of, 150 f.
Griffins, 179–80
Guanches, 242
Guano, 153

Hair, bewitching by locks of, 111 ff.
Hammock, 150
Harpokrates, 34
Heads, preserved, of New England, 281
Hebrides, inhabitants of, 286
Hot stones: baking with, 277; boiling with, 278–86
Humboldt, A. von: on connexion of Mexicans with Asia, 78, 339 ff.; on human degeneration, 162; on Mexican elephant-like head, 174

Husband, name not mentioned by wife, 119

Ideas, association with images and words, 91–127
Idiots, gesture language in education of, 66
Idols, 93–96
Images, 91–105
Indians of North America: gesture-language, 28–32; picture-writing, 69–77
Inventors and civilizers, legends of, 127–32, 168 ff., 243–44, 269
Irrigation, decline in art of, 159

Jack and the beanstalk, 209 ff.
Jonah, 205

Kafirs, 119, 125
Kamchadals, 188, 270, 281
Kang-hi, his Encyclopaedia, 178, 189
Kava, 155
Kettles, 284–89
King's and chief's names not mentioned, 122–23
Kissing, 44

Language: origin of, 9 f., 48–51, 55; Chinese myth of, 51; speech compared with gesture language, 51–57; predicative and demonstrative roots compared with two classes of gesture signs, 52–54; concretism, 55; verb roots, 56; syntax, 56; relation of speech to thought, 57–61; deaf-and-dumb, 60–62; lip-imitations of words, 61; attempts to discover by experiments on children, 66–68; modified by superstitions in Polynesia, 123, in Australia, 123, in Tasmania, 123; among Abipones, 124, Kafirs, 125, Yezidis, 125, English and Americans, 126; as evidence of progress in culture, 138–41
Letters; *see* Phonetic characters
Life, future, 4–6, 214–17
Little Red Riding-Hood, 206

Madagascar, 142 ff., 255
Magic and sorcery, 100–117

Malayo-Polynesians, 142, 153
Mammoths and extinct animals: recollections of, 172; myths derived from remains, 173–82
Man in the Moon, 194 ff.
Man swallowed by fish, 204–6
Map-making, 75–76
Mexico: picture-writing, 77–84, 173; calendars, 77–78, 339–40; von Humboldt on connexion with Asia, 78, 173, 199–200; phonetic characters, 79–83; Quetzalcohuatl and the Toltecs, 129–31; fire-drill, 254
Mirrors, pyrites and obsidian, 265, 276
Moslems, opinions on images, 104
Müller, Max, 53–54, 125
Myths: 171–231, 238; of origin of language, 51; connected with the shapes of rocks, stone circles, statues, 96–97; of footprints, 98–99; of sympathetic plants, 114; about sun, 128–31, 205–12, 224; of Quetzalcohuatl, 129–31; geographical distribution of, 193–231; common nature and character of among different races, 193–97; man in the moon, 194 f.; sun and moon brother and sister, 195; Castor and Pollux in Tasmania, 195–96; derived from Bible stories, 197–98; transmission of, 197–98; of America compared to those of Old World, 199–231; World-Tortoise, Tortoise Island, 200–204; man swallowed by fish, 204–6; Sun-Catcher, 206–12; Little Red Riding-Hood, 206; Tom Thumb, 206; Jack and the beanstalk, 209; ascent to Heaven by the Tree, 210–17; Swan-coat, 215; Bridge, River of Dead, 218–23; Fountain of Youth, 223–25; Tail-Fisher, 225–29; moon as cheese, 226; stumpy-tailed animals, 226–27; as historical evidence, 238–39; of Prometheus, 243, 271; of origin of fire in Polynesia, 244 ff.; of monstrous tribes, 247 ff.; growth of, 247; permanence of, 248; of Old World transferred to New, 266; Chinese, 269; Phoenicia, 270; *see also* Myths

of observations; Beast-fables; Traditions

Myths of observation, 167–92: petrified lentils, 175; sun hissing in sea, 175–76; rain of stones, 176–77; connected with fossil remains, 177–92; mammoths, 177–84; griffins, 179–80; rhinoceros horns, 179–80; animals out of caves, 181–82; creatures which die on seeing daylight, 178, 182; giants, 182–85; degeneration of man's stature, 185; bearing of fossils and remains of boats on Deluge traditions, 185–92; bones of whales on high mountains, 187

Nails, bewitching by, 111
Names: association with objects, 107–8; in magic, 108–11; concealed, 109; changed to deceive evil spirits, 109; exchanged in token of amity, 110; personal names, own, of others, of husbands, of parents-and-children-in-law, of either connexions, of kings and chiefs, of dead, of spirits, of superhuman beings, 117–27
Needfire, 271–76
New Zealanders, 164, 281
North American Indians: picture-writing, 69 ff., 77; calendars, 77 ff.; syllabarium of Cherokees, 88
Numa Pompilius, 265
Numerals: by gesture, 65–66; Roman, 104

Objective and subjective confused, 116–27
Ostyaks, images of dead, 93

Peru: New fire, 266; Virgins of Sun compared with Vestal Virgins of Rome, 267
Phonetic characters: of Mexicans, 79–84; Egyptian hieroglyphs, 83–87; Chinese, 85–86; of Central America, 85; alphabets and syllabaria, 87–90
Picture-writing: of North American Indians, 69–79; of Mexicans, 77–84; numerals, 89–90
Plants, sympathetic, 114

Polynesians, 119–23, 148, 168, 205 ff., 251, 281
Pottery, 149, 154, 280–84; transition vessels of, 284–89; Gogeut's theory of origin of, 286–89; gourd shapes, 287–88; ornamentation, 288–89
Prometheus, 243, 271
Puris and Coroados, 63–65
Pyrites, striking fire with, 263, 275

Quetzalcohuatl, 99, 129–31
Quipus, 132–36

Rainbow, bridge or ladder, 221
Rainmakers, 115
Reynard the Fox, 7, 212, 225
Rice, traditions of introduction of, 170–71, 215
Roasting and broiling food, 276 ff.

Sago, 154
Samovar, 140
Samson, 207
Sanchoniathon, cosmogony of, 270
Signatures, doctrine of, 106–7
Similarity in distant regions, 3–4, 116–17, 144, 191–92, 230–31, 276
Sneezing, customs related to, 238
Sorcerers, arts, 111–17
Soul, future life of, 4–9, 218–23
Sound and color, comparison of, 59
Spirits: of dead, affected through remains of bodies, 112; names not to be mentioned, 120 ff.
Steinthal, Prof., on gesture-language, 9
Stick-and-groove, 251
Stone-boiling, 171, 279–85
Stumpy-tailed animals, myths relating to, 225–26
Sugar, 179
Sun-myths, 128–31, 205–12
Supernatural beings, names not mentioned, 121, 125
Swan-coat, 215
Symbolic offerings, 105

Tabu, 141
Tail-fishing, 225–29
Tally, 141

Tea-urn, 140
Teeth: artificial, 148; stopping with gold, 148
Textile fabrics, 163–66
Toltecs, 129–31
Tom Thumb, 206 ff.
Tortoise-myth, 174, 201–4
Traditions: 167–75; of inventors and civilizers, 128–32; of quipu in China, 132, 167; of Polynesia, 167; Central America, 169; in tropics apparently belonging to high latitudes, 169; of introduction of rice, 170; first appearance of white men among North Western American tribe, 170–71; possible recollection of mammoth, colossal tortoise, great ape, 172–75; deluge, 185–92
Tree, Heaven, 209–17
Tribes: deficient in speech, 62–65; degraded, 159; fireless or no means of fire-making, 243–50

Utterance: not by speech only, 9; relation to thought, 57–62

Veddahs, 63–65, 253–54
Vei syllabarium, 87–88
Vessels: for stone boiling, 171, 279–85; for setting over fire, 284–87; of potstone, 285; pottery, 286–90; gourds plastered with clay, 288
Vestal Virgins, 265–67

Wattled cloth, 164
Weaving, 154, 164
Wild fire, 269
Words, superstitions concerning, 107–10, 117–26
World, conception of among lower races, 201, 217–18
Writing, in magic, 110; *see* Picture-writing; Phonetic characters

PHOENIX BOOKS
Sociology, Anthropology, and Archeology

P 2   *Edward Chiera:* They Wrote on Clay

P 7   *Louis Wirth:* The Ghetto

P 10 *Edwin H. Sutherland,* EDITOR: The Professional Thief, by a professional thief

P 11 *John A. Wilson:* The Culture of Ancient Egypt

P 20 *Kenneth P. Oakley:* Man the Tool-maker

P 21 *W. E. LeGros Clark:* History of the Primates

P 24 *B. A. Botkin,* EDITOR: Lay My Burden Down: A Folk History of Slavery

P 28 *David M. Potter:* People of Plenty: Economic Abundance and the American Character

P 31 *Peter H. Buck:* Vikings of the Pacific

P 32 *Diamond Jenness:* The People of the Twilight

P 45 *Weston La Barre:* The Human Animal

P 53 *Robert Redfield:* The Little Community *and* Peasant Society and Culture

P 55 *Julian A. Pitt-Rivers:* People of the Sierra

P 64 *Arnold van Gennep:* The Rites of Passage

P 71 *Nels Anderson:* The Hobo: The Sociology of the Homeless Man

P 82 *W. Lloyd Warner:* American Life: Dream and Reality

P 85 *William R. Bascom and Melville J. Herskovits,* EDITORS: Continuity and Change in African Cultures

P 86 *Robert Redfield and Alfonso Villa Rojas:* Chan Kom: A Maya Village

P 87 *Robert Redfield:* A Village That Chose Progress: Chan Kom Revisited

P 88 *Gordon R. Willey and Philip Phillips:* Method and Theory in American Archaeology

P 90 *Eric Wolf:* Sons of the Shaking Earth

P 92 *Joachim Wach:* Sociology of Religion

P 105 *Sol Tax,* EDITOR: Anthropology Today: Selections

P 108 *Horace Miner:* St. Denis: A French-Canadian Parish

P 117 *Herbert A. Thelen:* Dynamics of Groups at Work

P 124 *Margaret Mead and Martha Wolfenstein,* EDITORS: Childhood in Contemporary Cultures

P 125 *George Steindorff and Keith C. Seele:* When Egypt Ruled the East

P 129 *John P. Dean and Alex Rosen:* A Manual of Intergroup Relations

P 133 *Alexander Heidel:* The Babylonian Genesis

P 136 *Alexander Heidel:* The Gilgamesh Epic and Old Testament Parallels

P 138 *Frederic M. Thrasher:* The Gang: A Study of 1,313 Gangs in Chicago (Abridged)

P 139 *Everett C. Hughes:* French Canada in Transition

PHOENIX BOOKS
in History

P 2   *Edward Chiera:* They Wrote on Clay

P 11   *John A. Wilson:* The Culture of Ancient Egypt

P 13   *Ernest Staples Osgood:* The Day of the Cattleman

P 16   *Karl Löwith:* Meaning in History: The Theological Implications of the Philosophy of History

P 22   *Euclides da Cunha:* Rebellion in the Backlands

P 27   *Daniel J. Boorstin:* The Genius of American Politics

P 28   *David M. Potter:* People of Plenty: Economic Abundance and the American Character

P 29   *Eleanor Shipley Duckett:* Alfred the Great: The King and His England

P 36   *A. T. Olmstead:* History of the Persian Empire

P 40   *Giorgio de Santillana:* The Crime of Galileo

P 61   *Warren S. Tryon:* My Native Land: Life in America, 1790–1870

P 66   *Alan Simpson:* Puritanism in Old and New England

P 69   *Gustave E. von Grunebaum:* Medieval Islam

P 70   *Oscar Jászi:* Dissolution of the Habsburg Monarchy

P 73   *Howard H. Peckham:* Pontiac and the Indian Uprising

P 80   *Carl Bridenbaugh:* The Colonial Craftsman

P 125 *George Steindorff and Keith C. Seele:* When Egypt Ruled the East

P 144 *Forrest McDonald:* We the People: The Economic Origins of the Constitution

P 147 *Donald Culross Peattie:* Venice: Immortal Village

PHOENIX BOOKS
in Science

P 21   *W. E. LeGros Clark:* History of the Primates
P 35   *C. F. von Weizsäcker:* The History of Nature
P 40   *Giorgio de Santillana:* The Crime of Galileo
P 58   *Laura Fermi:* Atoms in the Family: Life with Enrico Fermi
P 126   *Alan Gregg:* For Future Doctors

PHOENIX SCIENCE SERIES

PSS 501 *Carey Croneis and William C. Krumbein:* Down to Earth: An Introduction to Geology
PSS 502 *Mayme I. Logsdon:* A Mathematician Explains
PSS 503 *Heinrich Klüver:* Behavior Mechanisms in Monkeys
PSS 504 *Gilbert A. Bliss:* Lectures on the Calculus of Variations
PSS 505 *Reginald J. Stephenson:* Exploring in Physics
PSS 506 *Harvey Brace Lemon:* From Galileo to the Nuclear Age
PSS 507 *A. Adrian Albert:* Fundamental Concepts of Higher Algebra
PSS 509 *Walter Bartky:* Highlights of Astronomy
PSS 510 *Frances W. Zweifel:* A Handbook of Biological Illustration
PSS 511 *Henry E. Sigerist:* Civilization and Disease
PSS 512 *Enrico Fermi:* Notes on Quantum Mechanics
PSS 513 *S. Chandrasekhar:* Plasma Physics
PSS 514 *A. A. Michelson:* Studies in Optics
PSS 515 *Gösta Ehrensvärd:* Life: Origin and Development
PSS 516 *Harold Oldroyd:* Insects and Their World
PSS 517 *A. Adrian Albert:* College Algebra
PSS 518 *Winthrop N. Kellogg:* Porpoises and Sonar
PSS 519 *H. G. Andrewartha:* Introduction to the Study of Animal Populations
PSS 520 *Otto Toeplitz:* The Calculus: A Genetic Approach
PSS 521 *David Greenhood:* Mapping
PSS 522 *Fritz Heide:* Meteorites
PSS 523 *Robert Andrews Millikan:* The Electron: Its Isolation and Measurements and the Determination of Some of Its Properties

PHOENIX BOOKS
in Philosophy and Religion

042439

42439

P 1   E   Renaissance Philoso-

P 5   Ja

P 6   A   : Selected Writings

P 8   T   to Plato

P 9   T   tle to Plotinus

P 16   K   the Philosophy of

P 17   T

P 18   T

P 19   P

P 30   R   dal Logic

P 34   M

P 44   R

P 67   Y

P 81   H   undations and the

P 92   Jo

P 95   A

P 110   M

P 112   L

P 114   L

P 128   M

P 131   P

P 137   L

P 141   S

P 142   C   God

P 143   K